Her Voice, Her Faith

8 95

Her Voice, Her Faith

WOMEN SPEAK
ON WORLD RELIGIONS

ARVIND SHARMA
KATHERINE K. YOUNG
EDITORS

A MEMBER OF THE PERSEUS BOOKS GROUP

Copyright © 2003 by Westview Press, A Member of the Perseus Books Group

Westview Press books are available at special discounts for bulk purchases in the United States by corporations, institutions, and other organizations. For more information, please contact the Special Markets Department at the Perseus Books Group, 11 Cambridge Center, Cambridge MA 02142, or call (617) 252–5298 or (800) 255-1514, or email special.markets@perseusbooks.com.

Hardcover first published in 2002 in the United States of America by Westview Press, 5500 Central Avenue, Boulder, Colorado 80301–2877, and in the United Kingdom by Westview Press, 12 Hid's Copse Road, Cumnor Hill, Oxford OX2 9JJ

Paperback first published in 2004 by Westview Press.

Find us on the World Wide Web at www.westviewpress.com

Library of Congress has catalogued the hardcover edition as follows:

Her voice, her faith: women speak on world religions / Arvind Sharma, Katherine K. Young, editors.
    p.   cm.
    Includes bibliographical references and index.
    ISBN 0-8133-6591-0 (hardcover: alk.paper)
    1. Women and religion.   I. Sharma, Arvind.   II. Young, Katherine K., 1944-
BL458.H45   2002
200'.82—dc21

                         2002015755

ISBN 0-8133-4257-0 (paperback)

10   9   8   7   6   5   4   3   2

Contents

Preface

To APPEAL TO ONE'S *common* humanity is to appeal to something profoundly moving. However profoundly moving though, it is not unambiguous, for although our common humanity inspires us, it also obscures one fundamental fact about humanity—its even split into men and women. When asked to respond simply as a human being, what if someone asked—as what, as a man or a woman? Of course one can speak with a common voice but it is not the same voice. Isn't one able to tell whether one is talking to a man or a woman by the voice alone?

To appeal to one's faith is also to appeal to something profoundly moving—but although it is profoundly moving, it too is not unambiguous. For although one's faith inspires, it also obscures another fundamental fact of humanity—that there are many faiths. Of course one could talk of what these faiths have in common but they are not the same, a fact that becomes even more obvious when the faithful begin to talk to each other.

Once it was possible to take men alone as the main sample of the human race and the Christian faith as the prime sample of all faiths. But what could be taken as axiomatic in the imperial and rationalistic glare of the nineteenth and twentieth centuries has become problematic in the discriminating dawn of the twenty-first, which reveals these samples as merely examples. To be a man is only one example of what it means to be a human being, and to be a Christian as only one example of what it means to be a person of faith.

Her Voice, Her Faith is an attempt to unite these two new perspectives, and its various chapters are the offspring of their union. In this book women rather than men give voice to different faiths—both Christian and non-Christian—and we hope you enjoy being a part of this valuable conversation.

ARVIND SHARMA

Introduction

Katherine K. Young

SOMETHING PHENOMENAL—Indeed, historically unprecedented—happened in the second half of the twentieth century. Women recovered their religious history and challenged negative stereotypes that had become so deeply embedded in the authority of scriptures and their commentaries that they seemed to be about female nature itself. The cutting-edge scholarly contributions were built upon solid knowledge of ancient languages, both scriptural and vernacular, the detective's eye for clues to the real world of women, scrutiny of male accounts for bias, and a relentless search for texts by women and about women that had been ignored, marginalized, or reinterpreted to disguise their creativity.

Because much of this development occurred in the United States (or was inspired by the women's movement there), I am tempted to call this, in the spirit of the history of American religion, "a great awakening," adding it to other great American awakenings such as the eighteenth century's awakening of religious piety and the nineteenth century's religious fervor that transcended sectarian and denominational lines. In our present context, the term "awakening" has been expanded to include women's awakening to their religious histories and practices and their awakening to the fact that now many religions are included in a new American religious movement that is challenging the idea that secularism is here to stay. In addition, the word "awakening" is apropos for our topic because it is a quintessentially spiritual term (used for the great moment of realization by Buddhas, Hindu yogis, Taoist immortals, Jewish kabbalists, Christian and Muslim Sufi mystics, and other spiritual adepts). The word brings our story directly to the context of *insiders* of the world religions—here as female spiritual seekers in their own right, as doers of family and community rituals, and as scholarly interpreters and leaders.

The United States has become a different religious place in the second half of the twentieth century, and into the twenty-first. Diasporic communities have transformed the religious landscape with mosques, Hindu temples, and Chinese Buddhist shrines—proud visual emblems of identity and sacrality.[1] And women, in turn, have participated in the women's movement, one of the great social transformations of our time. Women have also converted to religions such as Buddhism and Wicca. It is fitting, therefore, that *Her Voice, Her Faith* should celebrate this new vision of women and world religions in which personal epiphanies begin the journeys that help us to hear in a new way.

A lot of world history is covered in the following chapters. By way of introduction, permit me to set the scene with several broad historical strokes, which also helps us to understand where we are now.

Religions of large-scale societies covered in this book—Judaism, Christianity, Islam, Hinduism, Buddhism, Confucianism, and Taoism—have several distinguishing phases. First, they are influenced, either directly or indirectly, by early civilizations. This already tells us much about the frame of our story about women and world religions. Early civilizations are informed by a class-based society with social and economic inequalities in the form of social hierarchies: exploitation by the elite to extract surplus foods, goods, and labor; political power to maintain stability; symbols, usually drawn from religions, to conceptualize status and authority; and a professionalized memory either through written records or oral transmission. Men held most of the official and bureaucratic positions, including those in religions. Even though women still had some public visibility, they were subordinate to men both in public and, with respect to men's decision-making authority, sometimes within the home as well. As Bruce G. Trigger writes, "The early civilizations were societies in which inequality was accepted as a normal condition and injustice viewed as a personal rather than a systemic evil."[2] Hierarchy was dependent on common recognition of rank and for that status symbols were necessary: special clothing, jewels, multistoried dwellings, monumental architecture, and sophisticated art.[3] Hierarchy affected women by making some women superior and others inferior. In addition, when male high status was defined by having multiple women (as concubines or wives) and/or by secluding them (as non-laborers under male control), elite women's lives were profoundly affected. Hierarchy was rarely challenged because there were obvious benefits to the new state system and its tributary relationships including political protection from acquisitive and militarily aggressive neighbors and disruption in the means of production, mainly agriculture and trade, on which *all* lives depended. For women, this meant economic security and personal protection, something that had been sorely lacking in the chaotic transition from small-scale societies to the unbridled individualism of chiefdoms and fledgling kingdoms.

In early civilizations, there was no clear line between deities who personified natural forces and deceased ancestors; in other words, the supernatural mirrored much of the natural and social worlds.[4] The cosmos was simple: a small, short-lived, or unstable earth, sometimes surrounded by an ocean and one or more celestial and subterranean realms, all of which might be encompassed by an ocean or abyss or chaos. Deities, which included both gods and goddesses (though the latter were already being marginalized), were rarely omnipotent or omniscient, they were vulnerable to age, suffering, and loss of power. They were also jealous and could harm people. More importantly, they were dependent on human beings, especially for offerings and rituals.

The consolidation of these early civilizations had a major effect yet again on the lives of women. Male power was consolidated in the public realm. Whereas the previous phase still had some queens, female traders, businesswomen, and priestesses, these were even more marginalized or disappeared altogether.[5] Because early civilizations made specialized knowledge possible, it should not surprise us that the consolidation of male power in the public realm had as its corollary male control of education and literacy (where that had developed). What is striking is the *male exclusivity* of this domain. Whereas male dominance in war (because of male size and strength), agriculture (because of the upper-body strength needed to push the plough), and long-distance trade (because of freedom from pregnancy and lactation) is understandable, male exclusivity in education seems to be without good reason. Although women were told that because of their "nature" they were lacking in reason, we know this to be otherwise. The argument that education was not possible for women because of their reproductive role is not convincing (even childhood education was denied to many women and literacy could easily be combined with domestic roles). Rather, it seems that literacy, and by extension, specialized knowledge was especially important for urban men whose bodies no longer had a functional role and identity had to be defined in a new way. When mind replaced body for elite urban men, it became an expression of high status and was made exclusive by allowing literacy and specialized education only for boys and reserving roles such as scribe, bureaucrat, and philosopher only for men. The exclusivity of this new domain was buttressed by a rhetoric of female intellectual inferiority, rhetoric made convincing by the fact that without literacy and education women were indeed intellectually inferior—a feat of culture, however, not a dictum of nature. The prejudice went that women, as laborers and reproducers, had bodies, and that men, in turn, had minds. Of course, most men also paid the price of this hierarchical system. Many were conscripted by kings to wage battle with massive loss of male life, and defeated warriors were killed outright or forced into slave or indentured labor. Many were forced into arranged marriages, and many, even most, were illiterate, too. If the minds of elite men had prestige, the bodies of ordinary men, even when of functional importance for society, were controlled by others, and were fast declining in status.[6]

This basic frame of androcentrism, created mainly by elite men, became embedded in the religions of the day to provide ultimate authority. The turn to male gods was complemented by an increase in their independence and transcendence, sometimes resulting in monotheism and usually in a male priesthood that defined the values for society—including the roles for women and men. The worldview was now framed, by and large, through *his* eyes and the role of elite women became even more limited to motherhood (though it was eulogized—in positive appreciation of this essential role but also, no doubt, in compensation for opportunities and dignities denied). Because upward mobility meant imitating the elite, this hierarchical model became replicated as groups sought to increase their status.

But curiously, this frame, which has been dubbed patriarchy, was soon challenged by branches of some of the very religions that were providing authority for it (what started out as reforms occasionally resulting in new religions). Sometimes hierarchy was criticized—both Jesus and Buddha, for instance, befriended prostitutes and criticized the corruption of priests. Sometimes hierarchy was circumvented altogether by alternative lifestyles such as wandering asceticism or following a path believed to lead to another realm, such as heavens characterized by equality or a type of transgendered state altogether. The fact that specialization, built in part upon classification, had led to distinctions of nature, society, and the supernatural in Near Eastern, Graeco-Roman, Indian, and Chinese civilizations during the first millennium B.C.E. made the world more complex and created more possibilities. Some women, too, became ascetics. Some heeded the call to join monastic communities, which set themselves apart from the dominant hierarchical society and opened the doors to literacy and education. Some contacted deities directly through possession and prophesied. And some preserved goddess traditions. The pages of this book are filled with a new cast of actors in history. In short, the world religions discussed in this book have inherited both the patriarchal frame and its critique, which gave rise to countercultures or reforms. Even though some of these were short-lived, the emerging culture was sufficiently complex that it could always inspire new adaptations or reforms.[7] We could even argue that those religions that could no longer inspire the allegiance of women and undergo reforms died on the world scene. One major trait of the religions represented in this book, after all, is that they are still today *living* religions. And after two or more millennia that is no small feat.

All this has informed the story of women and world religions, but it could not be seen clearly through *women's* eyes until the modern period.[8] The Enlightenment's ideas of liberalism and egalitarianism inspired women's critique of hierarchy. Democracy, socialism, and Marxism subsequently inspired movements for national liberation in general and women's liberation in particular. The industrial revolution contributed machines that equalized the bodies of men and women in the labor force as did the development of birth control. Small families were valued in postindustrial societies, and this released women from all-consuming reproductive roles. Finally, and most importantly, from the 1960s large numbers of women went to university and many received Ph.D.s. At the same time, many traditional religious schools opened their doors to female students and religion departments educated others and then went on to hire them. The fact that they have been increasingly joined by women of diasporic communities is absolutely critical for the insights provided by this book.

Inclusion of the insider's perspective in the study of religion is just now coming of age.[9] This is the first book written exclusively by insider women (as scholars and practitioners) on the topic of women and world religions. This new perspective leads us to new understandings. In her chapter on Hinduism, for instance, Vasudha Narayanan talks about her favorite experiences growing up in an orthoprax Sri Vaishnava household in Chennai (Madras), India. Her lived experience inspires her to reorganize the vast, complex content of this religion to capture distinguishing features of contemporary Hinduism (especially as lived by women) rather than a romp through historical periods and philosophical systems that leaves one wondering just who a Hindu today might be. Rita M. Gross speaks frankly and eloquently about her "awakening" in 1973, which led her from teaching about Buddhism as a professor to actual practice of meditation. This awakening, however, was not without its existential problems because on the surface it appeared that women in Buddhism were in the background, a situation that conflicted with her own feminist concerns for the empowerment of women. This essay bears testimony to how scholarship can help to reconcile such apparent contradictions by finding more facts and meanings within a spiritual tradition that lead to deeper understandings and insights into what women need to recover from the past or what to revise for a faith of the future. Terry Woo takes us inside a poignant moment of her life that embodies a Confucian family tradition: her father's parting words of wisdom to her as she leaves Hong Kong for study in America. The journey is more than one of crossing continents. The further she travels away, the greater her search backward intellectually and spiritually to rediscover the roots of identity. Taking Confucianism seriously once again after decades of its being maligned by Communists (especially on the topic of women) is a daunting task. But here again the tools of scholarship help Woo to recover, understand, and sift the tradition for her future (and perhaps that of others within her community), thereby meeting her father's parting words that she must put back into the community what has been given to her. In her chapter on Taoism, Eva Wong speaks of her own spiritual practice (which at certain stages must be related specifically to female bodies) and knowledge of oral traditions through the female line of spiritual adepts of Taoist meditation to complement the textual (land largely male-oriented) sources. Susannah Heschel helps us to empathize with the experience of some Jewish women of being excluded in Orthodox circles from the recitation of key prayers at the sensitive time of mourning (though her chapter shows how other forms of modern Judaism have been inclusive). And the chapter on Christianity by Mary Gerhart deftly weaves the rich history of Roman Catholicism—the author's own tradition—which has been neglected in other accounts of women and Christianity with other branches of the religion. Riffat Hassan reminds us all how important mothers have been in encouraging their daughters to explore the educational opportunities of the modern world, which they themselves had been denied in the name of tradition. But easier said than done, Hassan reveals to us. Despite her upbringing with wealth and status, her journey through knowledge into freedom and personhood had its trials. It meant fierce debates and going back to the scriptures to find out for herself what they said and how they spoke about and to women. Sometimes it's mothers, sometimes it's a professor's students who point to new paths, and sometimes it's both. The latter was the case for Wendy Griffin, who accepted her student's invitation for the class to join a ritual celebrating the spring equinox. This led to research on Wicca and then into her gradual recognition that this orientation spoke to her in a spiritual way, a way that also seemed like going home, back into her childhood experiences of a summer girls' camp run by her mother. As in Wicca, there were meditations in nature, silent processions, and myths spoken around the campfire. Given that the authors have had to be ruthlessly selective for the space assigned, they have accomplished quite a feat: to give us entrance to religious worldviews, not to mention the insider women's take, and make us want to learn still more.

These developments have produced some intriguing paradoxes. Despite men's virtual control of the public sphere of religion over many centuries, we find that they have had to turn to women's knowledge on occasion for an authoritative voice. This reminds us that orality, too, is powerful and can be transmitted through the generations—in this case, mother to daughter or female guide to female student—contributing thereby to women's reputation as wise and knowledgeable. Another paradox is that women's entrance to mass literacy and scholarship has made possible the literate record of women's oral traditions. This is especially true of those scholars who use their training in the anthropology of religion to record women's memories of customs and wisdom and their actual rituals, spirit-possessions, and spiritual journeys.

In my estimation, it is important to present a nuanced picture of women and world religions in order to avoid the extremes of those who criticize the world religions as unredeemably patriarchal and blame all of women's and society's problems on the sheer malice of men—the seedbed of misandry.[10] This book shows how those women who are insiders to the world religions struggle with these issues. It also shows how they struggle with conflicts between continuity (encompassing both identity and spirituality) and discontinuity (the need for reforms, especially for inclusion not to mention leadership, in what were once exclusive male spheres). But this book also brings to attention the traditions of some marginalized religions where women once were or still are central to the vision of religion.

An enormous interest in primal religions of small-scale societies has emerged as women recover their macro-history. Goddesses abound in many of these religions, as do priestesses, female shamans, and other custodians of ritual and community identity. Many primal religions are marked by an integral worldview that deeply connects nature, society, and the supernatural. And some are also marked by a spirit of egalitarianism. All of this has become terribly relevant to women of contemporary Wiccan groups in their search to recover knowledge of women's religious lives and to learn from it when reforming the present.

Her Voice, Her Faith documents neglected voices. It was first necessary to get the "female" voice up to strength so it could really speak again. Now, curiously, this voice is so strong in some feminist circles that it is producing female-centered (gynocentric) worldviews to replace the old male (androcentric) ones. Despite their prevailing androcentrism, the latter were a mix of premodern, general human, and specific male (elite) perspectives. Some of us now recognize that there is still much to be learned about maleness (through modern science) and masculinities (through the phenomenology of private male experience, male embodiment, and societal role impositions). Ironically, the particular male voice needs to be strengthened today in some ways (just as women have had to do this for themselves so men must take up the task) and women need to empathize with the new insights that this has to offer. The goal, as I see it, is stereophonic sound. When both the male and female voice become of equal strength (in a balance that also considers the contributions of both insiders and outsiders), we may begin to see for the first time three-dimensional religious worlds—fully of the two genders (and multiple cultures) but also of the human dimension that transcends their particularities—and then we may begin to see the one world of us all. This goal, of stereophonic sound, I hope, will inform the religious voices of the future. And from them, of course, may come another great awakening!

I

Hinduism

By Vasudha Narayanan

WHEN I WAS A CHILD in South India, my favorite festival was Navaratri, dedicated to three goddesses, Sarasvati, Lakshmi, and Durga. Navaratri, which means "nine nights," begins on the new moon that falls between mid-September and mid-October and runs through ten days. A room in our house would be set apart and filled with exquisite dolls for plays about the goddesses. Elaborate tableaux were put in place to depict stories from thousands of years of Hindu texts. In the center of the room were large images and clay dolls of the goddesses. As we set up the many scenes, my aunts or my grandmother would narrate tales connected with the tableaux. Some Hindus celebrate Navaratri to mark the victory of the goddess Durga over the buffalo-demon Mahisha. Others, especially in northern India, think of it as the time when Rama, the divine incarnation of the Lord Vishnu, battled with the demon Ravana.

Every evening during this fall festival, women and children wearing soft, bright silks visited each other, admired the kolu, or display of dolls, played musical instruments, and sang songs in praise of one or another of many Hindu deities, from the repertoire of South Indian classical music. It was a joyous time of festivity, music, elegance, and beauty—a glorious celebration of womanhood. The last two days were dedicated to Sarasvati and Lakshmi. These were special holidays, and we did not have to go to school. Large pictures of the two, draped with garlands of fresh flowers, were kept in front of the display of dolls.

On the day dedicated to Sarasvati, we solemnly put in front of her all our musical instruments, writing devices, selected textbooks, and the kolu, to be blessed by her for the year to come. We did not read or write that day: we relaxed while Sarasvati did the work, blessing every pen and pencil, the lonely typewriter, the string instruments called vinas, and every one of our science, geography, and algebra books. The next day, the victorious tenth day (Vijaya Dashami), is dedicated to Lakshmi.

But first we had to finish Sarasvati's business. After a ritual bath early in the morning, we lit lamps and incense, bowed down before her, picked up our pens and wrote "Sri" to begin the new scholarly year (this was not the calendrical new year) with an auspicious word. New prayers and pieces of music were learned; new knowledge was to be acquired that day. Even as children, we knew that Sarasvati was the goddess of learning and Lakshmi was the goddess of all good fortune; and on the last days of the Navaratri festival, the fortune of learning, the wealth of wisdom, and the joy of music were given to us, every year, by the grace of the goddesses. Victory was ours, for the rest of the year. After the victorious tenth day, the dolls returned to their boxes in the attic, and the pictures of Lakshmi and Sarasvati went back up on the walls in the family room.

Most Hindus learn about their religion through stories, music, and dance, going to temples, and participating in rituals, festivals, and pilgrimages. These are the first entry points and, for many, all the religion that they will get in life. In general, most Hindus living in India do not worry about religious doctrines, fixed times of prayers, or a historical unfolding of events.

Many introductory texts on Hinduism take the reader through an important and standard list of topics. These include the origins, that is, the Indus Valley Civilization, the Indo-Aryans; the earliest religious compositions starting with the Vedas and the emphasis on sacrifice; philosophical enquiry in the Upanishads; the two epics; the Bhagavad Gita, which is part of one of the epics, law books, the caste system, stages of life, six systems of philosophy; the important philosophers of Vedanta (Shankara, Ramanuja, Madhva, et al.); the devotional (bhakti) movement; and then fast forward to reforms in the nineteenth and twentieth centuries. This conceptual system is not one that we can necessarily label as just "male"; the credit for this descriptive list is shared between the high-caste brahmin male scholars, well versed in Sanskrit, who collaborated with the British in the production of the Hindu traditions, and Western scholars influenced by Enlightenment paradigms of history and religion. These lists are neither wrong nor unimportant, but they do exclude the experiences of women and the millions whose knowledge of religious phenomena has not come through the Sanskrit language or Brahmanical modes of perception.

I write both as an academic and as a woman who was raised in a particular Hindu tradition, or sampradaya, called the Sri Vaishnava, theologically, and Ayyangar, socially. Having lived in a relatively orthoprax household in India, I found it difficult to reconcile my understanding of the Hindu tradition with the depictions of it in Western textbooks. Many studies of religious traditions in the West begin with questions of history, prophets, leaders, and beliefs. As a Sri Vaishnava Hindu woman, I grew up associating my tradition with culinary customs, distinctive names for foods, performing arts, rituals, and localized pilgrimage centers. In this chapter, we will look at rituals and situations that most Hindus will be familiar with in some manner and put them in perspective to enhance our understanding. The four sites I have chosen are homes, weddings, temples, and funerals.

Most Hindus are fond of the saying "Hinduism is more than a religion, it is a way of life," whereas most introductory texts and Western understandings of the tradition have focused on the "otherworldly" issues such as karma, reincarnation, and the idea of a Supreme Being. Hindus will tell you that the closest word in Sanskrit for religion is dharma. Dharma is more ambiguous and far reaching in scope than religion itself. Coming from the root dhr, meaning to support or to sustain, it is most popularly translated as righteousness or duty. And yet, in other contexts, it may mean the way to salvation or liberation (moksha), ethics, and much more. The M. Monier-Williams Sanskrit-English Dictionary gives seventeen meanings: religion, the customary observances of a caste or sect, law usage and practice, religious or moral merit, virtue, righteousness, duty, justice, piety, morality, sacrifice, and so forth. From a Western understanding, however, the many books on dharma containing these topics are often not considered part of religion. These topics include human behavior (acara), justice (vyavahara), and repentance/atonement rites (prayascitta). Other classifications are more elaborate. Pandurang Kane, the twentieth century's pre-eminent writer of the history of dharma, starts his second volume on the subject with the "Topics of Dharma Shastra" (Dharma

Shastra: texts on dharma) and includes the duties of the classes and castes of society and stages of life; sacraments from conception to death; the duties of the different stages of life; the days when one should not study the Vedas; marriage; the duties of women; the relationship between husband and wife; ritual purity and impurity; rites of death and rituals for ancestors; gifts and donations; crime and punishment; contacts; inheritance; activities done only at times of crises; mixed castes; and so on. Although this list is extensive, it does not exhaust the other areas that the term dharma covers (Kane, volume II, chapter 1, pp. 1–2).

Texts on dharma have always been only selectively followed, and local customs have tempered the rule of the books. In some parts of India, dharma texts such as the Manu Smriti were not well known, and certainly large parts of them were ignored (Kishwar). Although Hindu traditions are portrayed, and quite correctly in some instances, as being patriarchal, the system has built-in mechanisms to allow for dynamic reinterpretation. This wiggle room can serve to legitimatize progressive action. The Vedas, the tradition of the epics and puranas, actions of the righteous, and finally doing what is dear to one's soul—that is, to act after much thought and according to the dictates of one's conscience—all these are the sources of dharma (Kane volume I, part I, p. 7, 1968). The last of these allows women, or anyone who may feel marginalized, to appropriate or redefine rituals. Particular theologies of traditions or schools (sampradaya), which depend on historical theologians for the interpretation of sacred texts, may emphasize carefully argued worldviews. The succession of teachers in each school will espouse and teach the philosophy of that tradition. Thus, the teachers in the Sri Vaishnava community say that the universe is the "body" of God, teachers of Advaita assert that there is only one reality, and followers of Madhva declare that God and the soul are distinct. The theology may be nonnegotiable, but there will be more latitude in modes of prayer and worship, which can be redefined by women.

THE HOME FOR THE HINDU TRADITION

Many Hindu sacraments, rituals, and festivals are conducted at home, and from some perspectives a Hindu can be very religious without ever leaving the house. Spatially, there may be a special room, or at least an altar, set apart for worship (puja). Several days in a year may be spent in the celebration of major ritual festivals. Religious rituals associated with birth, puberty, pregnancy, and death take place at home. It is here that a child will first hear stories from the Hindu epics or encounter them through television broadcasts. It is here that the most enduring associations between religion and food will be made, the first prayers learned. It is in the home that Hindu tradition has been transmitted primarily for women.

A Hindu child's earliest exposure to her or his religious tradition comes from seeing daily rituals at the puja altar, with its many pictures and images of local gods and goddesses, as well as those brought as souvenirs on distant pilgrimages. Every day, or even twice a day, the mother may light an oil lamp in front of this altar. The women may draw symmetrical geometric designs with rice flour in front of the altar or in front of the house. These patterns are also drawn outside shrines in South Indian temples. Family members may recite prayers regularly; there may be copies of holy texts or prayer books that people may read or recite. Red powder, known as the kumkum, may be taken from the altar and placed on one's forehead. Flowers and fruits may be offered to the deities on the altar and then used by the devotee.

There are other simple acts that straddle the grey area between religion and culture. One of the first acts a child is taught when he or she is barely a year old is to join the palms together in an act of adoration. This act, which is common in the West only during acts of prayer, is called a namaskara or namaste (literally, "I bow before you") in India and used when greeting people or when praying. There are many other such practices that form part of this vast religious culture. Putting a mark on your forehead as part of your daily routine indicates auspiciousness or which Hindu community you belong to. You must eat, give, and receive with your right hand; it is disrespectful to give with your left hand—the right hand is used for all socially acceptable actions but the left for cleaning the body. You should bow down in front of elders and seek their blessings on important occasions. Elders should bless younger people with standard phrases or wish them all happiness. The list of rituals is long, and many of them are internalized by the time a child enters school, but it is through these simple acts that one participates in the larger Hindu culture.

DEITIES AND FESTIVALS

Hindus narrate stories about Vishnu, Shiva, or the goddesses, sing about them, and dance their stories in many cultural performances. The performing arts are one of the main vehicles for expressing Hindu religious culture. In the diaspora, learning classical dance like Bharata Natyam becomes one of the main ways in which the child learns about Hindu culture.

Birthdays for the gods Krishna and Rama and stories associated with their lives are most popular all over India. Hindus consider Rama and Krishna to be incarnations of the Lord Vishnu, one of the most important deities in India. Vishnu (the one who pervades) is mentioned in the earliest literature, the Vedas (ca. 1750 B.C.E.), but became popular at a later time. Many of the gods spoken about in the early Vedic hymns have now been forgotten. By the beginning of the Common Era, Vishnu was considered to have incarnated to earth several times. In the popular versions of these narratives, he is said to have come down nine times and is predicted to come again one more time at the end of this cycle of time. Vishnu's first incarnation in this series is said to be as a fish. In a story reminiscent of many flood narratives, Vishnu wanted to save Manu, a pious man, his family, and seven rishis (holy men) from a catastrophic flood. Manu gets all of them and the seeds of all animals into a boat, harnesses it to the divine fish, the form that Vishnu has taken, and rides out the flood (O'Flaherty, pp. 181–84).

Some of the most popular stories a child will hear, the songs she will learn, or the dances she will see will be connected with Rama and Krishna. The story of Rama is told in the Ramayana (The Way of Rama), a Sanskrit epic from the fifth century B.C.E. and an integral part of Hindu culture. Rama is married to Sita, a beautiful princess, popularly considered the incarnation of the Goddess Lakshmi. Because Lakshmi and Vishnu are inseparable, she incarnates every time Vishnu comes down to earth. Rama is exiled because of a family intrigue; Sita and Lakshmana, Rama's brother, accompany him to the forest. Here, Ravana, a king of Lanka, lusting after Sita, kidnaps her. After an epic battle, in which Rama is helped by Hanuman (a wise, divine monkey who is also a popular Hindu deity), Ravana is killed and Sita returns to Rama. Rama and Sita then return home to Ayodhya and are coronated. Rama's rule of the kingdom is held to be paradigmatic, as are his filial piety, the loyalty of Sita, and the devotion and service of Hanuman.

Krishna is considered the eighth or ninth incarnation of Vishnu, depending on which text you read, and is beloved in India and in many parts of the world, where members of the International Society of Krishna Consciousness (ISKCON, more popularly known as the Hare Krishnas) and other Hindus live. Children are told about Krishna's divine birth, his magical childhood, his mother's and foster mother's love for him, his mischievous pranks, his dancing the autumnal moonlit nights away with the young cowherd girls he grew up with, and his philosophical counsel to his cousin and peer, Arjuna, on the battlefield. The enchanting evenings of dance are emulated in autumn in some communities in India. The battle to destroy the forces of evil is celebrated annually. One such festival is Deepavali (Diwali), the festival of lights, celebrated with great enthusiasm by Hindus all over the world.

Deepavali and Navaratri are two of the best-known home celebrations. Deepavali (literally necklace of lamps) is celebrated on the eve of the new moon that falls between mid-October and mid-November. Although most Hindus observe it, the reasons for celebration differ among the various regions. Hindus from some parts of northern India believe that Lord Rama returned to Ayodhya after his victorious battle with the evil Ravana that day and that the kingdom lit lamps all over to mark the celebrations. In other parts of India, it is believed that Lord Krishna fought a long battle with Narakasura (demon of hell) and won the battle on the dawn of this new-moon day. To commemorate this victory of good over evil, Hindus in every home let off fireworks, mimicking the noise of Krishna's war against evil, and light lamps to celebrate the victory of light over the forces of darkness. Special sweets and candies are made at home; new clothes are bought and worn. In some parts of South India, Hindus believe that the sacred river Ganga is spiritually present in all water. Early on the morning of Deepavali, even before dawn, people take a special ritual bath using oil and fragrant herbs, and some communities greet each other with the rhetorical question: "Have you bathed in the waters of the Ganga?" Bathing in this river is said to purify a human being, and one begins this day with this physical and mental purity. Hindus from Gujarat celebrate their new year at this time (most others celebrate it in March or April).

Hindus from Punjab spend the nights in ritual gambling and invite Lakshmi, the goddess of good fortune, to their houses. In most parts of India, gifts of dried fruits and sweets are given to friends and cash bonuses are given to employees. In some states like Bengal and Kerala, the festival is the most important of the year.

In general, in most parts of India, goddesses are worshipped during Navaratri. The celebrations in Calcutta are communal and in honor of the Goddess Durga. Many Hindus who are devotees of her think that she is the manifestation of the Supreme Being. Like other rituals that are celebrated to mark particular stories, here too there is one that speaks about the victory of good over evil. The buffalo-demon Mahisha was terrorizing human beings, and none of the gods could subdue him. The energies of Brahma, Vishnu, and Shiva—the three male gods important in many of the Sanskrit texts—combined, and out of this power emerged Durga (unapproachable), the mighty Goddess. Beautiful and strong, she came striding on a lion. The demon tried to woo and marry her; she rejected him with contempt and after a battle lasting nine nights and ten days, she emerged victorious. This victory is celebrated on the last day of the festival, the Vijaya Dashami (the victorious tenth day). In Calcutta, it has become a practice for each part of the city to make a giant effigy of the goddess, usually set against a modern contextual background. For the days of the Durga Puja (worship of Durga), this effigy is thought to possess divine energy, and at the end of it, all the effigies are taken to the river Ganga and ritually immersed. There, her energies return to the universe.

In parts of South India, Sarasvati, Lakshmi, and Durga are all worshipped during the nine days. In the South Indian states of Tamilnadu, Karnataka, and Andhra Pradesh, the festival is very much a home celebration, and very much a women's celebration. Here, in some castes and some communities, women put up temporary altars in the largest room in the house. Several steps, usually seven or nine, of altars are set up in each house, covered with cloth to resemble gallery seats and adorned with beautiful dolls. Traditional clay dolls of deities intermingle with secular dolls. Once set up, the whole area becomes sacred. This display of dolls, the kolu (royal court), is said to be the divine court of the deities. Toy trains, mini-waterfalls, parks, tiny gardens are all created as works of art, all in the main room of the house. For the next nine days, this functions essentially as the family altar. Food offerings are made to the deities, and prayers said. Once the display is set up, the line between secular and sacred dolls is obliterated, and the whole area is sacred. Viewed from the locus of devotion, any space, any object can be seen as diffused with or as a container for the divine. And yet others consider these displays to have pedagogical or entertainment value; displays teach, instruct, offer pleasure and joy. Women go from house to house in the evenings to visit and admire the doll displays. Singers trained in classical music sing songs, in honor of the goddess. Through sight and sound, the goddess is glorified and praised.

The creative energies of the goddess are venerated in Gujarat, where she is celebrated in her non-iconic form, that of a flame that shines bright through a clay pot that has ornamental orifices. This is the garbha, or womb, and women sing joyous songs and dance around it all evening and night. Women do this dance every night of the Navaratri and during any auspicious ritual at home and in the community. The garbha is followed by the ras lila, a circular dance with sticks, performed by men and women. Whereas the garbha glorifies the goddess, the ras, which has been popular in the last few centuries, re-creates the magical atmosphere of the fall nights when Krishna danced with the cowherd girls. Both these dances are traditionally domestic in nature but over the years have become mega-events in local communities.

Durga and many other goddesses are worshipped all over India. Though the names and nature of the goddesses may have changed, some of these practices have likely survived for more than four millennia. The goddess and a buffalo figure (the antecedent of Mahisha) first appear in the Indus Valley Civilization, also known as the Harappa Culture, around 3000 B.C.E. The earliest archaeological evidence of Indian culture is found along the banks of the river Indus (which in Sanskrit is sindhu, the word from which both Hindu and India derive). The Indus Valley Civilization was contemporary with Mesopotamia and probably traded with it. Although the script of this civilization has not been deciphered to everyone's satisfaction, seals found in this area indicate that there was goddess worship and veneration of a deity who is later identified as Shiva. The Indus Valley Civilization died out around 1750 B.C.E., and it was at about this time that the Vedas, the earliest scriptures of the Hindu tradition, were composed. The worship of the goddess, therefore, likely had its origins in the earliest cultures of India.

PERFORMING ARTS

Over the millennia, educated Hindus have recognized four Vedas as authoritative. The Vedas were composed between 1750 to the sixth century B.C.E. and then transmitted orally over the generations. In the philosophical and ceremonial traditions in India, there has been a continuous tradition of using some sections of the Vedas as sources of authority and reciting some hymns daily for over three millennia. Music and dance are supposed to be derived from the ancient text Natya Shastra (Treatise on Dance) composed by Bharata Muni, at the beginning of the Common Era, and many consider it the Fifth Veda, a scripture that, when followed, will lead one to the supreme goal of salvation or liberation.

Most Hindus, however, have not generally been familiar with large tracts of the Vedas and many of the archaic deities mentioned in them. And so, over the centuries, a few other seminal texts have been considered to be the Fifth Veda. The epic Mahabharata (ca. 500 B.C.E. to 400 C.E.), which along with the Ramayana, recounts one of the most beloved narratives of the Hindus, and the Natya Shastra have been counted as the Fifth Veda by Hindus at various times.

Worship in the Hindu tradition includes music from the time of the Vedas. The mystical syllable om is considered the beginning of sound in the universe and a manifestation of the Supreme Being. Knowledge of the proper nature of sound and its expressions are therefore considered to be religious knowledge. The Vedas specify the different kinds of pitch and tone by which the verses are to be recited.

Classical music in South India has been for the most part religious in nature. Treatises on music speak of a divine line of teachers, beginning with Shiva and Parvati, and also mention worship of Sarasvati as the patron goddess of the fine arts. Some Hindu texts say that Vishnu and Sri are manifested as Nada Brahman or the Supreme Being in the form of sound. Sound, if properly controlled and articulated, can lead one to a mystical experience, and the sound of the music is considered as important as the lyrics. Nadopasana, meditation through sound, has become popular as one form of religious practice. The Supreme Being is supposed to manifest divinity on earth in the form of sound, just as an icon is a visual representation of the divine.

Singing and dancing can function in various ways to take one closer to a higher state of consciousness or even to communion with the deity. Some may understand the lyrics or the emotions conveyed in religious dances as giving rise to devotion in the audience; others may think of the "flavors" of emotions as heightening their consciousness; still others may think of just the pure movement and the music, even when devoid of any lyrics or emotions, as being divine. Dancers frequently depict stories from the Ramayana and the Mahabharata as well as the beloved narratives from later scriptures called the Puranas. The many Puranas (Purana means "ancient lore") were composed primarily in the first millennium of the Common Era. These books extol deities who had become very popular by then, including Vishnu, Shiva, and Devi, especially in her form as Durga.

THE LUNAR CALENDAR, FOOD, FEASTING, AND FASTING

Many of the festivals celebrated at home occur on dates calculated according to the phases of the moon. Hindu calendars are lunar but adjusted to the solar year, so, like Easter or Yom Kippur, they come at the same time of the year, though not on the same dates. Navaratri, in fact, coincides with the nine holy days starting with Rosh Hashanah of the Jewish calendar in most years, though occasionally they may occur one lunar cycle later. Apart from festivals, every lunar cycle is marked with days of fasting and feasting at home. On the eleventh day after the new moon (ekadashi), many people, especially the followers of the god Vishnu, stay away from grains. Fasts, like many rituals, come in various forms: some involve abstinence from all food and water or from grain only or certain vegetables like eggplant, which are considered to be filled with seeds, and therefore, potential life forms; or all sour foods. Other kinds of ritual fasts permit the eating of only fruits. Women in many parts of India observe special days of fasting and feasting in connection with votive rituals called vratas.

These rituals, which involve a day or more of strict fasting, are done in honor of specific goddesses and for various purposes (Pintchman). Women from Uttar Pradesh and Punjab, dressed in their wedding finery, observe the Karva Chauth fast, which usually comes soon after Navaratri. They fast from dawn to dusk and break their fast after seeing the rising moon. This fast is undertaken on the fourth day of the waning lunar cycle between October and November and is done to pray for and preserve conjugal happiness. Other fasts are done for the welfare of the family. There are regular fasts like Ekadashi, which men and women observe, and special ritual fasts that only women observe. Although some of these ritual fasts occur in a patriarchal context (prayers for the husband or son), some scholars see even these as empowering to women (Pintchman, McGee, Pearson).

Food is central to the practice of the Hindu tradition; next to weddings, food commands the most space and energy of the writers of the texts on dharma. In practice, specific lentils and vegetables have to be prepared for specific occasions. In Tamilnadu, for instance, these are prepared for happy (auspicious) occasions and others for inauspicious events and rituals such as those connected with death. Contrary to popular perception, most Hindus are not vegetarian, but certain castes and communities may avoid fish, fowl, or meat. Onions, garlic, and mushrooms are not considered to be part of a pure diet by many followers of Vishnu; early texts on dharma have a blanket decree against these foods. Right eating is not just what you can eat or avoid; in the texts on dharma as well as in orthoprax houses, it involves issues such as the caste and gender of the cook (preferably male and high caste, or the lady of the house, except at times when she is menstruating); the times you may eat (twice a day, not during twilight times, not during eclipses, and a wide variety of other instances); not eating food cooked the day before; and so on. In earlier times other directives were also in vogue; in detail, some of these equaled or even surpassed those given in many Confucian texts. The order of food courses in a meal, the direction in which the diner must sit (preferably facing east or north), how much you may eat (the number of morsels depending on the stage of life), the materials with which the eating vessels should be made, what is to be done with left-over food—were all topics for discussion. Many such directives, and some that were common to the local region, were followed for centuries.

There were several strict rules concerning with whom you may dine (and the ideal is to dine alone!). Silence was recommended for the time of dining except to inquire after a guest's needs. Most texts say—and this was followed till probably the mid-twentieth century—that one may dine only with people of the same caste and with people one knows. It was believed in many circles that one shares the sins of the people one dines with, especially if one sits in a single row with them. Even up to the time of India's independence, college food services in South India were divided along simplified caste lines—with dining halls for brahmins only, and separate ones for non-brahmin (vegetarian) and non-brahmin (non-vegetarian).

The greatest amount of discourse involved forbidden foods, which varied through the different time periods and among authors. It is generally agreed that most people ate meat, even beef, possibly up to the beginning of the Common Era. It is a matter of some controversy whether Indians ate beef during the time of the Vedas and whether the cow was a protected animal then, but it seems to be fairly well accepted that most Indians ate other kinds of meat and fowl. Several writers have noted that it is remarkable that a whole culture seems to have slowly given up meat eating or at least that meat eating ceased to be the norm after the first centuries of the Common Era. In popular understanding and by fitting a template from philosophical discourses on what we eat, food, like people and even deities, is said to tend toward three characteristics: purity (sattva), energy and passion (rajas), sloth and stupor (tamas). Although this is not clearly discussed in the early texts on dharma, most Hindus have tried to fit in food regulations with these categories.

The home is also the location of many domestic sacraments. The birth of a child is celebrated as an auspicious event, but the mother and the family are said to be in a state of "ritual pollution." Death is inauspicious and also ritually polluting to the family. Other rituals, such as those associated with pregnancy, are celebrated with joy at home. Among domestic sacraments, the wedding is treated at great length by the writers of dharma and is celebrated with considerable sanctity and social pomp.

THE HINDU WEDDING

Weekend newspapers in India have supplements devoted to matrimonial advertisements, which resemble, to some extent, the personal ads in the United States. The worldwide web has also gotten into the act, with sites for ads. Most ads are placed by the bride or bridegroom's parents and mention the potential bride or groom's physical attributes, education, occupation, horoscope, community, sub-caste, clan, and language. Let us examine two such ads, from the June 20, 2000, on-line edition of a newspaper.

> # 1 ALLIANCE INVITED for B.Tech. (Mech), MS (Engg. Mechanics), Project Engineer, Detroit, USA, H1-Visa Holder, Tamil Iyer, Parasara, Brahacharanam, Sadhayam, Suddha Jadhagam, 28/177, from Iyer girls, professionally qualified, articulate and good looking. Boy visiting India August 2000. Respond with horoscope, bio-data, family details. Box No. xxxx, Hyderabad- 500016.

> # 2 VADAGALAI ATHREYAM Poosam, 32/ 170/ 15,000, B.Com, owns business/house in Chennai with Mars (Eighth place) seeks suitable unemployed graduate girl from same sect only. Reply with horoscope, details to Box No. Chennai–600002.

The diligent South Indian reader will immediately recognize that the advertisers are looking for brides of the brahmin caste. The key words here are Iyer in the first ad and Vadagalai in the second. Iyer is a term used for brahmins from the Tamil-speaking area—specifically followers of the theologian Shankara (eighth to ninth centuries C.E). Vadagalai indicates that the family is Tamil-speaking brahmin and belongs to a community (sampradaya) that follows the theologian Ramanuja (eleventh century).

The caste system has been one of the main features of religion in South Asia. Caste is used as shorthand for thousands of stratified social communities that have developed over the centuries. The beginnings of the caste system can be seen in the Hymn to the Supreme Being that is part of the Rig Veda, one of the four Vedas (Purusa Sukta v. 12—Rig Veda 10.90). The Hymn enumerates the priestly, ruling, mercantile, and servant classes—the four varnas (literally, colors):

From his mouth came the priestly class,
from his arms, the rulers.
The producers came from his legs;
from his feet came the servant class.

Although the origins of the caste system can be seen in these verses from the Rig Veda, it is probable that, long before their composition, a stratification of society had already taken place. From the simple fourfold structure eventually arose a plethora of endogamous social and occupational divisions, so that today in India, there are more than 1,000 jatis (birth groups). The English word "caste" comes from the Portuguese, who used "casta" to refer to the various sections of Hindu society. The modern word signifies both the four broad varnas and the minutely divided jatis, although Western scholars sometimes translate varna as class and jati as caste.

By the first centuries of the Common Era, many treatises on the nature of righteousness, moral duty, and law had been written. These were the Dharma Shastras, and they form the basis for later Hindu laws. The most famous of these, the Manava Dharma Shastra, or the Laws of Manu, probably codified around the first century C.E., reflect the social norms of the time. We see the caste system firmly in place. Women had slipped to an inferior position from the relatively high status they had had in the Vedas.

When reading Manu, we must understand that the prescriptive behavior he records for the various castes was seldom followed strictly (Kishwar). In a similar vein, we have to take his pronouncements on women with a grain of salt.

According to texts on dharma, only the brahmins—the priestly class of society—had the authority to teach and learn the Vedas. The term "priestly," by the way, is used loosely here; not all members of this community were priests. Frequently, they were in the business of teaching and counseling; some specialized in domestic rituals; a few conducted temple services. Even when not engaged in religious pursuits, they held the power and prestige generally associated with spiritual learning. The monopoly that the brahmins exercised in teaching the Vedas orally was jealously guarded, and for centuries these hymns were not written down. The second caste in the traditional list is the rajanya or royal class. Kings and rulers emerged from this group. Eventually the term rajanya was replaced with the better-known word kshatriya. The men from this community were allowed to learn but not teach the Vedas. Their dharma was to protect the people and the country. The kshatriyas generally traced their ancestry either to the lineage of the sun (surya vamsha or solar dynasty) or the moon (chandra vamsha or lunar dynasty), both going back to the primeval progenitors of humanity—a classic instance of a ruling class seeking legitimacy by invoking divine antecedents. Even usurpers of thrones began to trace their ancestries in this way. In the Hindu tradition, both then and now, lines of claimed biological descent are all-important. The kshatriya families held the power of rulership and governance, and rituals of later Hinduism explicitly emphasized their connection with divine beings.

The mercantile class (vaishyas) was to be in charge of most commercial transactions. According to the codes of law, they, like the ruling class, had the authority to study but not teach the Vedas. They were to rear cattle, trade, and deal with agricultural work. The power of wealth and economic decisions lay with this community.

The last class mentioned formally by Manu and in the other texts on dharma is the shudras, generally translated as "servants." The Dharma Shastras say that the duty of a shudra is to serve the other classes, especially the brahmins. Shudras who desire to obtain good karma are advised to know their duty, to commit no sin, and to imitate the practice of virtuous men without reciting sacred texts. The shudra was not allowed to accumulate wealth. There was no area of power that the shudra could tap into; a shudra could be respected because of his or her old age and for no other reason. It is also important to note that the caste system is far more complex and flexible than the descriptions in the dharma texts—for example, a caste of wealthy landowners, the Vellalas, though technically a shudra caste, has wielded considerable economic and political power in the south.

There are hundreds of castes now in India and similarly, hundreds of communities. For instance, although the people in the first two ads are both from the brahmin caste, and both Tamil-speaking, they come from different social communities that follow different theological traditions and will not generally intermarry. The two communities follow two different theologians, Shankara and Ramanuja. The followers of Ramanuja worship Vishnu and Lakshmi (also known as Sri) and are called the Sri

Vaishnavas. Sri Vaishnava is the name of the community or theological tradition; members of it may be of different castes, and in the case of the advertisement above, happen to be brahmin. These brahmin Sri Vaishnavas are further subdivided along sectarian lines. The beginnings of this split came about through differing emphases in theological interpretations in the thirteenth and fourteenth centuries and again crystallized as different social groups (Vadagalai or northern sect and Tenkalai or southern sect). For some centuries, there was no intermarrying between these subgroups of the Sri Vaishnava community; only recently have intermarriages occurred. The person who has placed the advertisement is, however, conservative; having identified himself as a Vadagalai, he has invited correspondence only from the same sect.

Sometimes caste and community may conflate or community may be emphasized more than caste. Thus, communities like Vellala, Reddy, Kallar, or Nadar emphasize those names, and one may not be sure if these are castes or communities. Some of these caste/communities cross religious lines; in many parts of Gujarat and Rajasthan, one finds common castes between the mercantile communities of the Hindu and Jain traditions. Similarly, in South India, the Nadar and Vellala castes/communities are found among Hindus and Christians. The following advertisement in the same list as the earlier two is an example:

#3 C.S.I. NADAR, B.E. (Civil), 22/160 cms, very fair, beautiful, daughter of Senior Engineer seeks Doctors/ Engineers. Box xxxx

Here, CSI stands for Church of South India, an umbrella group that contains many Protestant denominations, and Nadar refers to the specific caste to which the potential bride (who is identified as having an undergraduate civil engineering degree, B.E.) belongs. Caste, therefore, is a strong institution among many religions of South Asia, including Hindus, Jains, and Christians.

There are groups that are technically "out" of this caste structure—people who, over the centuries, have been called outcastes or untouchables. The Sanskrit name for these many groups was panchama or "fifth [group]," the group outside the fourfold caste system. At various times, reformers have tried to integrate people from these groups into society. Ramanuja (c. 1017–1137), for instance, is said to have called them

Tirukuḷattar (sacred clan) and Mahatma Gandhi named them Harijan (Children of God). Since independence, the name "scheduled caste" (SC) has been the administrative and social category. Harijan is seen as patronizing and has been shaken off in favor of the term Dalit (protestor). These groups were, in the past centuries, discriminated against by other castes and frequently lived outside the villages. People from many such groups converted to Christianity, but the caste followed them; today there are SC Hindus and SC Christians. Government quotas in education and job opportunities have helped alleviate past inequities. In the following advertisement, again from the same crop of matrimonials, the potential bridegroom says he is SC:

#4 HINDU SC, AD, DGO, Doctor, 27/ 163, Employed- Private Hospital, Chennai, expects alliance as Doctor/Engineer/Govt. Executives. Send horoscope: Box xxx Chennai–600002.

The code AD stands for Adi Dravida, an umbrella term for people believed to have descended from the indigenous inhabitants of India. These "outcastes" are seen both as people who did not belong to the caste system, and also as those who did not belong to the four large (theoretical) divisions of the society. In the past, they had to perform the least desirable tasks in a village, tasks that were considered ritually polluting. In ancient Tamil society, for instance, those who beat the large village drums (parai) were considered to be polluted because the drums were made by stretching animal hides over large frames. The drummers (paraia) were considered to be outcastes; from them comes the English word pariah.

There is one final social classification that we need to take into account before we move to other issues that make up a Hindu's identity. This is a relatively minor one, but which, like much else in the Hindu tradition, goes back to the Vedic period and pertains to weddings, especially in the so-called higher castes. This is the notion of gotra. Gotra literally means cow-shed or cow-pen and is said to refer to a physical and spiritual joint family of followers of holy men (rishis or seers) who intuitively perceived the Vedas and transmitted them. There were seven such traditional rishis, and eventually an eighth one was added. Many high-caste people consider themselves to be part of these lineages and use the gotra name in all their sacraments and rituals to identify themselves. Gotra names have been transmitted through male descendants. Women have the gotras of their fathers and then their husbands. Marriages within the same gotra are forbidden by Hindu law. Originally a brahmin institution, gotras became part of the higher castes' identity for many centuries, but today in many parts of India, the concept is confined once again to brahmin communities. In some matrilineal communities such as the Bhants of Mangalore, gotras are not followed. In the first matrimonial advertisements above, the bridegroom is of the Parashara gotra, and in the second, the advertiser belongs to the Atreya gotra. Thus, only women belonging to non-Parashara gotra can apply to the first and non-Atreya gotra to the second.

Horoscope and Astrology

Jyotisha the (knowledge of the stars) was a form of astronomy-astrology to do with determining auspicious and inauspicious times, casting of horoscopes, and so forth. In ancient India, it was considered a distinct branch of knowledge ancillary to the study of the Vedas (vedanga). It is very much connected with the practice of the Hindu tradition. In many families, even now, a detailed horoscope is cast soon after a child's birth; in some castes and communities, this may be used in later years to be "matched" with a potential matrimonial mate. In some communities, the time and date of a child's birth is cross-referenced with the almanac, and the child's name may be chosen to have a numerical value or start with a syllable harmonious with this moment of birth. The movement of the planets and stars are studied in detail, and when a person experiences, say, a series of setbacks in her career, or is not able to find a right partner in life, an astrologer may be consulted. The astrologer will tell you that either Saturn (Sani) or Mars (Sanskrit: Mangala; Tamil: Chevvai) is positioned where it shouldn't be and then recommend a series of remedies to alleviate the problem. Many South Indian temples, following a custom that began to be popular toward the end of the first millennium C.E., have an altar with the personification of the Nine Planets (Nava Graha). Devotees propitiate these nine planets regularly in an effort to ward off evil influences and maximize good vibrations. The nine are not completely congruent with Western lists of planets; the Indian list excludes the Earth, and includes the sun, the moon, Venus, Mercury, Mars, Jupiter, Saturn, and two "planets" called Rahu and Ketu, identified as the ascending and descending nodes of the moon.

In orthoprax households, horoscopes of the potential bride and bride-groom are matched before they even meet. This is said to ensure compat-ibility of personalities and to balance out good times and bad in the course of the married life. The first such compatibility match is with the star that a person is born under. This is determined by where the moon is at the time of one's birth. Twenty-seven constellations are recognized as birth stars. If we look at the first two advertisements, the names Sadhayam and Poosam (referring to stars in the Aquarius and Cancer signs) denote the birth constellations. After negotiating the obstacle course of caste, community, subsect, and gotra, one then comes to the issue of compatibil-ity of stars. By a quick reckoning, one can figure out if the stars of the po-tential mates are compatible. If everything fits, then one takes it a step further to see if the horoscopes match in detail. Mars is the big offender in many of these wedding matters, and so in the first two advertisements, we see a shorthand reference to the principal feature of the person's horo-scope. "Shuddha jadagam" (clean horoscope) in the first advertisement and "Mars in the eighth house" in the second immediately alert the bride's family as to what kind of horoscope is needed to balance the bridegroom's birth chart.

With all that we have learned in the last few pages, let us deconstruct one of the two ads again. The words in brackets describe the information in the categories we have discussed.

2 VADAGALAI [This word is shorthand for three categories; the term indicates it is a subsect of the Sri Vaishnava community and that the person is a brahmin caste.] ATHREYAM [gotra] Poosam [birth star] 32/ 170/ 15,000 [personal details: bridegroom is 32 years old, is 170 centimeters tall, and earns 15,000 rupees a month], B.Com, owns business/house in Chennai [continuation of personal details: college degree, occupation, wealthy enough to own house] with Mars (Eighth place) [horoscope detail saying that Mars is hanging around a tricky house in the horoscope] seeks suitable unemployed graduate girl from same sect only. [The bride should be the same

subsect; i.e., Vadagalai, Sri Vaishnava community, brahmin caste] Reply with horoscope, details to Box No. Chennai–600002.

Once all the criteria are met, the young man and woman may meet under carefully chaperoned circumstances. If they like each other (either party can opt out easily at this stage) and decide to get married, the families proceed with the preparations for the ceremony. The number of rituals and the time frame involved in conducting weddings depend on the class, caste, community traditions, and economic factors. In the early twentieth century, rituals in brahmin weddings in South India lasted five days. In the early twenty-first, most of them last from a few hours to half a day, and in many urban families, a Western-style reception is added to the festivities.

The Wedding

In the Hindu tradition, the wedding ritual is a sacrament. The texts on dharma describe sacraments, starting with pregnancy rituals to death rituals. Many of them begin discussions on sacraments with the wedding. The Sanskrit word for sacrament is samskara, which means "to make perfect." A wedding is a kalyana, which means "happiness, good fortune, auspiciousness "; it is also known as vivaha (to lead home); in Tamil, it is known as manam, which means (union between two lovers). Although love is not generally a criterion in the choosing of a mate (as we saw in the matrimonial ads), many ancient texts speak about its beauty. Love was considered to be very important in ancient Tamil literature; in one poem, a young girl says:

> Bigger than earth, certainly
> higher than the sky,
> more unfathomable than the waters
> is my love for this man . . .
> Kuruntokai 3 (circa first–second century C.E.), in Ramanujan

The auspicious marriage is a way to fulfill obligations to society. The texts on dharma, which hold an upper-caste male as the norm, say that a man has an obligation in life to marry, raise children, and fulfill his debts to his community. According to these texts, a man is born with debts to the sages, the gods, and the ancestors. A wife helps repay these debts. With the performance of correct domestic and social rituals with—and only with—his wife, a man pays his debt to the gods; by having children, the debt to the ancestors is discharged. A wife is a man's partner in fulfilling dharma, and without her a man cannot fully perform his religious obligations. A woman and her husband are partners in fulfilling religious obligations, partners in the acquisition of wealth and fortune, partners in the enjoyment of sensual pleasures. Thus, through a marriage a man and a woman become companions in the pursuit of spiritual and material goals. Within the Hindu tradition, a man can only perform religious rituals if his wife is by his side.

Although the sacred texts mention dozens of wedding rituals (starting with the engagement/betrothal rites) and many more local and family customs have been added to these, only a few are absolutely crucial. Although some of the rituals performed today are common to most Hindus, a few are unique to individual communities. Let us look at the specific example of the Sri Vaishnava community of South India.

Pre-Wedding Rituals

Although the attendant rituals differ in many parts of India, most Hindus begin the wedding ceremony with a prayer, usually to Ganesha, for a smooth conduct of the ritual. In Sri Vaishnava weddings, however, Vishvaksena, the commander in chief of Lord Vishnu, is worshipped; offerings of incense, sandalwood, and flowers are made to ensure the success of the ceremony.

Before the start of rituals at home or in temples, participants recite important mantras for the evocation of purity. This ritual of purification (punyaha vachanam) is done to protect the primary participants in the rituals and for peace. The wedding rituals begin with a Vedic ritual called Aupasana Homa, the kindling of the household fire and the preparation for the daily domestic worship. This fire sacrifice is done during the householder stage of life. Fire (Agni) is important to the Hindu home.

Agni is therefore recipient of sacrificial offerings and the witness to all domestic rites and ceremonies. The priest invokes the presence of God, who is manifested in the Divine Light of Fire. He consecrates the fire with hymns, surrounds it with darbha grass (sacred grass), and chants. The bride's father makes offerings to Agni.

All significant Hindu sacraments take place near a sacred fire (agni: cognate with the English ignite). Its importance goes back to the time of the Vedas, more than 3,500 years ago. Early Vedic rituals were done around an altar of fire. The sacred fire is lit during those milestones of growth and aging—aging that begins in the prenatal state. Fire is the eternal witness to life and to the major sacraments of life. The fires are lit when a man is sixty years old, and again when he is eighty years old. In many parts of South India now, women also celebrate these birthdays with all the attendant homas or sacrifices.

Wedding Rituals

At the beginning of most Hindu rituals, the officiating priest and those performing the ritual formally declare the coordinates of the land and the time in which the rite takes place. These words are part of the sankalpa, or the declaration of intention to do the ritual. Such coordinates are in cosmic frameworks. The land is identified with one of the dvipas or islands in puranic cosmology, and the time span is given as a moment that occurs in a span of millions of years.

The celebrant first announces the name of the kalpa (a span of 4.32 billion human years, which is equal to one day in the life of the creator god Brahma) and then fine-tunes it to a shorter time period called the manavantara, a span of approximately 306,720,000 human years, named after the primeval man, Vaivasvata. The celebrant then notes that this is first part of the kali yuga (this immediate cycle of 432,000 years). The name of the year is mentioned (Hindu calendars go in sixty-year cycles and each year has a name), followed by a Sanskrit term to indicate whether the sun is in the northern or southern hemisphere—followed in turn by the zodiac sign, the season, the month, the phase of the moon, the week, and the particular stellar constellation where the moon is that day. Finally, the celebrant says that this day is an auspicious one, one fit for weddings. Thus, cosmic time, calendrical time, and auspicious times are all noted in the declaration of intention to complete the rituals with divine blessings.

The order of the rituals varies in different parts of India, but many rites are widely performed. In earlier days, the bride and bridegroom would be brought in by their maternal uncles. The couple now exchange garlands of fragrant flowers as a symbol of their sharing the fragrance of life. In epic narratives of svayamvara (the choosing of a bridegroom by the bride), the garlanding of a young man by a woman showed that she had chosen him as her husband. In the Sri Vaishnava tradition, the woman poet-saint Andal (eighth century C.E.) is said to have worn garlands and offered them to Lord Vishnu with love. The sharing of the garlands is a symbol of the intimacy to come as well as a symbol of the victorious garland worn by fortunate bridegrooms.

The bride and bridegroom sit on a decorated swing. As the swing gently sways, women sing melodious songs recalling the auspicious weddings of Sita, Gowri (Parvati), and other goddesses. In South India, this ritual ends with women circling the young couple with lighted lamps. They pour a thin thread of water as a protective boundary, to keep away evil influences. The women wave little balls of rice and throw them in different directions to ward off the evil eye and shield the couple from harm that may come from any direction. Following this, the bride and bridegroom tie amulets on their wrists, again for protection.

Many of the mantras recited during the wedding ritual are from the Rig Veda and have been used in Hindu weddings for over three thousand years. The bridegroom prays to the Vedic gods Varuna, Brihaspati, Indra, and Surya to remove all defects from the bride. Hindus do not worship these Vedic gods today, but many may believe that the God they worship manifests as these deities. In the Vedic mantra that is recited now, the bridegroom asks for a long marriage filled with love and children and tells the bride:

> May you never throw a fierce glance at [me] during your married life; do not be hostile to [me]. Let us not pull our oars in different directions. Be compassionate to animals; cheerful in your tasks as the mistress of the house; the mother of brave [children], blessed with

long life; the source of happiness in the house. May you bring prosperity to our livestock!

O Lord! make [my bride] blessed with children and fortune.
Giver her ten sons and may her husband become her eleventh one!

My bride! may you be as a queen [samrajni] to your father-in-
law, a queen to your mother-in-law, a queen to your sister- and
brother-in-law!

May all the guests present here unite our hearts! May we be calm
and united! May we be peaceful and unite together like the rivers
mingling [in the ocean and losing their separate identities]. May we
be like breaths united with the body. May we be united like the Lord
and his creation. May we be united like the teacher and his disciple.
May we love each other and be loyal to each other through our lives!
   (RigVeda 10.85.44–47)

The bridegroom then wipes the eyebrows of the bride with a piece of
darbha grass, symbolically wiping away all defects, saying "I cast away all
inauspicious influences [alakshmi] which may harm my life."

The bride's parents prepare to give her away. The bride's father asks
the bridegroom to sit facing east, the auspicious direction of the rising sun
and rising fortunes. He washes the bridegroom's feet and offers him a
mixture of sweet substances to eat (madhu parka). During the kanya dana,
or the "gifting of the young girl," the father of the bride sits down and
gives her away to the bridegroom reciting words from the Ramayana. In
this epic, the words were spoken by Janaka, the father who gives away his
daughter Sita in marriage to Rama:

This is Sita, my daughter; she will be your partner and companion in
all religious obligations, your companion in faith. Take her and be
blessed. Take her right hand in yours; she will be faithful to you, and
be as close to you as your shadow, forever.

Saying that, the bride's father gives her away by ritually pouring water
on the couple's hands. In South India, the bridegroom ties a sacred thread,
blessed by all the elders in the hall, around the bride's neck. This sacred,
auspicious thread (mangala sutra), which is sometimes called a wedding

necklace, is the equivalent of the wedding ring for the bride. The thread has gold pendants with emblems of Vishnu and Lakshmi on them. The bride will wear this wedding necklace for the rest of her life. As he ties it, the bridegroom says:

> This is a sacred thread [which is a symbol] of my long life. I fasten it around your neck. O beautiful lady! O lady with auspicious qualities! May you see a hundred autumns [with me].

In northern India, the bridegroom anoints the bride's forehead with a red powder called sindur; this is the symbol of her married status. The central ritual of the wedding itself is the holding of hands (panigrahana) and the taking of the seven steps around the fire (saptapadi). The bridegroom holds the bride's hand in his and recites mantras to various Vedic gods (Bhaga, Aryama, Savita, Indra, Agni, Surya, Vayu, and Sarasvati), while holding her hand. He prays that they enjoy longevity, children, prosperity, and harmony. He concludes this recitation by rejoicing thus:

> Agni, the Radiant One and other divine beings have given you to me so that we may, together, do what is right and what befits our station in life. . . .
> May the divine wind, he who blows in all directions and who is the friend of the golden fire on which we prepare our food, blow your thoughts in my direction. . .

In the most important rite of the wedding, the bride and the bridegroom take seven steps (saptapadi) around the fire together. The bridegroom says:

> Take the first step; the lord [Vishnu] will follow you. You will not want for food for the rest of your life. Take the second step. The lord will guard your health. Take the third step; the lord will follow you and see that you may observe all religious rituals. Take the fourth step; the lord, following you, will grant you happiness. Take the fifth step; the lord will follow and grant you prosperity with cattle and kine. Take the sixth step; let the lord follow you and let us enjoy the

pleasures of the season. Take the seventh step, the lord will follow you. We shall worship together.

Through these mantras, he asks Lord Vishnu to bless the bride with food, strength, piety, children, wealth, comfort, and health.

After taking the seven steps, the bridegroom says:

You have taken seven steps with me; be my friend. We who have taken seven steps together have become companions. I have attained your friendship; I shall not forsake that friendship. Do not discard our relationship.

Let us live together; let us think together. We have come to a right and fitting stage of our lives; let us be happy and prosperous, thinking good thoughts.

Let there be no difference in our hopes and efforts; let us attain our desires. And so we join ourselves [our lives]. Let us be of one mind, let us act together and enjoy through all our senses, without any difference.

You are the song [Sama], I am the lyric [Rig], I am the song, you are the lyric. I am the sky, you are the earth. I am the seed; you shall bear my seed. I am thought; you are speech.

I am the song, you are the lyric. Be conformable to me; O lady of clear, sweet words. You who are so precious, come with me; let us have children and attain prosperity together. May there be auspiciousness.

The bride and bridegroom are now officially married. The Laws of Manu say: "The Vedic mantras for the wedding ritual of the joining of hands mark the attainment of the wife; but wise people say that the [sacrament] is sealed in the seventh step" (Manu Smriti 8:227).

The couple sit on the western side of the sacred fire and conduct their first fire sacrifice together. The bride places her right hand on her husband's body so that she gets the full benefit of the ritual. There are prayers again to various Vedic gods to bless the marriage and asking for a long married life, health, wealth, children, and peace of mind, with freedom from worries. The bridegroom repeats a petition that has been enunciated earlier. He asks, with dry humor, that Indra bless them with ten children and muses that he will be the eleventh child of his bride in their old age: "Dashasyam putram dehi, patim ekadasham kriti!" Others interpret this line as indicating that the husband is born again through the wife.

The bridegroom then holds the right toe of his wife and gently places her leg on a flat grinding stone (ammi). Touching her right foot he says:

> Stand on this stone, be firm and steady as this stone. Stand conquering those who oppose you while you do your work according to tradition. Be firm about your rights, firm as this stone and be victorious. Be patient with those with whom you do not get along.

The bride, helped by her brother, feeds the flames of the fire with parched rice and prays for a long life for her husband; may he see a hundred autumns, she says again.

In the concluding rituals, the bride and the bridegroom are blessed by the elders of the community. A final, auspicious arati—the waving of a camphor light in a circle—is done to bless them. Later in the evening, the newly married couple are taken to see the stars in the sky. They are shown the polestar (dhruva). They pray that, just as the polestar stays constant and unmoving while the planets and stars swirl around it, they too remain constant and protected from enemies.

Next, they are shown a star in the sky known to Hindus as Arundhati. The constellation of the Great Bear is known in India as the seven sacred sages (rishis). Vasishtha is one of the seven sages. For most Hindu communities, Arundhati, his wife, is a symbol of fidelity. She is identified as a companion star to one of the seven that form the seven sages (Great Bear) constellation. Just as the companion stars remain close together through the years, the young couple is urged to stay together forever.

There is much in the wedding ceremony to show that the Vedic culture is largely patriarchal. A girl inherits her father's gotra ritually and adopts her husband's after her marriage. A father "gives away" his daughter, arguably with his wife by his side. In the Ramayana, Sita, Rama's wife, follows him to the forest; her parents have "gifted" her to Rama, and have to tell her to be his partner in dharma. Sita has been a model for many generations of women, a model that is being questioned now by many Hindus today. But just looking at the wedding rituals, we see that there is a great deal of companionship that is envisaged in the mantras; after the most important ritual of going around the fire, the bridegroom petitions that they live long as friends and as companions.

The wedding is supposed to be auspicious and refers to prosperity in this life. It is seen in terms of wealth and progeny, along with the symbols and rituals connected with these. Cattle, elephants, kings, married women with a potential for bearing children, and rituals connected with birth and marriage are said to be auspicious. These are connected with the promotion of three human goals—dharma (duty), artha (prosperity), and kama (sensual pleasure)—recognized by classical scripture. There is also a second level of auspiciousness connected with the fourth and ultimate goal, moksha (liberation), and the path leading to it. The two levels of auspiciousness have been implicit in Hindu religious literature and rituals. In many contexts, women have auspiciousness in different degrees, which determine the levels of their acceptance.

In the classical literature of the Dharma Shastras and in practice, it is auspicious to be married and fulfill one's dharmic obligations. A sumangali is the ideal woman with the ideal amount of auspiciousness, who can be a full partner in dharma, artha, and kama, through whom children are born, and through whom wealth and religious merit are accumulated. She is called grihalakshmi, or the goddess Lakshmi of the house. She is the most honored woman in traditional Hindu society, especially if she bears children, and is adorned in various rites. Conversely, in many sections of Hindu society, a widow has been considered inauspicious, a bad omen to anyone encountering her. Even in educated, reform-oriented circles, vestiges of this attitude remain. Traditionally, the higher the widow's social caste, the greater the discrimination. Till the middle of the twentieth century, South Indian brahmin widows underwent tonsure, a complete shaving of the head. The so-called higher castes were considered the trend setters in attitudes to women. Thus, the humane attitudes and freedom theoretically accorded by tradition to women in the lower castes were not always manifested in practice. In their eagerness to imitate the higher castes, the lower castes also subjected their women to negative treatment. As we keep noting, however, there are many exceptions even to these general practices regarding widowhood. Even though most high-caste widows in the last two thousand years did not remarry and were not allowed to remarry by the dictates of the texts of dharma, in some brahmin communities of Gujarat, widows regularly practiced remarriage (mehta) up to the nineteenth century. Many widows were great benefactors of temples and charitable institutions.

The nineteenth and twentieth centuries saw efforts to improve the lot of higher-caste widows. These have aimed to keep pace with legal reforms, such as the 1829 proscription of sati (the practice by which widows of some communities in India sometimes burnt themselves on their husband's pyre) and the 1856 legalization of widow remarriage. The efforts of Pandita Ramabai (1858–1922) and Mrs. ("Sister") Subbulaksmi were noteworthy, as were the editorial exhortations of several leading newspapers. The legal age of marriage has been raised, lessening the number of child widows. Education for all women, especially for young widows, has been encouraged, but acceptance and achievement of reform are painfully slow.

The Wedding: Theological Perspectives

In many Hindu theistic theological traditions, the Supreme Being is considered a male deity—generally envisaged as Vishnu, Krishna, Shiva, or Murugan, a popular, handsome South Indian deity. The human soul is portrayed in thousands of poems and songs as a young girl passionately in love with a young man (the deity) who plays fast and loose with her. There are brief moments of ecstatic union and long intervals of excruciating agony in separation. Modeled on classical Tamil poems of love and war written around the first few centuries of the Common Era, vernacular poems composed in South India between the sixth and seventh centuries C.E. portrayed the human soul as the lover waiting for the beloved.

These romantic sentiments are seen in the work of Andal, who in one poem recounts a dream in which she marries Vishnu. This poem is still recited in all weddings of the Sri Vaishnava community, and frequently the bride is dressed to look like Andal, with her distinctive hairstyle and garlands. Andal did not want to get married to a human being and treat her husband as God; she wanted God as her husband. She composed two poems, the Tiruppavai (The Sacred Lady or The Sacred Pavai Ritual) and the Nacchiyar Tirumoli (The Lady's Sacred Words). The rituals of the wedding are discussed in great detail, and many are still performed. According to the Sri Vaishnava tradition, Andal is said to have had her wishes fulfilled and indeed became the bride of Vishnu. But it is not only Andal who is the bride of Vishnu; in some theistic theologies, all souls are the bride of the Supreme Being. Male poets assume the stance of a woman speaking to the beloved. And most classical dances contain at least one or two pieces in which the performer shows "her" passion for the lover seen as Vishnu or his incarnation Krishna, Shiva, or Murugan.

The depiction of the Lord as the male lover and the soul as female has to be seen against other perspectives as well. There are Hindu traditions in which the Supreme Being is a woman, a goddess. In many poems and texts, the supreme goddess is hailed with fervor as "Mother." Unlike the male deity, in general, the Goddess is not addressed in a romantic way by the devotee. Do we then interpret situations where the devotee identifies himself as a lovesick woman as a projection of social patriarchy in the human-divine relationships? There is no doubt that many of the cultural tropes are held over in theological formulation. However, the picture is not quite so simple. To think of the theological relationship as a replication of a patriarchal culture is to miss the richness of the poetry and the drama of longing. The bonds between the divine and the human being imitate some human relationships without being limited to patriarchal structures. The Supreme Being can be conceptualized as male, female, half-man, half-woman, and beyond sexual identity. In some Shaiva traditions, Shiva is called Ardhanarishvara, the Lord who is half female. Iconographically, this form of the Supreme Being is seen as literally and physically half male and female; the left half of this form is female (the Goddess Parvati) and the right half is male (Shiva). Even in the long poems where the male poet identifies himself as a female, the Supreme Being is not always seen as a lover who must come and get the beloved. Sometimes, the "female" devotee identifies herself as the mother of Krishna or Rama and the Lord is seen as a child. So the Supreme Being is both gendered and beyond gender. Even when thought of as a male, he could be a child, a lover, a father, a mother, and a counselor.

Some texts say that while the human being is male or female, the essence of the soul is neither (Leslie). Thus, the lover-beloved relationship is only one of many possibilities in the play between the human being and the deity in the poetry of male and female devotees. Andal, Mira, and other women poets explore many of these relationships.

Andal is by no means the first woman poet in the Hindu tradition. In the Rig Veda we encounter Ghosa, Apala, and Lopamudra, who composed hymns to various deities. Starting with the eighth century, women poets like Andal, Karaikkal Ammaiyar, Akka Mahadevi, and others rejected married life and dedicated passionate poetry to Vishnu and Shiva. These saints have been honored and venerated in the Sri Vaishnava, Shaiva, and Vira Shaiva traditions in many Hindu communities. Over the centuries, many women have also been patrons of temples. Like homes, temples are nerve centers of the many Hindu traditions.

THE HINDU TEMPLE

The Hindu Temple of Atlanta, Georgia, is a majestic building with looming towers similar to many that one may encounter in South India. It is a place for worship, for eating blessed food, and meeting friends—a community center where one can learn classical dance and music. In the temple, there are inner shrines, each dedicated to a particular deity in the Hindu pantheon.

Between 1991 and 1992, Hindus coming from many states of the southeastern United States installed icons in the Atlanta temple with traditional rituals and fanfare. Once installed, the icons are considered divine presences of the deity. The priests, at various intervals or at the conclusion of every cycle of the rituals, wave a camphor light in a circle to illuminate the form of the deity. This central ritual of adoration, known as the arati, touches many chords in the worshipper. The flame reveals the visage of the deity whom they know is unknowable and has yet graciously descended to Earth. The light from the flame reminds some that the Supreme Being is pure light, and reality, consciousness, and bliss. Many Hindus recite a short Sanskrit prayer from the Upanishads (the last sections of the Vedas) composed around the seventh century B.C.E.:

Lead me from unreality to reality
Lead me from darkness to light
Lead me from death to immortality.

The texts from which this prayer is drawn identify the Supreme Being as the "light of lights" and as ineffable. And yet, over the centuries, most Hindus have preferred to think of the Supreme Being in a theistic mode, as one who makes himself accessible to human beings in a perceivable form. Thus, when seeing the arati flame, some Hindus, who think of the God Vishnu as the Supreme Being, may remember the verses composed around the seventh century C.E. by two poet-saints in Tamil. For centuries many orthodox people had held that the Sanskrit Vedas were only to be recited and learned by male members of the upper castes of society; the Tamil verses, however, could be recited by anyone:

With the earth as the lamp,
the sweeping oceans as melted butter,
and the sun with the fiery rays
as the flame;
I have woven a garland of words
for the feet of the Lord,
who bears the red flaming wheel,
so I can cross the ocean of grief.

    MUDAL TIRUVANTATI I
    (POYKAY ALVAR, CIRCA SEVENTH CENTURY)

The second poet transforms the metaphor so that the earth is not the lamp, it is his love; the fuel is not the melted, clarified butter (or ghee), but his love:

With love as the lamp,
passion as the ghee,
a mind melting with joy
as the wick,
with my soul dissolving,
I lit the blazing flame of wisdom
for Narana.
I, who desire the wisdom of Tamil.

    IRANDAM TIRUVANTATI (BHUTA ALVAR, CIRCA SEVENTH CENTURY)

Prayers in temples are frequently from Sanskrit texts, but, in some regions, local languages like Tamil have been used side by side with Sanskrit for many centuries, and some hymns like the ones quoted above have been considered to be the vernacular equivalent of the Sanskrit Vedas, that is, of trans-human origin. In these verses, the poets portray Vishnu as a deity worthy of devotion. The first verse shows him bearing a flaming wheel in his hand—a wheel used as a weapon against evil. It ends with the hope that the Lord's flaming discus-wheel will destroy the poet's ocean of grief. In many of the theistic traditions of Hinduism, grief is generally understood as stemming from not understanding the soul's true nature and as located in the continued cycle of birth and rebirth that every soul endures.

In Atlanta, as elsewhere in the diaspora, temples are set up by different communities from various parts of India, and the flavor of each is very different. A few miles away from the Hindu Temple of Atlanta is a temple called Shakti Mandir—devoted to various forms of a Supreme Being, the Goddess, and houses not one but many manifestations of the Goddess. The main deity in the Hindu Temple of Atlanta, however, is Venkateswara, a popular name for the Hindu God Vishnu in Tirupati, a famous pilgrimage center in South India. In many parts of India, a Hindu deity that has a generic name like Vishnu, Shiva, or Devi may also have a local name. The shrines inside the temple house Padmavati (She of the Lotus Flower), a local name for the Goddess Lakshmi, and Andal. In the Hindu Temple of Atlanta, as in the Hindu Temple at Pittsburgh, Andal is identified as an incarnation of the Earth Goddess. There are other shrines for the Goddess Durga and one for Ganesha, who shares his space with an icon of Lord Shiva. There is a little platform in a corner for the Nava Graha, the presiding deities of the Nine Planets. Saturn and Mars, particularly, are considered to have malefic potential, and special rituals have to be done for them if they happen to be transiting in some path that adversely affects one's horoscope. There are no congregational prayers in this temple; it seems to be more of a cafeteria-style approach, with devotees gathering near the deity of their choice and offering prayers either individually or through a priest. This is typical of many temples in India, although in some worship services, especially in the North American continent, some temples with devotees from northern India have chosen to adopt a congregation style of worship.

As part of the worship, the priests in the Hindu Temple of Atlanta recite the many names of the God or Goddess, each describing a divine at-
tribute or form, and offer the devotees fruits or flowers considered to be
blessed by the deity. In the other temples in Atlanta that attract devotees
from northern India, as the rituals conclude and the lamp is being waved
in front of the deity, devotees may sing a hymn that has recently become
popular, "Jaya jagadisha hare" (Victory, Victory to the Lord).

Most Hindus ask the deity for earthly and material favors such as
health, wealth (bhukti), and liberation (mukti). Frequently, in many of the
temples built by people from northern India, as the camphor flame is
waved in front of the deities and the song is in progress, a collection plate
is passed around. Donation (dana) is an important part of the religious rituals in the field of dharma.

The whole town surrounding any temple is said to be sacred. Every
tree, every stream near the precincts of the temple exudes this sense of sa-
credness. Bathing in a sea, river, stream, or pond near the temple is said to
grant salvation. In South India, every village temple will have a story of
how the Lord or the Goddess revealed him/herself in that place to a particular devotee. Pilgrims believe that they will receive divine grace by remembering the stories of the devotees whose wishes were fulfilled in the
past and in worshipping that local deity in a particular way. This grace will
eventually give one liberation from the cycle of life and death.

The temple itself is like a port of transit, a place from where a human
can "cross over" (tirtha) the ocean of life and death. Many temples and
holy places are near bodies of water—oceans, streams, rivers, and springs.
When such a body of water was not readily available, temple architects
dug a deep well or pool and used it for ritual purposes. Scholars note that
some of the places that seem to have been important in the earliest period
of Indian history—possibly around 3000 B.C.E.—are still considered to be
sacred sites charged with power. In other words, there is a continuity in
the palpable manifestation of the sacred. The sanctity of places, however, is
not frozen and immutable; while a few places like Srirangam and Varanasi
have been continuously sacred for almost two thousand years, the popularity of a place in the past was dependent on political expansions and the
caprice of emperors and royal patronage.

Another example of this dynamism and innovation is seen in the growth
of goddess temples in Tamilnadu. In the early 1970s, devotees belonging to

several Hindu sectarian traditions joined together in Besantnagar, a suburb of Madras, and built a temple devoted to eight forms of Lakshmi. This form of worship, glorifying female power, is rooted in tradition, but one that has a new life today, using a conventional framework that is also innovative. In this temple we do not find the customary separate shrines for Vishnu and Sri/Lakshmi. Rather, there are eight small shrines arranged in a clockwise circle, one of each of the eight Lakshmis, and in the ninth shrine we find Vishnu and Lakshmi together sharing the same space. In other words, Vishnu is the "consort," rather than the presiding deity in this temple. There is no other earlier example of such a temple in which Lakshmi has been given primary place.

Although traditionally Lakshmi is a popular deity, her being portrayed in eight iconographically different forms is a relatively new phenomenon. The eight Lakshmis are seen as manifestations of Sri, and some of them represent her powers. In a song that became popular at the same time as the temple was built, we see Sri as primeval (adi Lakshmi), as the goddess of grain (dhanya Lakshmi), as being fearless and giving fearlessness to her devotees (dhairya Lakshmi), as one who is worshipped by elephants (gaja Lakshmi), as giving one progeny through her favor (santana Lakshmi), as being victorious and making her devotees so (vijaya Lakshmi), and as bestowing knowledge and wealth (vidya Lakshmi and dhana Lakshmi). Although these attributes and descriptions of Sri are all found in traditional literature (along with a dozen others), the emergence of these eight in precisely this combination is quite new. Devotional songs on cassettes, poster pictures with the eight Lakshmis, prayer pamphlets with songs to her, and water pitchers with the Lakshmis carved around them have also made their appearances as support artifacts and are sold around the temple.

In the mid-1970s in Mel Maruvattur, a village about fifty miles from Madras, the temple of Adi Para Shakti (the Primordial Great Powerful Goddess) truly broke new ground for women. A revelation to a young man who lived in this village proclaimed that land to be the place where the Goddess abides. The Goddess, it is said, announced that although the skin of her devotees may be white, red, brown, or dark, the blood that runs in them is always red. To denote the equality among all devotees of the Goddess regardless of sex, caste, or race, her followers wear red when they worship her in the temple. For miles around the temple, one can see truckloads of worshippers or a solitary pilgrim walking sedately, all head-ing to the shrine of the Goddess, all wearing red. Nor does the innovation stop there; in contrast to most brahmanical temples, menstruating women can worship here.

Purity and Impurity

Rituals, places, and people are all considered to be auspicious or inauspicious, pure or impure. Some kinds of purity and impurity may be generic and more or less always associated with certain places; for instance, a cremation ground, because of its continuous association with corpses, is always impure. Death and things associated with it are usually impure. This impurity, when associated with people, is temporal; for instance, the family of a dead person is said to be in a state of impurity and cannot go to a temple or conduct normal rituals, but that impurity is lifted after a specific number of days.

Although death is inauspicious and impure, some events, like the birth of a child, are happy and auspicious but nevertheless impure. In other words, after the birth of a child, the extended family, drawn on patrilineal lines, is considered to be in a state of impurity for a varying number of days, depending both on the sex of the baby (a longer period of impurity with the birth of boys) and the proximity of blood connections of the family member to the parents of the child. Matters of purity and impurity associated with death and birth are discussed at length in the Dharma Shastras.

In addition to birth and death being associated with impurity, menstruating women are said to be impure. During menstruation, therefore, especially in the "upper castes," women are considered impure and are prohibited from participating in regular household work and ritual matters. In many communities, the woman used to be reintegrated into the household only after a purifying bath after four days. Most of these restrictions are no longer followed, especially in the diaspora. However, most Hindu women still do not go to the temple while menstruating. It is this prohibition that was lifted in the Mel Maruvattur temple.

While menstruation is connected with ritual impurity and women are not supposed to participate in religious activity but then, as usual, certain examples in Hindu tradition seem to be striking exceptions—for example, the story in the Mahabharata of Princess Draupadi's surrender to Krishna.

Draupadi is married to the five Pandava brothers. The oldest, Yud-hishthira, gambles away his kingdom in a game of dice. He finally stakes the freedom of his other brothers, himself, and his wife and loses it all to his foes, the Kaurava brothers. Dusshasana, one of the Kauravas, then drags Draupadi into the royal court. Draupadi is menstruating. The Kaurava brothers declare her to be their slave and viciously try to remove her clothes, which technically belong to them. Draupadi asks for justice, chal-lenging the elders in the court, but no one comes to her aid. Her five hus-bands, all heroes of the epic, seem powerless. The third brother, Arjuna, arguably one of the best warriors of India, stands by helpless as the Kau-ravas begin to strip his wife. Draupadi sees no help against this abuse; in despair, she throws up her arms and surrenders herself to Krishna, seeking his protection. Krishna miraculously appears to her, and her garment seems to be never ending even as the wicked Dusshasana tries to pull it off of her.

The thirteenth-century theologian Pillai Lokacarya sees Draupadi's surrender to the Lord as paradigmatic. In speaking about the ritual of pra-patti, or surrendering to Vishnu, he says that one does not have to seek rit-ual purity, such as having a special cleansing bath. He cites two examples and then showcases the incident of Draupadi. If one takes Draupadi's sur-render as a model, we see in the Hindu tradition a way of bypassing the ritual injunctions if one has devotion for the Supreme Being. Although the restrictions concerning menstruation may seem to rise from the patri-archal discipline of the Dharma Shastras, an epic as early as the Maha-bharata shows a way in which devotion overrides the ritual injunctions of texts.

Patrons of Temples

Women, especially those from royal families, were liberal benefactors of temples and other institutions. In the year 966, in Tiru Venkatam (Tiru-pati), Samavai endowed money to celebrate some festivals and conse-crate a processional image of the Lord, a silver replica of the main deity.

A record of her endowment is inscribed in stone; it concludes with the phrase "Sri Vaishnava raksai" (by the protection of the Sri Vaishnavas). Within a short time, Samavai endowed two different parcels of land, one of 4 hectares (10 acres) and the other 5.4 hectares (13.3 acres), and ordered that the revenues derived from these were to be used for major festivals. She also gave a large number of jewels to the temple and asked that these be used to adorn the image of the Lord. Of all temples in India today, the temple at Tirupati has the largest endowments and sources of revenue.

And Samavai was not an isolated example. The queens of the Chola dynasty (c. 846–1279) were enthusiastic patrons of temples and religious causes for the Shaiva community of South India around the tenth century. At that time, a South Indian queen, Sembiyan Mahadevi, gave major endowments to many Shiva temples. Such generosity implies a certain independence of lifestyle and finances. Apart from queens and royalty, many other kinds of women also endowed temples. Obviously, the record of such activities has to be integrated with our reading of scripture and hagiography to get a more complete vision of women's religious roles (Orr).

Although most Hindu communities worship in temples, not all do. The Vira Shaiva tradition, for instance, which reveres the eleventh-century teacher Basava, rejects the importance of temples. In the nineteenth century, Ram Mohun Roy and Dayanand Saraswati, leaders of new movements within the Hindu tradition, also rejected the worship of the Supreme Being in iconic forms in temples.

Who are the religious leaders in the Hindu tradition? Are they male or female? Traditionally, the priests in the temples were male brahmins, and they performed prayers on behalf of devotees and celebrated rituals for the community. Most of them simply trained by apprenticeship. Another specialization for some of these male brahmin priests was to serve their "clients" at home and perform domestic sacraments. In most cases these priests were not theologians or philosophers; nor did they have a ministerial role to play for people who came to the temples. They were, and are, specialists in ritual.

Most Hindus may point to gurus or teachers (acaryas, who practice in traditional lineages) or even learned narrators of epics (who weave theology and ethics into their expositions) as leaders. Although these were, in the past, largely men, in recent years women have been evident in all these fields. There are web pages for many women gurus and harikathas (narrators of Vishnu stories). Women like Anandamayi Ma and Ammachi have been powerful gurus in the twentieth century. Devotees of these gurus argue that the teachers are not teachers by choice; they are either highly evolved or enlightened souls or an incarnation of divine being. Thus, the question of gender is, they say, not relevant.

Many women gurus preach from Hindu temples in the diaspora. In India, they tend to work from their own ashrams or sanctuaries and frequently attract hundreds or thousands of devotees each day. These devotees come to get a glimpse of their teacher or hear her. The gurus teach about how one can get detached from one's family, friends, and career and achieve mental equanimity. Detachment from life and attachment to a deity is frequently stressed; these, they say, will lead you to moksha.

DEATH AND LIBERATION

Although weddings are auspicious from the viewpoint of most Hindus, death and funeral rituals are all inauspicious and impure. The ritual impurity is contagious if there is a death in the family; even if you go to a funeral, your are considered to be impure. A cleansing bath or pouring water over your head will ritually cleanse you of this impurity. Although the texts on dharma wax eloquent on this purity and pollution and one observes it in practice, from the viewpoint of one who wants liberation, death is indeed auspicious.

Funeral Rituals

Most Hindus cremate the dead. Cremation takes place very soon after death—in many cases within a day. The body is washed by the women in the house and the forehead is anointed with sacred marks. The dead body is laid on a bier, and the family priest begins the rituals at home itself. Family and friends garland the body and frequently bow down in respect, facing south, which is considered the direction of death. At the cremation ground, the pyre is lit; the ashes are collected the next day and eventually immersed in the ocean or in the Ganges.

In almost all cases, it is the son, or a close male relative, who does the funeral rites. In some areas, women do not even go into the cremation ground. However, as in so much else, there are exceptions. In families without sons, daughters do the funeral rites. Although this custom was hardly ever followed in the last two millennia, it is more and more common. Such behavior, moreover, is not without precedent in Vedic times, when a man sometimes appointed a daughter as a putrika, a daughter who functions like a son in ritual matters. This daughter, or sometimes her son, officiated at funerals. Rig Vedic verse (Rig III.31.1), which is rather difficult in structure, can be interpreted to mean that there is a practice of declaring a daughter to be one's son (Kane, vol. 2, part 1, pp. 435–36). Although this does not take away from the patriarchal structure and norm, it shows that, in this ritual, gender issues were fluid.

Even if a man did not so appoint a daughter, the traditional sources of dharma or righteous action are flexible enough to allow room for innovative action. The Vedas, the tradition of the Epics and Puranas, actions of the righteous, and finally doing "what is dear to one's soul" (atmatushti)— that is, acting after much thought and according to the dictates of one's conscience—these are the stuff of which dharma is made. Thus, while the son is favored in many of the texts and in practice in many communities, the sources of dharma allow reasonable interpretations by which a woman can go far beyond the dictates of the text.

Most Hindus believe that the soul is immortal. The soul is encased in a human body that perishes; but the atma, or soul, is imperishable. At death, one merely discards one's body and eventually takes on another. The classical location of this doctrine is in the Bhagavad Gita.

The Bhagavad Gita
and the Ways to Liberation

The Bhagavad Gita, one of the holiest books in the Hindu tradition, speaks of loving devotion to the lord and the importance of selfless action. In it, Krishna instructs his cousin Arjuna (who is generally understood to represent any human soul who seeks spiritual guidance) on the nature of the human soul and God and how one can reach liberation. Written around 200 B.C.E., the Bhagavad Gita eventually became part of the Mahabharata. It is frequently printed separately, and many people own a copy. For centuries people learned it by heart.

In verses that are still recited at a Hindu's funeral, Krishna describes the human soul as being beyond the reach of human senses and thought; it is not affected by the sense organs or physical nature. Just as a human being casts off old clothes and wears new ones, so too does a soul discard bodies and assume new ones. This process continues through the ages until the soul is finally liberated from the cycle of birth and death. The soul does not die when the body dies; it is never born and never killed. In later centuries, people have interpreted the soul as being beyond gender.

In the Gita, Krishna describes three ways to liberation (or as some Hindus believe, three aspects of one way to liberation) from the cycle of births and death: (1) the way of action, (2) the way of knowledge, and (3) the way of devotion. Each way (marga) is spoken of also as a discipline (yoga). The way of action (karma yoga) entails the path of unselfish action; one must do one's duty, but it should not be done either for fear of punishment or hope of reward. The right action should be done without expectation of praise or blame. For example, one is to study or do good acts because it is correct to do so—because it is one's duty (dharma) to do so, not because other people will reward and praise one for it.

Acting with the expectation of future reward leads to bondage and unhappiness. On one level, such actions instigate further action, and thus further karma is incurred, for one is never satisfied when one reaches a goal. One may long for a promotion, for more money, or to be loved by a particular person, and when one acts with these goals in mind, one may meet with disappointment and react with anger or grief. Even if one is temporarily successful, the goal that has been reached is replaced with another. Thus the thirst for material success is never quenched. Instead, one succeeds only in accumulating more karma, which leads to further rebirth.

Indeed, on one level (according to other books of the time), even the karma one gets from performing good deeds is ultimately bad and causes bondage because to enjoy the good karma, one has to be reborn. One Hindu philosopher calls good karma "golden handcuffs." Therefore, one is to act according to one's dharma. Krishna urges Arjuna to act without any attachment to the consequences. Then evil will not touch such a person, just as water does not stick to a lotus leaf. All actions are to be offered to Krishna. By discarding the fruits of one's action, one attains abiding peace.

Krishna also talks of the way of knowledge (jnana yoga): through the means of attaining scriptural knowledge, one may achieve a transforming wisdom that destroys one's past karma. True knowledge is an insight into the real nature of the universe, divine power, and the human soul. Later philosophers say that when one hears scripture, asks questions, clarifies doubts, and eventually meditates on this knowledge, one achieves liberation. Krishna tells Arjuna that just as fire reduces firewood to ashes, so, too, does the fire of knowledge reduce all karma (actions) to ashes.

The third way is the most emphasized throughout the Bhagavad Gita: the way of devotion (bhakti yoga). If there is a general amnesty program offered to those who sin, those who have a karmic overload, it is through the way of devotion:

> Even if a sinful person adores me with exclusive devotion
> He must be regarded as righteous . . .
> Quickly his soul becomes righteous and
> He gets eternal peace . . .
> My devotee is never lost. . . .
> (Bhagavad Gita 9:30–1)

Ultimately, Krishna makes his promise to Arjuna; if one were to surrender to the Lord, he will forgive the human being all sins:

> Letting go all dharma, take refuge in me alone;
> I shall deliver you from all sins; do not grieve.
> (Bhagavad Gita 18:66)

These are held to be "almost the last words" of the Bhagavad Gita, and thus the ultimate teaching of this work. Absolute surrender to Krishna is advocated, and the karma built up over many lifetimes will be erased by his grace.

The Bhagavad Gita is one of the most popular Sanskrit texts, and its popularity is attested to by the number of imitations it has spawned. The

Isvara Gita is very similar but casts Shiva as the supreme deity. The Devi Gita commends surrender to the Goddess. Such works have never attained the status of the Bhagavad Gita.

Although devotion is exalted in the Bhagavad Gita and many other texts, some philosophers like Shankara have held that it is knowledge that leads one to liberation. Of the many well-known theologians in the Hindu tradition, most are male. However, a careful look at Hindu history will reveal not only many women poets (such as Tarigonda Venkamamba, circa 1800–1866) but many women who wrote prose treatises or seem to have participated in discussions or even debates on philosophy. These women sought the ultimate knowledge that would lead them to immortality.

There are also many women philosophers. In the Upanishads, Maitreyi, the wife of the philosopher Yajavalkya, questions him in depth about the nature of reality. Gargi Vacaknavi, a woman philosopher, challenges him with questions in a public debate. There were probably more women composers and philosophers, but they are not noted in the texts. In time, possibly because the Vedas were transmitted orally, many parts of the text, including verses composed by women, were lost. It is also possible that the women's compositions that came after the Vedas were suppressed when literature became more androcentric, but women continued to be involved with poetry and philosophy.

Tirukkoneri Dasyai, a woman philosopher who is not much known in India, lived in the thirteenth or fourteenth centuries and wrote a beautiful commentary, Garland of Words, on the ninth-century Tamil poem Tiruvaymoli (Sacred Utterance), which the Sri Vaishnava community considers to be revealed. In her commentary, written in the manipravala style (a combination of Sanskrit and Tamil), she quotes the Vedas and the other Sanskrit texts profusely. Although a lot of these quotations may have been learned through ritual usage and commentarial exposition, the juxtaposition of vernacular and Sanskrit revelation along with ritual and commentary seems to have provided a milieu where men and women in Tirukkoneri Dasyai's community, but presumably elsewhere too, had extensive access at least to those parts of the Vedas that had theological and salvific import. Tirukkoneri Dasyai had access to this vast learning and was able to express herself creatively; this alone makes her a felicitous example of a learned and articulate woman from one prominent Hindu tradition. In her work, she reiterates over and over again the idea that

> Samsara is a vast ocean that no one can cross. You Great Lord should make sure we cross it. [The Lord] stands as a surety for those who have transferred their burden of salvation [to him or their teachers], he is the raft, the ferryman who takes them across [the sea of life and death]. He will alleviate the burden of all. (Tirukkoneri Dasyai: Comment on Tiruvaymoli 2.8.1; 42)

The paths of devotion, knowledge, and selfless action are open to the human being. Yet, from the viewpoint of devotion, it is the Supreme Being who is said, as in the verse above, to deliver a person from the endless cycle of samsara. In matters of liberation, it does not matter if one is a man or woman; all are eligible for it.

REFLECTIONS

Reflecting upon Jewish feminist writings, Davidman and Tenenbaum speak about three stages. They identify the first as when women scholars examine traditional wisdom from the standpoint of women and establish the groundwork for the critique. In the second stage, there is an attempt to fill in the gaps of our knowledge of women by studying their lives according to the categories created by traditional male scholarship. This is based on the assumption that traditional categories of analysis will be adequate for the understanding of women's experiences. However, most women scholars now believe that these concepts and theoretical frames miss out on what is distinctive about women's experiences. Many women simply did not or were not allowed to do traditionally male tasks. Consequently many women remained invisible. Davidman and Tenenbaum say, "Thus, correcting for this invisibility of women involves not simply 'adding women and stirring,' but reconstructing the model of scholarship in each discipline and across disciplines" (Davidman and Tenenbaum, p. 2). The third stage of feminist knowledge is the development of a scholarship that begins with women's experiences, focuses on women, and places them at the center, not the margins. The stages are not sequential but continuous and spiraling.

This approach involves asking new questions and reconceptualizing conventional categories. It is based on using gender as a crucial analytic tool. The notion of gender presupposed here is constructed and interpreted in many ways now, some of which challenge the feminist enterprise that Davidman and Tenenbaum are involved in. But if we accept for now the framework that they propose and use it as a template for understanding Hindu traditions, we can see where we are in the production and interpretation of knowledge.

The task is compounded for the study of Hindu traditions because we are critiquing categories and materials that have come from two sources—categories of religion based on Enlightenment models as well as traditional Hindu literature, most of which was composed by men who believed they were of a high caste—and also dealing with Western expectations that these texts are to be taken seriously. To study Hindu traditions, we can start with internal categories, but these need not necessarily be women-friendly. And using feminist strategies for interpretation may not fit the Indian cultures.

Many recent articles have critiqued Hindu traditions and have gone into the issues of "adding women and stirring" (Young, Patton, Findly, Dehejia, Kishwar, McGee, Narayanan 1999 and 2001, and above all Tharu and Lalita). Many others, including Kishwar, Pintchman, and Patton, also challenge the paradigms and begin to place women centerstage in studying the Hindu tradition as a religious tradition. The entire process is still in the early stages, and, as Davidson and Tenenbaum note, the stages are not sequential but continuous and spiraling.

There are many areas in the Hindu tradition to which a woman can look for encouragement and hope. The first is the historical factor. After patient researching, one can find women who made a mark in traditionally male spheres. Thus, the list of women poets, philosophers, and patrons grows longer by the year. And we are finding more and more evidence of women who performed rituals normally thought done only by men.

The second is in the philosophical sphere. According to at least some texts, the soul is without gender, and so, ultimately, in the quest for liberation, gender is irrelevant. In some literature and the performing arts, souls, whether they belong to male or female bodies, may be gendered as female, leveling the field in the potential for liberation.

And finally there is the sphere of social institutions, and it is here that we look to the field of dharma. Although the traditional lists of the sources of dharma point to various sacred texts, the fourth source is of crucial importance for us. These are actions that would be sanctioned by appeal to atmatushti, or the happiness of one's soul, an appeal to one's conscience. This alone, even if we did not have earlier precedents for women, gives institutional room for women to live their religious lives to the fullest potential. Hindus have, over the centuries, been able to keep their tradition vibrant, to interpret sacred texts, and assimilate and adapt practices from the ancient Indus Valley Civilization to the age of the Internet. The articulation of a faith with the voicing of a full range of possibilities and opportunities for men and women is the need of the day.

Classical Hindu texts give the impression of being immutable, but Hindu practices have been fluid and flexible, allowing for adaptations, assimilation, and adjustments. Concepts, rituals, even gods and goddesses have evolved and faded away; others have endured for millennia. Devotion and wisdom are still sought-after goals, even as they were three thousand years ago.

Since Vedic times, Sarasvati has captured the devotion of human beings who long for knowledge and, ultimately, transformative, experiential wisdom. As a personification of the sacred river Sarasvati, she cleanses and purifies sullied bodies and confused minds; as a goddess she grants the joy of learning, the pleasures of music, the power of knowledge, and the bliss of devotional wisdom. Every fall, during Navaratri, as I place her picture on the altar of the kolu, along with Lakshmi, the radiant goddess who bestows enjoyment and liberation, and instead of the pens and pencils put my floppy disks in front of them, I have the peace of knowing that all chips of knowledge become the goddess's abode, become blessed by them. All knowledge and transformative wisdom are said to flow as gifts from the goddess Lakshmi. As Sarasvati continues to flow through time, she clarifies and uplifts, and as the river of knowledge that is ever moving and ever growing, she will someday gently transport us to the other shore.

2

Buddhism

By Rita M. Gross

STORIES ABOUT the Buddha's life are lovingly retold in all Buddhist cultures. Among those stories, none is more frequently remembered than how Siddhartha Gautama, soon to become a Buddha (Enlightened Being), sat under the Bodhi Tree, defeated all the assaults of Mara, the Buddhist Tempter and Spoiler, and attained enlightenment. This story often includes an incident in which Mara taunts Gautama, claiming that he has not practiced generosity in the past and has no right to his seat. Mara's hosts testified for their leader, but being alone, Gautama had no one to witness for him. Touching the earth with the fingertips of one hand, he called upon the Earth Goddess to testify to his generosity in countless previous lifetimes. She rose up and squeezed an ocean of water from her hair as testimony, whereupon Mara and his armies withdrew. To this day, a favorite icon of the Buddha shows him sitting under the Bodhi Tree in this Earth Touching Mudra gesture. Another icon, popular in Southeast Asian Buddhist countries, depicts the Earth Goddess wringing out her long hair.

This story, with the Buddha in the foreground and the Earth Goddess in the background, is typical of most Buddhist records. Most people know of the Buddha, who attained enlightenment and founded the Buddhist religion, but even many Buddhists do not know how he called upon the Earth Goddess at that crucial moment or how she helped him. Buddhism's foreground highlights men, historical events, and philosophical thought, explaining why many people think of Buddhism as a male-dominated religion.

I studied Buddhism for years before I became interested in practicing Buddhism. I was already teaching university courses on Buddhism when it occurred to me, in the midst of immense personal anguish, that this religion might actually be "true" because its explanations of why so much suffering occurs and what could be done about it were so cogent. This awakening occurred in 1973. By then, I had already written some of the earliest work on women and religion in the current feminist movement, and women's issues were my most existential concern. A religion in which women were so much in the background was not initially appealing. But its dharma (central teachings) took hold and explained my life to me as nothing else ever had. As I began to explore Buddhism more personally, I realized that I was hooked by this dharma, that its relevance and power to make sense of things far overpowered Buddhism's unimpressive record on gender equity. I also realized that eventually I would have to reconcile the relevance of Buddhist teachings with its historical male dominance, a task I undertook in *Buddhism After Patriarchy: A Feminist History, Analysis, and Reconstruction of Buddhism* and other writings.

My years of study and reflection upon Buddhist history and ideas have yielded two generalizations. Buddhist teachings and symbols are gender-inclusive and gender-neutral or gender-free, rather than male-dominant or female-dominant. Nevertheless, throughout Buddhist history, its institutional setup has favored men over women as teachers, students, monastics, and meditators, the pursuits most valued and honored in Buddhist cultures. These two conclusions will be apparent time after time as we survey Buddhist history and teachings. The story of the Buddha and the Earth Goddess has been repeated over and over in the history of Buddhism. But without the Earth Goddess, the Buddha would have had no witness to his generosity. Without women, Buddhism would not have survived, not simply because women give birth, but because their presence is essential to every Buddhist context. As with every religion, about half of all Buddhists have always been women. For most Buddhist women, life consisted of motherhood, housework, and pious lay devotional practices, a situation no different from all major religions of the last three thousand years. Women were more essential as mothers and donors than as students or teachers of the dharma. Often, their main religious activity was giving food to monks seeking daily alms, but if women, who are in charge of domestic affairs, do not give food to the monks, the monks would starve because monastic rules prohibit them from farming or handling money.

The most important Buddhist ritual in a woman's life would be her monastic ordination, if she took monastic vows. But relatively few women became nuns; many more men became monks. Nevertheless, the institution was there—an escape hatch from unbearable domestic situations, a point to which we will return in the final section. Women with a genuine spiritual calling faced greater difficulties than those faced by men. Women were usually discouraged from following a spiritual calling, whereas men were encouraged to follow it. But, as we will see, some women did persevere and became highly respected practitioners, especially in early Indian Buddhism and in Vajrayana Buddhism, in India and in Tibet. Interestingly, almost all named Buddhist women are from these two periods and places. Many fewer named women exist in the records of Mahayana Buddhism in India or East Asia, or in Southeast Asian Theravada Buddhism. Earlier Western accounts of Buddhism totally omitted women, intensifying the impression that Buddhism is a male religion. In such a situation, it is difficult to know how much of women's invisibility is due to Western scholarship on Buddhism and how much is due to Buddhism itself.

Recently, another element has entered the picture. All forms of Buddhism are now being practiced in the West by Westerners. Among Western converts to Buddhism, women and men participate on a relatively equal basis in all aspects of Buddhism. The sole exception is that senior Western teachers are more often men than women, though there are some women senior teachers in all forms of Buddhism. Buddhism became popular in the midst of a strong feminist movement. Like myself, many women were attracted to Buddhism by its philosophies and meditation practices, but repelled by its seemingly male dominance and male chauvinism. Those who chose to pursue Buddhist disciplines nevertheless began to look more critically at conventional Buddhist practices than had ever been done before. Many troubling things were found, leading many to ask how a religion with such lofty views and practices could have so overlooked half its members. But critique and construction go hand in hand. Western Buddhists not only discuss what is found wanting but suggest how to rectify the situation. A relatively small but influential body of such literature had grown up around these topics.

Western and Asian Buddhism are in close contact. Asian Buddhists, pressed to explain why women had been so overlooked, began to look more critically at their own practices. A Buddhist women's movement advocating reform is now in place in most of the Asian Buddhist world. For many Asians, the most obvious issue is restoring the nuns' full ordination in countries where it has been lost. Better support and education for nuns is also an important agenda.

I: BUDDHISM IN INDIA AND BEYOND: HISTORICAL AND INTELLECTUAL DEVELOPMENTS

Though subject to some discussion, the Buddha's dates are usually given as 563–483 B.C.E. Born into a royal family, he lived a life of ease and luxury until becoming disturbed by the suffering his indulgent lifestyle masked. He abandoned his family and future career as king to seek liberation, to seek contentment beyond suffering and understand the riddle of life. After six unsuccessful years and many teachers, he finally sat under the Bodhi Tree and, as narrated above, attained enlightenment on the May full moon night of his thirty-fifth year. For the rest of his long life, he was a monastic wandering teacher, gathering a large following of disciples, monastic and lay, male and female. Given the long-term impact of his movement, he would have to be judged one of the most important people ever to have lived.

A: Early Indian Buddhism

Like any long-lived religious tradition practiced in various cultural settings, the many forms of Buddhism are significantly different from each other. Early Indian Buddhism is an important foundation for all of them. Monasticism, still central to most Buddhist cultures, goes back to Buddhism's beginnings. World renunciation—leaving behind the ties, cares, and privileges of one's family and career—was common and controversial in India of the Buddha's time. Prince Siddhartha was by no means the only young man to do what he had done; he was only the most successful. When Buddha became so enlightened, he was a celibate, propertyless world renouncer, and most who achieved enlightenment under his guidance were also world renouncers or became so immediately. It was taken for granted in ancient India that anyone, male or female, caught up in the busyness, emotional bondage, and stress of family and career could not find spiritual liberation or ultimate peace. However, the monastic community remained in close contact with the lay community. Daily alms rounds provided economic survival for the monks and nuns, and monastics provided religious instruction to the lay community.

However, the nuns' community was not immediately established. Though the Buddha did not observe caste restrictions, allowing men from any caste to join his community, and although the contemporary Jain movement already included women world renouncers, the Buddha did not initially welcome female monastics. Three years after his movement began, the Buddha's foster mother asked to be admitted to the order. She was refused, with the comment that it is inappropriate for women to renounce the world. She and her followers persisted, cutting off their hair and donning the ochre robes characteristic of the monastic community. They then walked barefoot until they found the Buddha and his monks. They were again refused ordination, but the Buddha's attendant Ananda took pity on them, noting their sincerity; these were court ladies unaccustomed to physical distress and their barefoot walk left them in rough shape. He took their case to the Buddha, asking him if women could attain the liberated state. When the Buddha answered positively, Ananda asked why, if women could be liberated, they would not benefit by renouncing the world? The Buddha then relented, though the texts add a vicious coda. Nuns were ordained only on condition of accepting eight special rules in addition to the monastic code. These rules formally subordinate all nuns to all monks without regard for seniority or attainments. Furthermore, it was said that because women had been accepted into the monastic sangha, the Buddhist religion would last only half as long as it would otherwise. Contemporary scholars debate whether these comments actually came from the Buddha or from later monk editors, given that the earliest Buddhist texts were not written down for about three hundred years. Whether or not these edicts actually came from the Buddha, they have influenced how Buddhists thought about and treated female monastics for millennia.

The stories of early Buddhism depict a wandering community; only later did monks and nuns settle in permanent dwellings. Monastic rules of discipline emerged gradually in response to predicaments in which monks and nuns found themselves. The Buddha frequently taught both monastics and lay people, giving rise to the large earliest Buddhist canon. Among these works are the Theragatha—the Songs of the (Male) Elders—and the Therighata—the Songs of the (Female) Elders. The latter text, attributed to nuns of the Buddha's day, may be the only canonical text written by women in world religious literature.

The social forms and teachings of early Indian Buddhism spread throughout the Indian subcontinent and beyond India into Sri Lanka by the third century B.C.E. One of the most famous Buddhists of this era was Emperor Ashoka, who ruled from 270 to 230 B.C.E. He was not born a Buddhist, but converted after winning a bloody war to consolidate and extend his kingdom. The carnage and suffering he saw caused a change of heart, after which he renounced warfare and hunting, promoted religions in general and Buddhism in particular; historical evidence suggests that he was genuinely concerned about the well-being of his subjects. He is also credited with sending Buddhist missionaries around the then-known world, including some to the Middle East. No historical records of missionaries to the West have been found, but scholars have long speculated about their possible influence on some strands of Western thought. In any case, other missionaries were more successful; the Sri Lankan Buddhist community traces its origins to Ashoka's son and daughter, who founded the monks' and the nuns' orders, respectively. From this evidence, we know the nuns' sangha was a routine part of Buddhism at this time; seemingly, it was expected that if a monks' sangha was begun, a nuns' sangha would also begin.

At this time, and some centuries later, Buddhism in India was undergoing the profound intellectual changes that led to the development of Mahayana Buddhism. But these newer movements did not succeed in Sri Lanka. The older forms of Buddhism eventually spread to the rest of Southeast Asia: Burma, Thailand, Laos, South Vietnam, and Cambodia. But through the vicissitudes of history, the nuns' ordination lineage eventually died out both in Sri Lanka and in India.[1] A nuns' order may once have existed in Burma, but it died out centuries ago; there are no records of fully ordained Buddhist nuns in any other Theravadin Buddhist countries.

Buddha's teachings have few, if any, direct applications to gender. In themselves, they are not more appropriate for or relevant to men than women. Women, like men, have been attracted to these teachings for millennia. To understand why women are attracted to Buddhism, we must know the basics of these teachings.

The key teachings of early Buddhism consist of the Four Noble Truths, the Three Marks, and Interdependence (pratityasamutpada). The words "suffering," "ignorance," and "grasping" appear repeatedly in all of these formulations of dharma. Suffering is the First Truth and the first mark; ignorance is at the root of the Second Truth and is the first of the twelve links of interdependence; grasping, as the cause of suffering, is the second Noble Truth and is a key link in the twelve links of Interdependence. In keeping with Indian thought in general, Buddhism sees ignorance as leading to grasping, which causes suffering. Thus, the fundamental liberating option offered by Buddhism is to overcome ignorance and thus end suffering, for oneself, but also, ultimately, for all sentient beings.

These key teachings are unique to Buddhism, but to understand them fully, one must remember that Buddhism adopted much of the world view already dominant in India of the sixth century B.C.E. Samsara, often translated as "cyclic existence," involves the claim that the universe is without beginning or end but goes through countless cycles of emergence and destruction. There is no resting place in this eternal cyclic existence, for everything in samsara is always changing. Everything changes in accord with karma, the unalterable law of cause and effect, which in Indian thought pertains to both the moral and physical universes. Karma could be likened to a bank account; one makes deposits of good and bad deeds and withdrawals consisting of good or bad fortune. Positive deeds result in a more fortunate rebirth, as a human being, for example, while negative deeds result in a less fortunate rebirth, as a hell-being, for example. Countless numbers of sentient beings migrate continuously through the various realms of samsara in accord with their karma. All Indian religions, including Buddhism, also teach that there is a way to undo this eternal roaming. Buddha's distinctive teachings, the Three Marks, the Four Noble Truths, and Interdependence, deal with how to undo endless wandering in samsara.

Because both the First Truth and the First Mark are about suffering, Buddhism has often been accused of being a "pessimistic" religion. Buddhists counter that this focus on suffering is not pessimistic but realistic. But suffering is not regarded as the essential trait of existence, a mistaken interpretation often made by those whose understanding of Buddhism is superficial. Buddhists emphasize that it is *conventional* ways of living, based on grasping and self-cherishing, that are inevitably permeated with suffering, not living itself. If grasping and ego-fixation are left behind, one will experience contentment and bliss. Suffering is the byproduct of grasping, which occurs only because of ignorance. Thus, the most important word in the fundamental Buddhist analysis of existence is not "suffering," but "ignorance." Ignorance of what? Ignorance of impermanence, of the lack of a permanent abiding self, ignorance that there is no essence, soul, or entity that endures through all the flux of experience. Because of this fundamental ignorance, which results in grasping for security and permanence and for assurance that personal identity is everlasting, suffering occurs. When it is fully realized that everything is impermanent, including personal identity, there is no grasping, and, hence, no suffering.

These Buddhist insights are most easily understood through thorough contemplation of the Three Marks, or fundamental characteristics, of all existence: impermanence, suffering, and egolessness. It is easiest to begin with impermanence because impermanence is so undeniable and so obvious; everything is subject to "birth, old age, sickness, and death," as a common Buddhist formula puts it. The fact of unending impermanence is easily conceded intellectually, but resisted emotionally, psychologically, and spiritually. Herein lies the genesis of suffering. Buddhists have never claimed that there is no pleasure, contrary to popular caricatures of Buddhism; instead, it is claimed that there is no *permanent* or *lasting* pleasure—a critical difference.

This cycle of suffering caused by grasping for permanence despite pervasive impermanence reaches its culmination in the thirst for personal immortality, in the desire to find a permanent abiding self that survives death or travels from one life to the next. The mark of egolessness, the lack of any permanent abiding self, is one of the most difficult Buddhist assertions to comprehend and assimilate; it goes completely against the grain of habitual psychology and most religious teaching. Buddhism claims that if we look carefully and dispassionately into our experience, we find only an assemblage of various parts, not a coherent, unchanging whole. These parts, called the Five Skandhas, are form (the body), feeling (pre-conceptual reactions of attraction, aversion, or indifference), perception, mental formations (basic mental patterns), and consciousness. The last of these five is most often taken to be the self, but it is easy to point out that consciousness is exceedingly impermanent, lasting only a fraction of a second and utterly irretrievable thereafter. Buddhists suggest that if one wants to look for permanence in human experience, the body is more enduring than any of the mental factors, but no one would pin their permanent enduring self to their body, which so obviously changes and dies. To argue even more pointedly, one might ask of the believer in personal immortality, "If you are immortal, tell me which one of you is going to be immortal? The one you are now? The one you will be when you die? The one you are at your best moment in life?"

According to Buddhism, it is not that we *become* egoless when we attain enlightenment. Egolessness is the basic reality of our existence, but unable to abide in that open expanse, we constantly try to create a self, which continually falls apart, but which we, nevertheless, think needs protection. So we set aside territory for ourselves and defend it against others. This cycle, unless broken by enlightenment, goes on forever. (Buddhists do assume the continuity of karma in past and future lives despite the lack of a permanent unchanging self.) To contemplate this claim thoroughly will show that, if Buddhists are correct, all suffering, from the sting of being insulted to all-out warfare, is due to self-cherishing.

These same ideas are repeated, but also amplified, by the other most basic Buddhist credo—the Four Noble Truths. The First Noble Truth is that suffering is inevitable in conventional life—a life characterized by self-cherishing. The Second Noble Truth is that suffering is caused by desire, by grasping, clinging, compulsion, or addiction to self and to pleasure. But, because suffering has a clearly identifiable cause—clinging—suffering ceases when its cause is abandoned. This is the Third Noble Truth, the truth of cessation. Experienced as a gap in the rush of self-perpetuation, a glimpse of unconditioned ease and contentment, Buddhist spiritual disciplines are about making this openness more familiar and more habitable, until one rests there continuously. Nirvana and nibbana are the Sanskrit and Pali terms applied to this state of egolessness.

The Fourth Noble Truth maps the path for the practitioner who wants to quell the fires of self-cherishing and find contentment and peace in unadorned, naked reality. The Eight-fold Noble Path consists of Right View, Right Intention, Right Speech, Right Action, Right Livelihood, Right Effort, Right Mindfulness, and Right Concentration. These eight are often summarized as the practice of Wisdom, Morality, and Meditation. They are the essentials of the Buddhist way of life.

Moral conduct is the basis upon which the rest of the path must be built and consists of not harming other beings in so far as that is possible. For example, Right Livelihood requires one not to engage in any occupation that causes harm to others—a precept that, if taken seriously, would significantly impact how global capitalism is practiced. Right Action involves basic commandments found in all religions, and Right Speech involves avoiding many misuses of speech more subtle than out and out lying—gossip and idle chatter, for example.

Although morality is universally expected of Buddhists, in traditional settings, meditation is more often a specialty of the monastic community, though lay meditation movements are now gaining strength. Its meditation practices make Buddhism distinctive among world religions and attractive to many Westerners. In most forms of Buddhism, meditation is considered essential for attaining any level of realization, any stabilization of the basic awake state beneath ego-grasping. There are many varieties of meditation, and all meditation teachers stress that meditation is better learned from a living teacher than from a book, but some generalities can be provided. The student is first instructed to place the body in the correct posture, usually an upright, cross-legged posture (though meditation can be done in a chair). In meditation, the mind is given an object upon which to stabilize, usually one's breath. One is instructed to place one's attention on the object of meditation and to return to that object when the focus is lost. Finally, meditation instruction involves knowing what to do with the seemingly ceaseless thought process. Contrary to many peoples' expectations, meditation is not about stopping thoughts, which is impossible, but about not being totally at the mercy of one's willy-nilly thought process. When thoughts occur, one returns to the object of meditation rather than pursuing, judging, or entertaining the thought. Slowly, slowly, the mind stabilizes and can stay put. The calming effect of this process can be used for anything from simple relaxation for better health to providing the basis for seeing the nature of ultimate reality.

Morality and meditation practice are the necessary prerequisites for developing Wisdom (prajna). In Buddhist perspective, wisdom is not a static body of knowledge to be memorized and recited, but genuine insight into the nature of things. In the context of early Indian Buddhism, prajna consists of tasting egolessness personally and knowing the peace of mind that it brings, rather than simply providing flawless intellectual arguments proving the truth of egolessness.

The final building block of early Buddhist teaching is Interdependence, the twelve links of pratityasamutpada, or the inexorability of cause and effect. Once the cause has been activated, the result will inevitably follow. This teaching is also about the possibility of reversing the process of cause and effect, of shutting down the ever-turning wheel of samsara by not activating the causes, by not making the leap from feeling to grasping. Most important, this teaching demonstrates that nothing in samsara stands by itself, independent of the whole conditioning network of all other phenomena. Everything is interdependent with everything else and nothing is independent. In contemporary times, this teaching has been used as the basis for a Buddhist environmental ethic and a global economic and political ethic.

Clearly, these early, basic Buddhist teachings are gender neutral and gender inclusive. Some feminists have claimed that the teachings about ego and egolessness are irrelevant to women living under patriarchal conditions because such women need "more ego" not "less ego." But this claim totally misses the Buddhist meaning of the terms often translated as "ego" and "egolessness." Egolessness has to do with an open-ended, nonforceful, spontaneous way of being beyond our usual boundaries; ego has to do with any style of being in the world, whether of self-aggrandizement or of self-effacement, that blocks such freedom and openness. In Buddhist terms, even a self-effacing victim has an ego—the ego of a self-effacing victim—and the solution is not to develop "more ego," as some feminists would think, but to drop self-effacement in favor of true egolessness.

On the other hand, these basic teachings contain a devastating critique of any system of gender hierarchy, including those perpetuated by

Buddhism throughout its long history. How can clinging to privileges conferred by gender or concepts of what it means to be a woman or a man be anything except the self-cherishing that basic Buddhist teachings so thoroughly critique? The Buddha saw through the self-cherishing of economic or racial caste privilege. But he let stand the self-cherishing involved in fixed ideas about gender and the ways in which women were limited by those fixed ideas. That a religion so thoroughly devoted to dismantling conventional ego would be blind to the way in which fixed and limiting ideas about gender reinforce ego is shocking.

B. Mahayana Buddhism

By five hundred years after the time of the Buddha, a new Buddhist movement, calling itself Mahayana (Large Vehicle) Buddhism, became established in India and was spreading to East Asia. This form of Buddhism is (or was) dominant in China, Tibet, Japan, Korea, and North Vietnam. Though historians would not accept the claim, Mahayana legends state that the Buddha himself taught Mahayana doctrines, but arranged for them to be hidden for five hundred years when he realized that most of his followers did not have the spiritual development required to understand these doctrines. Mahayanists take this legend quite seriously. The beloved Heart Sutra is the text about which this story is told, and the place where he gave this short discourse is a pilgrimage site. The meaning behind the legends is more important in the long run; Mahayanists insist that whether or not the historical Buddha taught the Mahayana, its innovations are a logical outgrowth of the Buddha's early teachings.

The central Mahayana innovations involve an ethical ideal—the bodhisattva path—and a series of philosophical proclamations—the Madhyamika and Yogacara schools. Mahayana Buddhism also developed a new understanding of Buddhahood, the Trikaya (Three Bodies of Buddha) doctrine, which led to the development of a vast pantheon of mythological Buddhas and Bodhisattvas and profoundly affected Buddhist art, ritual, and popular religious practices.

The Bodhisattva is someone who vows to attain "complete perfect enlightenment" for the sake of all sentient beings. Packed into that phrase is an array of claims and aspirations. The Bodhisattva is not practicing primarily to end future rebirths in samsara. According to early Buddhism, once one fully overcame the causes of suffering—grasping and ignorance—one would not be reborn but would instead experience nirvana—a state that Buddhists refused to define further. Mahayanists decried this ideal as still based on self-cherishing, claiming that it would be more self-less and compassionate for an Awakened One to remain in samsara, helping those who do not understand why their lives are so pain filled and unsatisfactory to discover the dharma. The Bodhisattva vows to remain in samsara for as long as samsara lasts, for the sake of the peace and well-being of all sentient beings. Furthermore, according to Mahayana Buddhism, this resolve is in accord with basic human nature. Despite countless lifetimes of ego-filled imprinting, humans still retain as their most basic heritage, the longing (bodhicitta) to benefit beings, themselves included. Thus compassion, a more active practice, comes to have the same importance in Buddhist ethics as does non-harming, the primary virtue of early Buddhist ethics. In Mahayana thought, this Bodhisattva path became incredibly long, with many detailed stages of practice and realization.

Mahayana Buddhism claims to open the Buddhist sangha more widely. Though monasticism continued to be central to all Mahayana Buddhist societies, Mahayana social ethics proclaim that dharma is fully available to one and all, lay or monastic, male or female. These statements suggest that the Indian Buddhist community had become rather male and monk dominated, a supposition borne out by the many anti-women comments that had become common in Buddhist writings. It is unclear if Mahayana writings actually reflect a social reality that respected women and lay people more highly or in which they had more opportunities, but many Mahayana sutras center on a lay hero, and women and girls are often represented as being more knowledgeable about dharma than their male interlocutors. In many sutras, a female demonstrates her highly realized state by changing instantaneously into a male. However, in one of the most famous incidents, a woman instead changes her male taunter into a woman and then asks him (now her) to find the essence of the femaleness that would limit her ability to understand the dharma. (We will analyze this story in depth in the concluding section.) Two thousand years ago, some Mahayanists clearly recognized that one implication of Buddhism's doctrine of egolessness is that, if there is no fixed *personal* self, then certainly there can be no fixed *female* or *male* self that limits and determines what men or women can or cannot do spiritually and intellectually.

Mahayana philosophical teachings have a similarly expansive quality. Early Buddhist thought had focused on the lack of a personal self or soul beneath the changing currents of karma. Mahayana teachings expand that analysis to cover all phenomena with their doctrine of emptiness (shunyata). Emptiness, Mahayanists point out, is not some mysterious vague nonsubstance, but only the logical extension of the analysis that led early Buddhists to posit egolessness. Things, thought of as entities or substances, disappear under rigorous analysis, whether that analysis pertains to the self or to the phenomenal world "outside" the self. Despite the potential that its teachings, wrongly understood, could easily lead to nihilism, Mahayana Buddhism posited universal emptiness. Mahayana thought fearlessly proclaims that nothing exists at all, if by "existence" we mean that something is independent of causes and conditions, unchanging, and permanent. Rather, everything really *is* interdependent with everything else, which means nothing does or can exist in and of itself. Thus the most famous line of the Heart Sutra, perhaps the most famous line of Mahayana Buddhist thought proclaims, "Form is emptiness; emptiness is also form. Form is no other than emptiness; emptiness is no other than form. In the same way, feeling, perception, formation, and consciousness are empty." Finally, the Heart Sutra draws the ultimate logical, but scary conclusion. There is "no suffering, no origin of suffering, no cessation of suffering, no path, no wisdom, no attainment and no non-attainment." No wonder Mahayana legends say that when the historical Buddha proclaimed this sutra many of his disciples had heart attacks, which is why he decided to keep these teachings hidden until later. In the Buddhist context, such teachings were not meant merely as abstract philosophical analyses. These teachings promote ultimate freedom from grasping and suffering. Religious people often cling fiercely to ideology, to religious "truths," and such clinging causes immense suffering. Therefore, even the most basic teachings of Buddhism are said to be empty. Far from being depressing or nihilistically promoting a lifestyle of "nothing matters, anything goes," emptiness, properly contemplated, brings a sense of openness, freshness, ease, and appreciation into life. It becomes the echo that puts every experience into perspective.

Mahayana refinements of the meaning of emptiness were the speciality of the Madhyamika school of thought. Almost as old as the Madhyamika school is the Yogacara or "mind-only" school, which complements Madhyamika by discussing how the mind and the phenomenal world work in the context of emptiness. This school especially focuses on consciousness and meditation practice. The Yogacara school minutely analyzes how the eight consciousnesses create samsara when operating in their confused or fixated mode, and how meditation practices can undo those distortions. Equally important to this school is the reality that after one thoroughly assimilates emptiness into one's being and gives up making one's self and the world substantial, experience still continues. Emptiness is not a mere negation or blank. Rather, an enlightened mind experiences without distortion or grasping. Yogacara explorations of "pure perception"—how an empty perceiver perceives an empty world—are of central importance to even later developments in Buddhist thought and practice in Vajrayana Buddhism.

Many other ideas important to Mahayana Buddhism originated with the Yogacarins. They first developed the idea of Trikaya—usually translated as the "Three Bodies of the Buddha," but much less misleading if understood as "three levels of Buddhahood." As already mentioned, this concept had major implications for Buddhist art and popular religion. According to this teaching, the historical Buddha was an instance of one kind of Buddhahood (nirmanakaya), the kind that is a human being who perfects the practice of the path and can serve other human beings as a visible example of the possibility of liberation. He was not the first nor the last such Buddha. Another level of Buddhahood could aptly be referred to as "mythical Buddhas and Bodhisattvas" as the term "myth" is used in religious studies. These sambhogakaya beings are quite advanced on the path; the Buddhas are already enlightened and have conjured their Buddha-realms as a result of their infinite merit, whereas the Bodhisattvas (who have taken the Bodhisattva vow) are well beyond the level of humans in the six realms of samsara. These various beings are also visible, though to most humans, they are visible only through art or visualization practices. They personify the primary Mahayana virtues of wisdom and compassion. And this is one of the places in which feminine imagery enters Buddhist art and practice. Some of the most important and beloved sambhogakaya Bodhisattvas are female—Prajnaparamita, Kwan-yin, and Tara. Finally, there is the abstract dharmakaya level of Buddhahood. Impersonal and all-pervading, this ultimate level of Buddhahood is synonymous with emptiness and suchness.

Another concept that originates with the Yogacara school is essential for tying the whole vast project of the Mahayana together. Why would human beings, so burdened with their samsara-filled lives, even aspire to be concerned for other beings or to expend the money, time, and energy that is required to practice the spiritual disciplines that lead to experiencing emptiness? The answer is Buddha-nature (tathagatagarbha), the inherent pull toward sane, compassionate living that Mahayana Buddhism claims as the fundamental birthright of all existence. Without conviction of that indwelling Buddhahood, very little else of the Mahayana Buddhist project makes sense. And one can ask why, if that indwelling Buddhahood pertains to the whole of existence, women have been treated as second-class, inferior beings incapable of serious Buddhist practice in so many traditional Buddhist social settings.

Like earlier forms of Buddhism, Mahayana Buddhism spread beyond India, first to China, eventually to Korea, and finally to Japan. Buddhism probably made its way into China by the beginning of the common era, spreading very slowly at first. China already had a highly developed literate culture and its own religious traditions of Taoism and Confucianism; Buddhism did not seem to fill any gaps in Chinese culture or religion. However, after 320 C.E., when northern China was overrun by invaders and the Chinese court moved south, Buddhism began to flourish in both parts of the divided kingdom. When China was reunited in 581, Buddhism became one of the most important cultural forces in the new dynasty. The next three hundred years represent the heyday of Buddhism in China, the period when the great schools of Chinese Buddhism developed and when Buddhism was the dominant cultural and religious force. Buddhist fortunes suffered a reversal in 842–845, when a rabidly anti-Buddhist emperor tried to exterminate the religion by destroying temples and shrines and forcing thousands of monks and nuns into lay life. Though he did not succeed in wiping out Buddhism, the religion never regained much influence among the elite classes, which returned to Taoism and renewed Confucianism. Buddhism did remain significant as a popular religion, however.

Once Buddhism became truly established in Chinese culture, Chinese schools of Buddhism developed. The major Chinese innovation involved forming separate schools from the many strands in the complex mosaic of Indian Buddhism. Thus, Chinese schools of Buddhism were much more specialized than their Indian predecessors had been.

One major tactic of Chinese Buddhist schools was systematizing the great mass of sometimes mutually exclusive Buddhist teachings and texts inherited from India. Called the "eclectic" schools, the T'ien T'ai and Hua-yen movements divided the Buddha's teaching career into stages and correlated various important texts with different periods of his teaching career. Why had the Buddha taught different things at different times? Simple. He was a skilled teacher who knew how much his students could assimilate without being overwhelmed, and he taught appropriately. Both T'ien T'ai and Hua-yen selected a text claimed to be the Buddha's definitive teaching.

The Meditation School, better known by its Japanese name—Zen— than its Chinese name—Ch'an—is a second specialization in Chinese Buddhism. This school, founded by Bodhidharma (470–520), a semi-legendary Indian meditation master, is famous for its paradoxical questions, for innovative teaching techniques, and for insistence on direct experience of emptiness over philosophical knowledge of the treatises on emptiness. This school also stresses that each being is fundamentally Buddha, but must awaken to that fact. Meditation is regarded as the most effective method to promote that goal.

Finally, devotional Buddhism, Pure Land Buddhism, became an important part of Chinese popular religion. This is a Buddhism of "other power," not "self power," the "other power being Buddha Amitabha," an already enlightened Buddha whose Buddha-field is called the Western paradise. His Bodhisattva vow included the aspiration, after becoming enlightened, to use his great store of merit to create a "Pure Land" into which rebirth would be easy, requiring only devoted chanting of Amitabha's name, and in which reaching enlightenment would be easy. Furthermore, there would be no unfortunate rebirths in this Pure Land. As a result, all who were reborn there would be reborn as males; female rebirth was thought to be unfortunate, an idea to be discussed later in depth.

As in Sri Lanka, monastic institutions for both men and women were introduced relatively early. Because monks cannot confer monastic ordination on women by themselves, it was necessary to bring Buddhist nuns from abroad for the first ordinations. In 429 and 433, nuns from Sri Lanka traveled to China to help ordain thousands of Chinese nuns. This ordination lineage, unbroken to the present day, is important for attempts to renew nuns' ordination in Buddhist traditions that have lost it. Today, in Chinese communities outside mainland China, the nuns' orders are flourishing, with many more women than men currently being ordained as monastics.

The Chinese practice of not demanding exclusive loyalty to one religion led to an interesting practice among elite classes. Traditional Chinese mores dictated strict separation between men and women; men ran the public world and women dominated private realms. After 845, Chinese men of the elite classes were overwhelmingly trained in Confucian classics and were taught to reject Buddhism. But women from these same classes often became ardent Buddhists; that religion offered them much more than did male-dominated Confucianism. These women were often especially devoted to Kwan-yin, the female personification of compassion.

Buddhism spread from China to Korea in the fourth century, where its story is quite similar. It spread very slowly at first, became quite dominant in the period 935–1392, and then was repressed by the government for the next five centuries. The Meditation School became the dominant form of Buddhism in Korea. Interestingly, despite repression of Korean Buddhism for many centuries, the Korean nuns' order survives to the present day. Chinese influence was also significant in Vietnam, especially North Vietnam. Again, the Meditation School is the most important school, and the nuns' ordination lineages are still alive.

Though Japanese Buddhism also came from China, initially by way of Korea, distinctive forms of Buddhism developed there. Buddhism did not enter Japan until 552 C.E.; it came as part of a diplomatic gift from a Korean king, who highly recommended Buddhism to the Japanese court as a religion that, if practiced, would safeguard the Japanese nation. A major Japanese clan immediately sought to implement the Buddhist practice, including making arrangements for Japanese monks and nuns to be ordained. When a plague broke out, Buddhist practice was forcibly discontinued. But when that did not quell the plague, Buddhists were allowed to resume their practice. During the regency of Prince Shotoku (573–622), Buddhism became well established.

Two themes predominate in Japanese Buddhism. First, Buddhism developed a complementary relationship with the indigenous Shinto traditions, which meant that the constant tension between indigenous and imported traditions so destructive to Chinese Buddhism was significantly mitigated. Today, most Japanese people would accept the slogan "Born Shinto, die Buddhist." Buddhism has become the religion dealing with death and ancestorhood—predominant concerns in Japanese religion. As such, it has a place in the lives of most Japanese, even if they do not regularly practice Buddhist disciplines. Second, distinctive Japanese schools of Buddhism developed, usually with some initial impetus from Japanese who had studied in China. The first major development occurred when Saicho (767–822), a monk fleeing corruption at established Buddhist centers in Nara, founded a new monastery on Mount Hei, northwest of Kyoto, the new capital. Saicho returned from advanced studies in China as the major Japanese promoter of T'ien T'ai, or Tendai in Japanese. This sect flourishes to the present day, and newer movements in Japanese Buddhism frequently sprang from it. The common practice of banning women from Japan's holy mountains, not lifted until the nineteenth century, began at this time. Its purpose was to ensure monks' celibacy, but its effect was to popularize beliefs that women are spiritually inferior, polluting, and perpetrate lack of celibacy among monks.

Shingon Buddhism, the Japanese form of Tantric Buddhism (to be discussed in the next section), was also introduced at this time. Kukai (774–835), one of the most brilliant, prolific, and beloved Japanese Buddhist teachers, went to China the same year as Saicho (804), but he found the ultimate teachings of the Buddha in Tantric Buddhism. (Tantric Buddhism existed in China at that time, but soon died out there.) He came back to Japan to found his monastery on Mount Koya, southwest of Kyoto and much more remote.[2] Though prolific as a scholar, he was also a religious pilgrim and helped make religious pilgrimage an important practice in Japan.

Political changes in Japan in 1185 led to the next period of creative development in Japanese Buddhism. During this period, the final three most important movements in Japanese Buddhism—Zen, Pure Land, and Nichiren—developed. All three schools were founded by monks who began their training on Mount Hei, became disillusioned by the rampant corruption that had developed there and left to start three very different reform movements.

Though he did not found the first Zen temple in Japan, the most famous and important person in the development of Japanese Zen is Dogen (1200–1253). Orphaned at the age of seven, he resolved to become a monk when the reality of impermanence impressed him deeply as he watched incense smoke rising at his mother's funeral. At the age of fourteen he was ordained on Mount Hei and quickly mastered everything they taught but still felt that his quest for understanding was incomplete. He could find no one in Japan to answer his questions, so in 1223, he left for China. Finally he found a Ch'an master whom he trusted and began intensive Ch'an practice. After experiencing the Awakening so central to Zen practice, which he called "the dropping away of body and mind," he returned to Japan in 1227 and began to teach Zen. Eventually, he was forced to move to Eihei-ji, the remote site that is still a principle training monastery of Soto Zen Buddhism.[3] Dogen, one of Japan's most important Buddhist thinkers, wrote eloquently of the spiritual equality of women and men, even suggesting that monks should become the disciples of nuns who were already awakened. This advice was largely ignored, however.

The basis for Pure Land teachings has already been discussed. However, in Japan, this school became more distinct than it was in China and made important innovations in Japanese religious life. The practice of reciting Amitabha's name far predates the development of Pure Land as a separate school. It is part of Tendai practice and popular Buddhism in general. But in Pure Land Buddhism, it is to be one's only practice; nothing else is necessary, and it is even presumptuous to think that one's own study, meditation, or merit-making could save one. It is necessary only to have faith in the Primal Vow of Amida (already discussed) and recite his name in utter faith and devotion. Two men who were once monks on Mount Hei were prominent in establishing Pure Land as a distinct school: Honen (1133–1212) and Shinran (1173–1262). Of the two, Shinran's innovations were more decisive. After many years of frustration with celibacy, he experienced a vision of Kannon (Kwan-yin) telling him he should marry and that she would help him in his new ministry. After he married, he refused to become an ordinary lay practitioner. He continued to teach and preach, claiming that all Pure Land practitioners are "neither monk nor lay." Some centuries later, Shinran's innovations became standard Japanese practice in all denominations.

Japanese Buddhist priests usually undergo a period of monastic training, after which they return to serve a local temple inherited from their fathers, expecting their sons to succeed them eventually. Many would consider Pure Land Buddhism to be *the* prototypically Japanese form of Buddhism.

Finally, the Nichiren denomination was founded by Nichiren (1222–1282). He too initially studied on Mount Hei but broke with the Tendai school. He taught that the Lotus Sutra alone should be regarded as Buddha's true teaching, whereas Tendai Buddhism studies and respects many other sutras, even though the Lotus Sutra is regarded as the Buddha's ultimate teaching. Nichiren also taught his followers to recite the phrase "Homage to the Lotus Sutra" as their major religious practice. Nichiren taught that this form of Buddhism alone is true and that all other forms should be prohibited. He predicted that Japan would become a Buddha-land on earth, from which true Buddhism would spread over the entire world if his recommendations were followed. These views brought him opposition, and he was exiled and almost executed. His sect survived, however, and in the twentieth century has given rise to one of the most successful "new religions" of Japan.

Apparently, there have always been Japanese nuns, even though a nun's ordination in accord with the ancient Indian monastic rules has never been performed in Japan. However, men's ordination in accord with those ancient rules also died out, making the lack of formal women's ordination much less problematic. In Japan, ordination ceremonies and vows are identical for men and women, though it is said that nuns usually keep the precepts more strictly than monks. They usually do not marry or drink alcohol, whereas monks usually do. Nuns can and do head temples and perform all the ceremonies of their tradition, but they have a harder time getting the economic support required to maintain a temple. In addition, priests' wives live in the temples with their husbands and can be involved in many temple activities.

C: Vajrayana Buddhism

Meanwhile, back in India, Buddhism was still developing, as Vajrayana or Tantric Buddhism slowly emerged. Some would argue that this is the most "feminine" form of Buddhism. Certainly it has more overtly positive female symbolism than any other form of Buddhism. Its history also records significant numbers of highly revered women, though many more men than women are remembered. Many essential Tantric teachings and practices are secret, to be revealed only to qualified students, making it the most difficult form of Buddhism to study accurately. Vajrayana portrays a world that seems so imaginary and yet unimaginable, a world that makes little sense in a rational context. The Vajrayana mythical universe is exceedingly full, well beyond that of Mahayana Buddhism; every imaginable kind of being resides there. Vajrayana is a fanciful and fantastic world, dense with symbolism. The key to that symbolism, conferred in initiation and the practices that follow initiation, makes the Vajrayana world make sense. Without that key, one could easily be quite lost.

The first step to accurate understanding of Vajrayana Buddhism is remembering that it exists in the context of Mahayana Buddhism. Every Vajrayana ceremony begins with renewing the Bodhisattva vow to become enlightened for the sake of all sentient beings and ends with dedicating to all sentient beings the merit earned by doing the ceremony. The belief system of Vajrayana Buddhism is almost identical with that of Mahayana Buddhism. It is often said that the point of Vajrayana Buddhism is to speed up one's progress on the Bodhisattva path, which is eons long in the Mahayana view. What distinguishes Vajrayana is its symbolism and its meditation-rituals, both of which are significantly different from anything found anywhere else in the Buddhist world. Both can be shocking and incomprehensible to outsiders, and Vajrayana Buddhism is often viewed negatively, both in other parts of the Buddhist world and by Western scholars. However, the prestige of the Dalai Lama, frequent visits to the West by Tibetan teachers, and a recent outpouring of accurate books on Vajrayana Buddhism have changed this stereotype considerably.

Without a doubt, Tantric Buddhism is best known for its use of explicit sexual symbolism, but uninitiated voyeurs usually draw wildly inaccurate conclusions about "tantric sex." Graphic sexual symbolism is central to all forms of Vajrayana Buddhism. Practices in which one visualizes oneself as deities in sexual union are common. Physical sexuality has been used as practice in Vajrayana Buddhism. But it is an advanced secret practice that is incomprehensible outside the complete context of Vajrayana. The sexual symbolism that so piques the curiosity of outsiders is quite straightforward. The feminine principle represents Wisdom while the masculine principle represents Compassion. Their union represents the inseparability of Wisdom and Compassion, which need to be developed equally. Their twoness represents duality—always the mistaken conventional understanding of things that cause all suffering, but their oneness as a couple transcends that duality into non-duality, reality as it is. However, non-duality is not monism. Oneness does not mean that distinctiveness disappears into a bland gray expanse. Rather, this is what scholars of religion call "two-in-one" symbolism—a flash of insight that is actually impossible to put into words, but which is communicated quite well by this central Vajrayana symbolism of dyadic unity. Sexual union is only the most obvious symbol for such dyadic unity, which Vajrayana Buddhism claims is found in all facets of experience.

Vajrayana meditation is also different from other forms of Buddhist meditation. The quiet sitting that most people associate with Buddhist meditation is basic in Vajrayana. In addition more colorful forms of meditation have developed. They include chanting and a ritual orchestra. As they chant, the meditators are visualizing—a meditation technique that is omnipresent in Vajrayana Buddhism. When the chanting stops, usually the meditators pick up a mala (a string of beads with which one can keep count of the numbers of recitations) and begin to recite mantras. Mantras, also common in Hinduism, are short, non-rational formulae that invoke the essential meaning and power of the deity being visualized. Finally, this form of meditation involves ritual implements and various gestures (*mudras*). The two hands hold two primary ritual implements, a bell and a scepter. The bell held in the left hand is feminine Wisdom and the scepter is masculine Compassion; when the hands cross in a mudra, that represents union.

The origins of Vajrayana Buddhism are difficult to ascertain. As with Mahayana Buddhism, Vajrayana legends say that the historical Buddha himself taught Vajrayana, but only to a select group of students, who passed it down their lineage until the times were right for Vajrayana to be more widely disseminated. Some legends say Buddha taught Vajrayana Buddhism at some point after his enlightenment experience, but others say that Buddha was actually enlightened through Vajrayana methods *before* his experiences under the Bodhi Tree. He then displayed his renunciation, battle with Mara, and enlightenment at Bodhgaya because he realized that

that was the only example with which most people could relate. Some accounts even state that he became enlightened while still living in the palace, as he engaged in ritual sexual intercourse with his wife. Why would such legends be important to Vajrayana Buddhists? Like Mahayana stories, they make the essential point that these practices are not innovations, but the full unfolding of the implications of the Buddha's teachings. No form of Vajrayana Buddhism has ever taught that Vajrayana can stand alone.

Historians, who do not accept these legends, find evidence that some form of Vajrayana Buddhism existed by the second century C.E. The so-called lower Tantras were being committed to writing by the sixth century, while the so-called higher Tantras, the ones usually practiced in contemporary Vajrayana Buddhism, only began to be written down in the eighth century. Vajrayana Buddhism undoubtedly began as a radical lay movement that included women and all social strata, from the most to the least respected. The movement was radical also in its rituals, deliberately flaunting well-established Indian religious practices such as not eating meat or drinking liquor. Practitioners are said to have met in charnel grounds and other ritually impure places, where they included sexuality in their repertoire of religious methods, sometimes claiming that sexual experience is necessary to the experience of realization. Most scholars suggest that the Buddhist Tantric movement borrowed heavily from Hinduism. Vajrayana Buddhists stress that the two Tantric movements may look similar but are fundamentally different. Nevertheless, the influence of Hinduism on Tantric Buddhism is undeniable to anyone who knows both traditions.

A major figure in the early development of this movement was Princess Lakshminkara, who led a Tantric circle of male and female disciples from all levels of society. Married off into an unsatisfactory marriage, she finally escaped by feigning insanity and took refuge in a cremation ground where she meditated. As is typical for Tantric legends about important founders, she had visions of the Buddhas and Bodhisattvas and was initiated personally by them. She then returned to her homeland to present the teachings they had given her. Soon similar circles were widespread and by the eleventh century many Siddhas (accomplished ones) wandered through India. A collection of legends about eighty-four especially prominent Siddhas is still important to Tantric practitioners. By the eleventh century, most Siddhas upon whom the legends focus were men. Most of them practiced with a female companion who is not portrayed as a mere ritual implement. Usually the story ends when they go together to the "realm of the dakinis"; one does get to the realm of the dakinis on the basis of someone else's achievements. This phrase is further evidence of the importance of females—both mythical and human—in Vajrayana Buddhism. Dakinis are enlightened female energies; the term is used for both humans and those who rule the "realm of the dakinis," a celestial realm that figures in many Vajrayana legends. Most important, most male Vajrayana leaders of this early period were initiated by females, sometimes human, sometimes celestial.

In its last flourish of glory before dying out in India, Buddhism gave rise to great monastic universities, the most famous being Nalanda. The curriculum focused on complex and subtle systems of Mahayana philosophy while the discipline was strictly monastic. Wandering lay Yogins (another common term for Siddhas), who often viewed scholarly learning as an impediment to realization and practiced sexual yoga, had no place in these universities. Nevertheless, the popularity and profundity of Vajrayana Buddhism eventually led to syntheses between the monastic curriculum and the most esoteric and flagrantly sexual Tantric texts. Scholars claim that in the context of monastic Vajrayana Buddhism, the practice of visualizing sexual union was substituted for the real thing, because monks could not engage in literal sex. It is also claimed that for a good meditator, there would be no difference between the two. If sexuality was not surrounded by deep and profound symbolism before this development (and I suspect it was), such symbolism certainly developed in this context and continues in the contemporary practice of Vajrayana.

This tension and synthesis between yogic and monastic Vajrayana Buddhism, the last development within Indian Buddhism, was being taken to Tibet at this time, just ahead of Muslim invaders who burned Nalanda University and assured the demise of Buddhism in India. This form of Buddhism became the lifeblood of Tibetan culture until the mid-twentieth century when China took over Tibet and curtailed Buddhist practice.

Buddhism first came to Tibet with the Chinese and Nepali co-wives of an early king. But Buddhism gained only a toehold at this time. In the eighth century, Buddhism become more firmly established when Tibet's first monastery, Samye, was built in Lhasa. The story demonstrates well the synthesis of monastic and yogic Buddhism typical of Tibet. A great Indian scholar from Nalanda University, Shantarakshita, was invited to preside over building the monastery, but natural disasters, attributed by the local population to the displeasure of local deities, occurred and construction was stopped. Shantarakshita went back to India, sending in his place the famous Indian Siddha Padmasambhava to tame the local deities. This plan worked; Padmasambhava subdued the hostile local deities and construction was completed.

Up to this point Tibetan accounts of what happened and accounts by Western historians agree; after this point they diverge radically. According to Western accounts, Padmasambhava stayed in Tibet only a few years and was forced to leave Tibet due to the court's displeasure. Tibetan accounts are vastly different; Padmasambhava is magnified into one of the most important figures in the history of Tibetan Buddhism, a second Buddha, who introduced numerous Vajrayana initiations and practices into Tibet, gained twenty-five major disciples, composed and buried many hidden "treasure texts" (terma) to be discovered later when needed, and lived in Tibet for many years before his body ascended into the light. Tibetan stories about Guru Rinpoche (his Tibetan name) also tell of his foremost student and consort, Yeshe Tsogyel. According to lengthy accounts of her life, she is as remarkable as he is. She is rarely mentioned in Western historical accounts of early Tibetan Buddhism, but Tibetans could not imagine telling the story of Guru Rinpoche while omitting that of Yeshe Tsogyel. If there is no historical woman behind these texts, it is remarkable that Tibetans would have developed such rich stories about her.

Whichever story is told, both agree that this was the "first propagation." In the ninth century, the growing power and influence of Buddhist monasteries led the king to try to limit their power. In the power struggle that ensued, the king was assassinated by a monk and political chaos resulted. The monasteries were deserted. For a period of about a hundred years, some Buddhists continued to practice, but with little cohesiveness or organization.

The "second propagation" began with a familiar theme; the great Indian scholar Atisha (982–1054) was invited from an Indian university to rejuvenate Buddhism. He and his Tibetan students founded the Kadam monastic order, a strict scholastic order important in the later development of Tibetan Buddhism. From this time until the end of Indian Buddhism, there was a good deal of traffic between Tibet and India. The traffic went both ways; Indians came to Tibet to teach, and Tibetans went to India in search of teachings. Two Tibetans are especially important because the texts and practices they brought back quickly generated two of the four main orders of Tibetan Buddhism. Drokmi's (972–1074) texts and teachings eventually became the basis of the Sakya order and Marpa's (1012–1096) of the Kagyu order.

Marpa's primary student, Milarepa (1040–1123) is one of Tibet's most beloved figures, rivaling Padmasambhava in popularity. His story is striking. As a young man he successfully learned black magic and totally destroyed the household of his uncle, who had usurped Milarepa's mother's property. He realized that killing so many people, for any reason, would bring very bad karma. Only expiating the bad karma during this life and then attaining realization would avert this fate. His quest for a competent teacher took him to Marpa, but instead of immediately granting him initiation, Marpa subjected Milarepa to hard labor for six years. These stories are among the most often retold by Tibetan Buddhists. Milarepa was at the point of suicide several times before Marpa finally granted him initiations and sent him off to practice in remote caves high in the mountains. (Long solitary retreats in remote caves became an important practice in Tibetan Buddhism.) He survived on nettles, turned green, and almost died of starvation, but he persevered. A gifted poet, he wrote many poems about meditation and the state of realization. Collected as the *Hundred Thousand Songs of Milarepa,* they are among the beloved Tibetan literature.

Eventually, Milarepa became famous as a highly realized Yogin and attracted many students. His principal student, Gampopa (1079–1154) was a Kadam monk before he became Milarepa's student. As Milarepa's student, he studied Tantric teachings going back to Naropa through Marpa. Gampopa, who held both the scholastic and the yogic lineages, is the founder of the Kagyu order, which includes both monastics and Yogins. The third of the four orders, the Nyingma (Old Order) was systematized at this point. It stems from lay practitioners who claimed to have retained the practices and teachings of the first propagation. Therefore, they claim Padmasambhava as their founder. In this order celibacy is not especially promoted and most of its great adepts had wives or consorts, a practice that continues to the present day.

To complete the story, the last major player to enter the scene was the Gelug order, founded by Tsongkhapa (1357–1419), one of Tibet's greatest philosophical minds and author of many treatises on emptiness. He was a reformer; by then many monks had wives or consorts and he was disgusted with what he saw as lack of respect for Buddhist ethical principles. Because he was ordained as a Kadam monk, the Gelug order combines the Kadam school's strict discipline with rigorous study of teachings on emptiness. Today the Gelug school is best known for its spiritual head, the Dalai Lama, Tibet's most famous Tulku. The uniquely Tibetan practice of finding young boys said to be incarnations (Tulkus) of recently deceased masters and training them from early childhood to fill that role was well in place by the time of Tsongkhapa, declared later to be the third Dalai Lama.

The period of the second propagation included one important woman teacher, Machig Labdron (1055–1145). Though she did not found her own lineage, she discovered a uniquely Tantric practice, chod (cutting). In this practice, done alone at night in frightening places, meditators visualize themselves being cut to pieces as an offering to needy hungry sentient beings. The purpose of the practice is a radical cutting off of any remaining ego clinging. Chod is said to be the only practice that originated in Tibet and was later taken to India, reversing the usual flow of teachings. Several versions of Machig's story can be found, but all agree that for a time, she took a consort and had several children.

As for less renowned women, the four Tibetan orders included monastic institutions for women. The nuns' full ordination did not reach Tibet, but the novice ordination did. Because the clothing worn by Tibetan novices is not noticeably different from that of fully ordained monastics, lack of full ordination for nuns is nowhere nearly as apparent as in Theravada Buddhist countries. As in most other parts of the Buddhist world, the support, respect, and training given to nuns was inferior to that given monks. But the tradition of solitary yogic practice also was available to women; in these situations, women were more on a par with men, and advanced, skilled women meditators were respected and could be sought out as teachers, though usually people studied with male Yogins. Finally, the mothers of Tulkus were highly respected and treated very well.

II: IS BUDDHISM MISOGYNIST OR PRO-WOMEN, NEITHER, OR BOTH?: THE PROBLEMS AND POLITICS OF INTERPRETATION

Having surveyed the historical and intellectual development of Buddhism, we are now in a position to discuss the problems and politics of interpreting what Buddhism actually says about gender. In the contemporary world, religions usually claim they treat women well. Because the treatment of women has become a highly contested issue, no religion declares that it mistreats women or wants to be perceived as if it did. But claims are made about every religion, by both insiders and outsiders, that its women face real obstacles and difficulties. Often the same religious phenomenon is evaluated both as an obstacle to women and as evidence that their tradition has their best interests at heart. Or it may be claimed that a specific practice has nothing to do with intentionally obstructing women, that given nature and biology, no alternatives are possible. Claims about whether a religion treats women well or poorly depend upon the values and perceptions of those making the claims. Thus, the often-asked question of whether Buddhism is good or bad for women has no real answer. In this section, we will examine several important Buddhist teachings, texts, or practices that affect women directly, and explore in more depth what are the limits and the possibilities of the Buddhist tradition.

A: The Woes of Female Rebirth

Most Buddhists throughout history probably believed that it is "bad karma" to be reborn a woman. But what does this mean?

We have already emphasized that the Buddha accepted pan-Indian ideas of karma and samsara without question. For traditional Buddhists, the question is not whether rebirth occurs but how it works. Good conduct produces fortunate rebirths and negative deeds unfortunate ones. So the statement that it is bad karma to be reborn as a woman contains two assumptions. First, to be a woman is less fortunate than to be a man. Second, this less fortunate rebirth is due to negative deeds in past lives.

When most people, especially women, not already familiar with this statement first hear it, they regard it as a very hurtful, negative statement about women. Many hear it as meaning that something is fundamentally wrong with women. Anger or frustration, especially on the part of people personally interested in Buddhism, is common. The statement seems to be in accord with the generalization that Buddhism favors men over women.

But what is claimed? What makes female rebirth woeful? Is there something wrong with women, or is there something wrong with the cultural conditions under which women are forced to live? Are *women* bad? Or do women have *difficult lives?* If they have difficult lives, is that because of inherent female biology, or because of the social context within which they live? All these possibilities have been proposed in Buddhist texts.

Definitely, female rebirth was sometimes thought to be negative because women were thought to be inferior. Common Indian stereotypes persisting to this day expect women not to be interested in spiritual matters, to be more materialistic, and definitely more lustful than men. In the Buddhist value system, this means women are inferior beings. Both women's bodies and women's minds were said to be inadequate and defective. Diana Y. Paul, quotes *The Sutra on Changing the Female Sex.* The Buddha is speaking:

> The female's defects—greed, hate, and delusion and other defilements—are greater
> than the male's . . . You [women] therefore should have such an intention. . . . Because
> I wish to be freed from the impurities of the woman's body, I will acquire the
> beautiful and fresh body of a man.[4]

Because of supposed inherent inferiority of women, it was claimed the Buddha would never be a woman, nor could a woman become a Buddha while in her woman's body. Asanga, an important Mahayana thinker, explained why. "All women are by nature full of defilement and of weak intelligence. And not by one who is full of defilement and of weak intelligence is completely perfected Buddhahood attained."[5]

However, the dominant view is, not that women are *bad,* but that women are *unfortunate.* These misfortunes were classified as the "five woes" and the "three subserviences." The five woes are "that she must leave her family at marriage; that she must suffer the pain of menstruation, pregnancy, and childbirth; and that she must always work hard taking care of her husband."[6] The "three subserviences" were common to both Indian and Chinese culture. A woman was never to be independent; she must always be subservient to some man: in youth, her father, in maturity, her husband, and in old age, her son. Both these lists concede that part of what makes a woman's life so difficult is *male dominance,* not *womanhood* itself. This insight did not need to wait for twentieth century feminism; the ancient Buddhist idea of the misfortune attending female rebirth includes that assessment. Concerning the evaluations that female physiology is woeful, these assessments were made by men; many women might not agree that menstruation, pregnancy, and childbirth are always woeful.

An unsentimental portrayal of women's lives in societies that produced this assessment of the woes of female rebirth could hardly draw any other conclusion. Married off young and without birth control, women experienced numerous pregnancies that often ended with a dead infant or young child. Infant mortality rates were high and so were maternal death rates. Upper-class women lived among many co-wives and mistresses, while lower-class women worked very hard at the family occupation. Daughters were less welcome than sons, were not educated, and were taught that they were morally weak and without spiritual potential. Men always controlled them. The physical difficulties of their lives were probably unavoidable, given the technology of that time. But the cultural and social negativities added to their physical difficulties would make life truly unbearable. Merely living in a society with cultural stereotypes of women as inherently "full of defilement and of weak intelligence" would make life woeful.

Because Buddhism emphasizes compassion, the Buddhist religion sought to ameliorate the pain of women's existence. But ancient Buddhism saw no way of doing so within this lifetime. Rather, to experience a better life, women needed to be reborn as men and this need was addressed. How? Women needed to fulfill the obligations put upon them in this life as women and be careful about their moral conduct. Religious piety and devotion were also means to that goal, and in some cases, women were given specific practices that would promote male rebirth. Most important, however, was the compassion of various mythic Buddhas and Bodhisattvas who took care that in their Buddha-lands, women's conditions would be unwoeful. Amida's Primal Vow, so important to Pure Land Buddhism, was the most famous such promise. In his vow he aspires that in the paradise he creates after he is enlightened, women could be free of female rebirth.

> Blessed One, may I not awaken to unsurpassable, perfect full
> awakening if,
> after I attain awakening it is the case that women in measureless,
> countless,
> inconceivable, incomparable, and limitless Buddha-fields in all
> regions of universe
> upon hearing my name have serene thoughts of faith, generate in
> the mind the
> aspiration to attain awakening, feel disgust at their female nature and
> yet are reborn
> again as women when they leave their present birth.[7]

It is common for male-dominant religions to regard male dominance positively, to claim that it improves not only men's but also women's lives. But classical Buddhism already contains a "feminist" position concerning the value of male dominance, recognizing that male dominance is one of the conditions that make women's lives woeful. Western Buddhists have added another suggestion to the problem of solving the woes of female rebirth. Western Buddhists are uncomfortable, not with the judgment that women's lives under present circumstances are woeful, but with the traditional solution to that problem. Instead of changing females into males in the *future,* why not change the predominant condition that make female rebirth woeful in the *present,* male dominance?

By looking closely, we see how subtle a seemingly simple statement can be. We also see how a statement that first strikes most people as negative toward women can be quite the opposite—a powerful tool for critiquing the system that makes women's lives more difficult than they need to be because of a social system that favors men over women.

B: Monasticism: Does It Help or Hinder Women?

Throughout Buddhist history, the monastic lifestyle was regarded as the most appropriate, if not the only possible way to pursue serious Buddhist practice. The curriculum of practice and study required for significant progress toward liberation requires time commitments unavailable to lay people busy with family and careers. The one-pointed, serene state of mind needed to pursue that curriculum is more easily attained in the disciplined environment of a monastery than anywhere else. For those with families and careers to worry about, distractions abound, and distraction is the opposite state of mind from one-pointed calmness. These values developed in ancient India, where they were not unique to Buddhism, but they have been transferred to every culture to which Buddhism has spread. (They were significantly modified in Japan, and it remains to be seen whether monasticism becomes common in Western Buddhism.)

The virtues of the monastic lifestyle are not readily apparent to many contemporary people. Many think that monasticism involves self-denial, and that monks and nuns regard sexuality and ordinary economic activities as "bad" and monasticism as morally superior. Many claim that the lifestyle would be extremely uncomfortable and unpleasant, and that celibacy would be the most unpleasant aspect of monasticism. (Many monastics do not regard celibacy as a great deprivation.) Why would anyone do this to themselves, many have often wondered!

In Western cultures, women thinking about what it would be like to be a nun are especially quick to dismiss the values of that lifestyle. They remark that because monastics don't have sex, they must be hostile to women. They can easily fuel their case with numerous misogynistic quotes from male monastics, both Christian and Buddhist. They often claim that abolishing monasticism improves women's status and that women have higher status in religions that do not include monasticism. Both assertions are questionable. Buddhist nuns have not fared as well as Buddhist monks in any period of Buddhist history, though in contemporary Taiwan, that generalization is being tested. It is more important, however, to consider nuns in comparison to *laywomen,* not in comparison to monks, and to ask what women's lives in traditional cultures are like with and without the monastic option.

A negative side effect of some monasticism is virulently misogynist attitudes. Men experiencing difficulties with celibacy, or even monks experiencing sexual arousal but not tempted to break their vows, often project their sexual feelings and desires onto women, who are then blamed for arousing them. Their logic seems to be "if it weren't for women, I wouldn't feel this way—it's their fault." The Buddha said that nothing is "so enticing, so desirable, so intoxicating, so binding, so distracting . . . such a hindrance to winning the unsurpassed peace as a woman's form."[8] (He also said the same about women's attraction to men.)

To counteract enticement provided by their form, women are vilified. An early Buddhist monk who saw a dancing girl while seeking alms proclaimed, "I had gone into town for alms and was going along when I saw her—ornamented, nicely dressed, laid out like a snare of Mara."[9] Buddha says to a monk who had sexual intercourse with his former wife only to beget an heir for his parents:

> It would have been better, confused man, had you put your male organ inside the mouth
> of a terrible and poisonous snake than inside the vagina of a woman. It would have
> been better, confused man, had you put your male organ inside the mouth of a black
> snake than inside the vagina of a woman. It would have been better, confused man,
> had you put your male organ inside a blazing hot charcoal pit than inside the vagina
> of a woman.[10]

The self-reflection so central to monastic culture encourages men to realize that *they* are the ones who are tempted by women. Therefore, it is up to them to acknowledge their own vulnerability to what is fundamentally an internal experience. Finally, it is up to the individual monk whether he experiences undistracted tranquillity, or agitation and distraction. It is the *monk* who experiences the enticement of the female form. To read these passages as being about *women* misses the point. They are about *monks'* desires and frustrations. In many passages though, monks do take responsibility for their own attraction to women. It is clear from such texts that language about male desire and about women is inextricably woven. Because monks are struggling with their desire, the *object* of their desire must be made unattractive. How much this has to with *women themselves* rather than male desire is a moot point.

Furthermore, such projections are not unique to monks, undercutting the argument that monasticism breeds misogyny. In many cultures, with or without monasticism, women are held responsible for male sexual arousal, which makes women, shrouded in heavy clothing and behind walls, the keepers of sexual morality for the whole society. In many contexts, including the modern West, women have been blamed for sexual infractions. While it is no longer common to say of a rape victim that "she was asking for it," until quite recently it was not uncommon. If in *nonmonastic* settings, women are held responsible for men's sexual feelings, it is not surprising that horny monks would draw the same conclusion. Whether or not women live in religious contexts that include monasticism, the results of being the object of male desire are the same. She is told to go away, cover up, become invisible, stop tempting men, or suffer the consequences.

To my knowledge, there is no parallel literature written by women or nuns, in which celibate women lust after men. This fact is especially interesting, given that women were thought to be more sensual than men in many Buddhist contexts and men often portrayed women as the sexual aggressors. But Buddhist women wryly comment that it makes no sense to favor male monastics over female monastics or to oppose the reintroduction of nuns' ordination. Women, they say, are the natural monastics because they have far fewer problems with celibacy than do men!

For women, the major problems are whether a nuns' community is available and gaining permission to become a nun. Many women would like to take vows, but the ordination lineages have died out or there may be no nunnery in their community or no economic support for them. Even if the lineages and the nunneries exist, women's families may be reluctant to let them be ordained. The family would lose the woman's economic value without gaining much in return. If a son becomes a monk, the family earns prestige and respect, but having a nun in the family brings little status. Widespread stereotypes that women lack spiritual interest or ability also play their part. If women believe these stereotypes, they will not even think of becoming a nun, but more often a woman would be pressured to be realistic about her abilities and get married instead. In the stories of women who become nuns or solitary renunciants, the motif of struggle to begin their vocation is common.

The scant literature about nuns that recounts their inner life is filled with expressions of relief and freedom. This, in itself, is not surprising; in a setting that recorded little about women's religious lives, probably no one would bother to write the autobiography of a disgruntled nun. These expressions of relief and freedom are crucial to understanding what monasticism can do for women. One nun named Mutta, whose story is in the early text called The Songs of the Women Elders, exclaims:

> I'm free. Ecstatically free
> I'm free from three crooked things:
> the mortar
> the pestle
> and my hunchbacked husband
> All that drags me back is cut—cut!

In the same text, another nun, identified only as Sumangala's mother rejoices:

> I'm free
> Free from kitchen drudgery
> No longer a slave among my dirty cooking pots
> (My pot smelled like an old water snake)
> And I'm through with my brutal husband
> And his tiresome sunshades
> I purge lust with a sizzling sound—*pop*
> "O happiness," meditate upon
> this as happiness.[11]

These two poems express very well the pain of these women's lives before they became nuns. They faced hard, boring work they had not chosen, and domestic violence, at least on the part of Sumangala's mother. Becoming a nun frees women from both, giving them the time and the instruction to develop their own gifts, including spiritual ones. Though these poems do not discuss it, becoming a nun also liberates women from the prospect of unwanted pregnancies. Younger nuns often remark that they appreciate their lives as nuns because otherwise they would already have several children. Women in modern cultures, who have many options and can remain single and economically independent, often do not appreciate how liberating becoming a nun could be. In almost every cultural situation until recently, nunhood was women's *only* alternative to marriage. In traditional religious cultures that do not include monasticism, women have no options. They *will* marry, usually to a man who is chosen for them, and they *will* remain in that marriage no matter how difficult it is for them—unless their husbands abandon them, in which case their economic situation will be difficult indeed.

The final justification for a women's sangha is that women experience the same genuine spiritual vocation that leads men to become monks. The story of how the nuns' order was founded clearly demonstrates this motivation. It would be inaccurate to portray the nuns' sangha merely as a refuge from domestic problems, nor would it survive if that were its only reason for existence. Providing options for women is important; central among these options is the ability to live out a spiritual vocation rather than to be forced to abandon it simply because one is a woman. All things considered, the existence of monasticism seems to be more positive than negative for women. The major negative spinoff of monasticism—misogyny—is equally present in non-monastic contexts. The positive function of providing more options for women, especially the option to pursue a spiritual vocation, far outweighs the negative spinoff.

C: Are Women Capable of Enlightenment?: Shariputra and the Goddess

Mahayana Buddhist texts detail a raging battle over the question of how far women could go on the Bodhisattva path. Buddhists often thought that the solution to women's problems was future rebirth as a man. It was also argued that a woman could go only so far on the path toward enlightenment, after which she would have to become a man. But that point was subject to dispute. Many texts suggest that a woman is already enlightened as a woman, but because people will not take her seriously, she must change herself into a man.[12] In these cases, the flaw is with society, not the woman. However, in one of the best-known texts of Mahayana Buddhism, the Vimalakirtinirdesha Sutra, the woman challenged by a male elder demonstrates that *she* does not have to become a man to be enlightened. The setting for this dialogue is Vimalakirti's palace, where a "goddess," meaning only "revered female," is debating with Shariputra, one of the elders among Buddha's first disciples. They have been debating for some time, and Shariputra is impressed with the goddess's understanding of the most difficult Buddhist teachings. So he issues a challenge:

SHARIPUTRA: "Why don't you change your female sex?"
GODDESS: "I've been here twelve years and have looked for the innate characteristics of the female sex and haven't been able to find them. How can I change them? Just as a magician creates an illusion of a woman, if someone asks why don't you change your female sex, what is he asking?"
SHARIPUTRA: "But an illusion is without any determinate innate characteristics so how could it be changed?"
GODDESS: "All things are also without any determinate innate characteristics, so how can you ask, 'why don't you change your female sex?'"

Then the Goddess, by supernatural power, changed Shariputra into a likeness of herself and herself into a likeness of Shariputra and asked: "Why don't you change your female sex?"

Shariputra, in the form of a goddess, answered: "I do not know how I changed nor how I changed into a female form."

Goddess: "Shariputra, if you can change into a female form, then all women [in mental state] can also change. Just as you are not really a woman but appear to be female in form, all women also appear to be female in form but are not really women. Therefore the Buddha said all are not really men or women."

Then the Goddess, by her supernatural power, changed Shariputra back into his own form. The Goddess questioned Shriputra: "Where are the female form and innate characteristics now?"

Shariputra: "The female form and innate characteristics neither exist nor do not exist." [13]

Though the Mahayana ideas about emptiness that underlie this interchange may be difficult, the basic point is easy to grasp. One cannot infer anything about levels of intellectual or spiritual attainment from physiological sex. In fact, women only appear to be women and men only appear to men, as is demonstrated by Shariputra's experience of being changed from a man to a woman and then back again.

The key phrase in understanding this dialogue is "innate characteristics." The key to understanding emptiness is understanding that nothing exists by itself, or is "innate." Today, people might say there is no "essence" underlying what we experience. Everything exists only in a matrix of interdependence and impermanence, constantly shifting and changing. Something that is "innate" is uncaused and always stays the same. So for women or men to have "innate" female or male characteristics would mean that there is something invariant, some trait that all men but no women always have, and vice versa. (The text is not talking about biology; it is talking about psychology and intellectual or spiritual capacities.) Furthermore, this "innate" characteristic could not be the result of culture or social conditions; it would have to exist, uncaused, in all men but no women, and vice versa. But that nothing whatsoever possesses innate, inherent existence is the whole point of the Mahayana teaching of emptiness. If nothing whatsoever possesses inherent, innate existence, then by definition, women and men could not possess "innate" traits that define and limit them, that hold them forever in the same position. That is why Shariputra can be changed into a woman and back again. And he is the one who needs to experience this lack of "determinate innate characteristics," because he is the one who believes in them. Though the Goddess could have changed herself into a man, as did many other female heroes of Mahayana texts who were placed in her position by men skeptical of women's abilities, she did not take the burden of male skepticism upon herself.

III: BUDDHISM IN THE FUTURE

When one studies the history of any religion, one is impressed by the amount of change a religion can undergo, its "shape-shifting" possibilities.

Buddhism has changed significantly in its long history. Due to many new influences and challenges, Buddhism stands poised to develop even more as it moves into a new cultural setting, and as the interactions between Asian and Western Buddhists increase.

Not only is Buddhism in a new world. So are women and men, especially in terms of how they relate with each other and the possibilities for each gender. Inevitably, new patterns of gender relationships will interact with Buddhism in this new phase. Among Western Buddhists, significant attention is placed directly on Buddhism and gender. But even without conscious attention to the issue of gender, changes are inevitable, simply because both men's and women's lives are changing. The Buddhist worldview helps because it is fundamentally open regarding gender. The story of Shariputra and the goddess represents the basic Buddhist view of gender. Like all else, sex, gender roles, and stereotypes are without inherent, innate, fixed characteristics. Buddhist institutions and popular thought, however, are another matter. Gender roles and ideas about gender have been quite fixed and rigid. Some pessimists and conservatives claim that such institutions can not or will not change. But the evidence of the history of religions is the opposite. There is no inherent, essential reason that Buddhism can not change in the direction of greater gender equity in the future. Furthermore, since change is inevitable in any case, why not direct change in a direction that brings Buddhist institutions more in line with its vision, rather than the other way around?

3

Confucianism

By Terry Woo

IT WAS 1971. I was nineteen. My father and I were riding the Star Ferry across the harbor in Hong Kong. Usually very much the quietly responsible Confucian patriarch of few words, my father surprised me with this bit of family education or *chia-chiao* before I left for Beaver College in Philadelphia:

"You're going abroad to study soon. I have given you the best that I have been able to. It is as if I've kept you in a cage, feeding you, teaching you how to be in the world. Now, it is as if I'm opening up the door of the cage; I'm letting you fly out into the larger world. I won't be there, by your side, to take care of you anymore. I've taught you the basic notions of how to treat people well and be loyal to your friends. But now I'm telling you that sometimes these rules will not hold. In the future, there will be occasions when you will believe and/or do something that your friends, family, and the other people around you will disagree with or deem wrong. If only one or two people tell you it's wrong, think again but go ahead and do it. If many people tell you that it's wrong, you should listen to them carefully and reconsider your position and only then go ahead and do as you intended. And if everyone you know thinks you're wrong, but if you've seriously considered the merits of their opinions and you still think you are right then you should go ahead and do what you had decided. But you should be very careful in thinking your own position through."

He then went on to say: "I don't know how your life will turn out. On the chance that you will be successful, you must always remember where you come from. You must put back into the community what has been given up to you." Only lately have I realized how Confucian my father's words were. He valued independent judgment through study and reciprocity through the remembrance and respect for elders in the form of ancestors, parents, teachers, and friends. In this remembering, humility is necessarily recognized through our indebtedness. Further, as my father put it when referring to my work: "Many philosophers have tackled the questions you are now working on. They haven't been able to reach a consensus or come up with one right answer. Who do you think you are that you should have an answer?"

And so it is with a sense of immense indebtedness that I dedicate this exploratory essay on Confucianism and women to my father specifically, my elders more generally, and my communities past and present.

INTRODUCTION: RITUAL OBSERVATION OF FILIAL PIETY OR HSIAO THROUGH ANCESTOR VENERATION

It is difficult to know what sort of uniformity, if any, there was in the performance of rituals pertaining to hsiao across time and geography. The primary festival days for ancestor veneration or pai tsu-hsien[1] remain marked on the Chinese lunar calendar even to our time, but the rituals themselves have in many cases been abandoned. Rituals pertaining to formal and public performances of ancestor veneration, chronologically traced through the lunar calendar, begin with the celebration of New Year, which begins on New Year's Eve with the all-important annual family dinner or t'uan-nien fan.[2] No married daughters are to be present;[3] they would have visited the day before, and were expected to be with their husband's family on the last and most ritually significant meal of the year.

At midnight, the patriarch and matriarch of the family receive ritualized gestures of respect in the form of prostrations or bows and good wishes for the New Year from all the junior members of the household. This ritual of hsiao is continued on New Year's Day with the presentation of family members to ancestors who are understood to be present symbolically through ancestral tablets. The ancestral tablet is a vertical stand on a broad base; it is sometimes mounted into the wall in temples. It is typically not more than eight inches high and four inches wide; it always has an inscribed name and sometimes a photograph of the deceased. Women were not allowed to participate in parts of this ritual in late dynastic China. When and why the exclusion came about is unclear. The Buddhist notion of women's impurity may have influenced the performance of this Confucian ritual.[4]

The Clear and Bright Festival, or Ching-ming, which occurs on the third day of the third month, is the first of three times during the year when descendants enact rituals of veneration in public by visiting their ancestors' graves, where food and flowers are often offered and the sites cleaned. I am not aware of special prayers that would be rendered to one's ancestors on these occasions; the attitude of sincerity or ch'eng and reverence or ching is what is considered to be of primary importance. The seventh day of the seventh month, which is known as the Festival of Ghosts or kuei chieh, is the second occasion for visiting the graves of one's ancestors. The universal aspect of ancestor veneration is marked during this time by offerings to souls, often women who were unmarried or had no sons and who therefore would have received no ancestral offerings. They are believed to be wandering in a realm that impacts on the living when the gates of purgatory are opened on this day—it is believed that the ghosts can harm the living.[5] The first day of the tenth month is the third occasion in which the ancestors' graves are attended to. Paper effigies of warm clothes in addition to mock paper money are provided so that one's ancestors will not have to go without them during the winter months in the spirit world.

It is difficult to say to what extent these practices have been continued; and I know of no effort to re-conceive and modernize these rituals. Only time will tell how and when, or if, these popular practices and the literary tradition will come together to bring forward a re-energized and revitalized Confucianism.

CONFUCIANISM IN MODERN TIMES

Confucianism is a tradition under stress. It is under stress because an aspiring chün-tzu (exemplary person) who wants to enact rituals[6] in addition to those described above, which reflect her exercise of cultivation of the mind/heart or self-cultivation, hsiu-hsin, and the investigation of things, ko-wu, no longer has the extended family and the state intact, Confucianism's two most significant theaters in which to continue her performance.

If construed in the spirit of self-cultivation, this exercise of examining women and the practice of filial piety, hsiao, can be understood as an engagement in the investigation of things.[7] A Confucian who is aspiring to be an exemplary person[8] would traditionally try to practice these two disciplines everywhere, at all times, and especially within the family and state, ultimately for the benefit of all. The very acts of scholarship, of studying, and that of the academic "ritual" of researching, questioning, analyzing, and writing can be seen as one form of these two Confucian practices; and as Fingarette might have it, it is one aspect of the Confucian "sacred" that overlaps with the Western-defined "secular."[9]

Self-cultivation, prevalent and omnipresent in Confucianism, is one of the threads weaving early and late Confucians together "not only for aesthetic development, but for moral strength, the social good, and spiritual insight."[10] The ideal traditional Confucian teacher teaches her students how to get on in the world; her duty goes beyond merely describing and singularly conveying information about the world; she nurtures foremost the practice of reciprocity, an element core to the development of Confucian social values. The focus on self-cultivation for a Confucian woman through work, careful speech, right behavior, and modest appearance ensures a practice that is firmly rooted in the self, the family, and the community; the secular practice is based, however, on the belief in an all-pervasive Way or Tao, which is immanent in the world but yet transcends it.[11]

To understand Confucian practice more carefully, I will analyze the elemental idea of filial piety as found in The Classic on Filial Piety for Women or Nü Hsiao Ching. The Classic is introduced with the fundamental five tuan or beginnings, and heart-minds or hsin, influenced by Mencius: that of benevolence or jen, righteousness or i, ritual or li, wisdom or chih, and trustworthiness or hsin. Other documents will also be used; and for the sake of easier reading, it will be assumed that filial piety is a central, unbroken, and uncut thread that can be traced through the cloth of Confucian teachings.[12] The definition of hsiao in the Book of History or Shu Ching is stated as "simply being kind as to a younger ·sibling."[13] This evolved over two millennia into Wang Yang-ming's (1472–1529) universal understanding that "the clear character of filial piety will be manifested" only when one loves all parents.[14]

Even though the individual thread of filial piety continues to be strong, two other threads within the tapestry of Chinese ritual tradition for women have been cut and removed. First, the empress, who was the symbolic head of Confucian womanhood, no longer exists because of the historical overthrow of the feudal government and creation of a modern Chinese government in the twentieth century. Second, the extended family has in many cases disintegrated and been replaced by the nuclear family, undermining the importance and power of older women in their roles as grandmothers. For this reason, unfortunately, writing about women and the practice of Confucianism cannot be straightforward; it cannot be "What Confucianism Said About and Prescribed for Women."

Without community and state rituals, women's contributions to society are not formally integrated and recognized. In dynastic China, the empress embodied the importance of women's work by the performance of the Ritual of Silkworms or Ts'an-li. This ritual symbolized the value of women to the empire as providers of cloth and related goods through their cultivation of mulberry trees, nurturing of silkworms, and manufacturing of silk. Moreover, without the broader framework, Confucianism can only remain a "personal" choice in philosophy and is irrelevant to the larger society in which an aspiring chün-tzu lives. For Confucianism to function fully as a religion, it needs to be determined if rituals can be made central to social interactions again and how and what kinds of rituals should be proposed and developed.

It is unclear to me what being a modern[15] Confucian woman means when she is disestablished from a Confucian state and family. First, as noted earlier, there is no longer an empress who participates in rituals such as the Ritual of Silkworms, which established the primary and essential place and role of women in a Confucian empire,[16] as the yin within the complementary polarities of yin and yang. Second, within the family, also central to the performance of rituals, the disappearance of the empress is echoed by a parallel disappearance of the once pervasive ancestral tablet. This domestic ritual of veneration, of paying respect to one's mother and/or grandmother with incense, flowers, and fruits is performed on different occasions like the common celebration of New Year but also on special occasions like the presentation of a new bride into the family.

With the slow disappearance of the once ubiquitous ancestral tablet comes a diminished sense of ancestral continuity, particularly in the role of the mother, grandmother, and great grandmother at the heart of the family. The real flesh-and-blood presence of mothers and/or mothers-in-law within families clearly continues to mark the biological fact of female ancestry. What I refer to here is the ritually unacknowledged importance of women as the roots of the family, specifically as the first teachers of children and the ministers of the inner realm of the extended family and clan. It is difficult to say how many Chinese families around the globe still maintain their ancestral tablets. It is clear, however, that many factors have contributed to the demise of these tablets, which symbolize the presence of ancestors.

The causes of this discontinuity are complex. Oddly, there is the sense of cultural inferiority and national self-loathing that was most evident in the May Fourth Movement in 1919. The May Fourth Movement is considered to be the Chinese Enlightenment. It was during this period that Confucianism came to be seen as the li chiao (ritual teaching) that cannibalized human beings. Ibsen's Nora, from A Doll's House, was adopted as a symbol for all the oppressed in China, both men and women. The popularity of Christianity, which is ambivalent about ancestor veneration, has also contributed to this demise. Political upheaval[17] caused by movements like the Cultural Revolution have displaced and separated family members, making it impossible to maintain the familial structure so necessary to the performance of certain rituals. Economic migration, like political upheaval, also changes or destroys the familial structure, most often through Western cultural influences present in the countries of choice like Canada and the United States. Finally, advances in the high-tech industries, which favor and reward the skills of the young, change the economic power relations within a family and disrupt traditional structures.

The breakdown of state and family rituals has special repercussions for women. Unlike the male literary tradition that has a rich textual tradition, there are relatively few texts for women.[18] A woman's Confucian tradition is one of attending to family members high and low, old and young, far and wide, by making sure that they are clothed and fed properly. It is also a practice of caring for the family altar, offering incense and fruits, and preparing for feast days. Therefore, a woman's Confucianism is more one of doing and devotion than of study and exegesis even though the foundational principles of the teaching are the same for women and men alike.

The erosion of formal and institutional foundations is not the only element threatening the survival of Confucianism. It has a dubious status as a religion in part because of the absence of a revealed canon, and finally its quasi-philosophy is seen as pedestrian when compared to its Greek counterpart.[19] In defense, Mou Tsung-san, a self-confessed modern-day Confucian, writes that the "Confucian emphasis was never on God and prayer" and hence did not develop along the lines common to religions that are based on emotional cries for help. (33–35) Even if there is no divinity in the Western sense of creator and final arbiter, there is certainly a notion of an all-powerful Heaven and Earth or Tien/Ti in Classical Confucianism,[20] which was replaced by the concept of the Supreme Ultimate or T'ai-chi in eleventh-century Neo-Confucianism. Moreover, scholars such as James Legge, David Nivison, Roger Ames, and Julia Ching have pointed out that the concerns of Confucians are recognizable as religious. Most pertinent is Fingarette's belief that what Western religions accept and divide into secular and sacred does not hold for Confucianism; as the title of his book suggests, Confucius and the tradition based on his teachings conceive of the secular as sacred.

Addressing the issue of whether Confucianism is a religion, Mou writes that the fact that

> Confucianism can provide a guide for daily life means that it fulfils one of the duties which make it a religion. But this is not the only function of religion. It still has another and more important function. A religion must serve as a motive force for the upward movement of the human spirit, and as a guide to the life of the spirit. (Mou 26)

The pervasiveness of Confucian rituals marked life's passages like birth, adolescence, marriage, and death; encompassed specific elements within society like the affairs of the military; included also the etiquette of everyday life that defined the parameters of hospitality and elements such as the veneration of ancestors and worship of spirits. All these, Mou suggests, meant that religious rules were not devised in addition to secular rules. This is the reason why China has no special religious ceremonies.[21]

This is, of course, not exactly right. A Confucian can simultaneously be a Buddhist or Taoist, participating in the numerous special religious ceremonies. And, perhaps, this Confucian acceptance of difference is one of its most important and attractive features; a characteristic that should be maintained and encouraged, especially in a world filled with religious strife.[22]

Although it remains a point of interest whether a person[23] was ever exclusively a Confucian—that is, the adherent of only one religion or teaching, as the Chinese term chiao is understood—it is important to stress that Confucianism's acceptance of hierarchical plurality and its lack of a divinely sanctioned dogma stand in contrast to the Western sensibilities of exclusivity[24] and equality.[25] Because of this, Confucianism is often challenged to define itself and forced to accommodate itself to another teaching. Historically this happened during Confucianism's first encounter with Buddhism when the latter was imported from South Asia.

Contemporary Euro–West Asian religious ideologies like Buddhism have enjoyed a certain success and have posed the crucial question to Confucianism and those who believe: What is Confucianism's relevance to the modern world? Of course, the question is not for me to answer. We are just at the start of the incursion of the Far West, which is most conveniently captured in its Greco-Judeo-Christian values, into Chinese culture; this violent burst of the Far West into Chinese cultural space is a watershed in Chinese history. From here on in, it is and will be very difficult, if not impossible, for Chinese teachings to be credibly evaluated apart from Western teachings. As to the issue of women, suffice it to say that much work needs to be done in order that Chinese women be rescued from scholarly exotica.[26] It is important to note here that no self-professed Confucian woman has written confessionally from inside the tradition.

Okada Takehito, a Japanese Confucian, thinks that the name of a tradition or more pointedly, the survival of its name in relation to its content, is unimportant. What is important is that "true understanding of human nature is the object of religion in the modern world, and this is the role for Confucianism as well." To him, the two are synonymous. He believes that without religious depth,

Humankind cannot know its true character. Without this possibility of knowing the true character, it will build its world and meaning from the self-directed and self-centred motives that are a part of human consciousness, the (human heart or) jen-hsin, rather than the root and foundation of such consciousness, the Tao-hsin [heart of the Way or in West Asian terms, God's Way]. Under these conditions the very survival of humankind is at risk. (Taylor 1990, 145)

Mou shares Okada's perspective. He writes that Confucianism calls upon human beings to fulfill their nature, for if human beings do not fulfill their nature, they fall and become as beasts. (32) Here is a potential point of contention for a contemporary Confucian woman; the teaching has understood the natures of women and men to be different. For example, women were deemed to be like Earth while men were like Heaven. This kind of thinking has had a tremendous impact on the understanding of the nature of woman in China. For example, a woman would be categorized under yin and associated with the night, cold, winter, moon, passivity, and so on.

These notions are encouraged and reinforced by an important text, The Book of Changes or I Ching, which describes the Heaven or ch'ien hexagram as "creative" (Wilhelm 3) and the Earth or k'un as "receptive." (Wilhelm 10) These are the first two hexagrams in the book and represent male and female respectively. Being associated with Earth, women were seen to be passive and multiple; men, on the contrary, being associated with Heaven, were thought to be active and singular. These notions therefore justified polygyny, the practice of one man having many wives.

Mou then goes on to describe another feature in Confucianism that is presumably the same for men and women; he writes that Confucians

see human existence as a process of moral perfection, its final goal being sagehood and the attainment of goodness. Its teachings, therefore, are not developed with deity as their central theme. Rather they are developed on the basis of how [a human being] is to embody and manifest the Way of Heaven in order to perfect [her] virtue.

T'ang Chun-i, another modern self-professed Confucian like Mou, has a somewhat different view. He criticizes later Confucianism for being "too centred on human beings to the detriment of having neglected the understanding of the material world and the exercise of control over it." He believes that the "significance, for Confucius, of combining (human beings)[27] with Heaven and Earth, and of regarding (them) as having access to both, was that Confucius was able to encompass the spirit of Jesus, Sakyamuni, and science." (T'ang 52) One might imagine T'ang to be sympathetic to historical developments that have lessened the burdens of human beings, in particular for women, for whom improved material circumstances translate directly into easier lives because they no longer need to bear so many children, die in childbirth, and suffer from sundry gynecological illnesses.

Confucianism admits no revealed scriptures even though it embraces the ultimate supremacy of Heaven and Earth over human beings.[28] Mencius (ca. 372–289 B.C.E.) is recorded as saying that "If one believed everything in The Book of History, it would have been better for the History not to have existed at all."[29] This statement of skepticism recognizes human fallibility; Heaven and Earth may be omnipotent and omniscient, but human beings are not. So ultimate authority does not rest in the books recorded by humans. In addition to this Mencian declaration, Hsün Tzu (310–238 B.C.E.) elaborates on the varying degrees of human fallacy. On the subject of ritual, he has this to say:

> . . . the sacrificial rites[30] originate in the emotions of remembrance and longing, express the highest degree of loyalty, love, and reverence, and embody what is finest in ritual conduct and formal bearing. Only a sage can fully understand them. The sage understands, the [exemplary person][31] finds comfort in carrying them out, the officials are careful to maintain them, and the common people accept them as custom. To the [exemplary person] they are a part of the way of man; to the common people they are something pertaining to the spirits. (Watson 110)

Hsün Tzu states clearly that all human beings do not share the same quality of intelligence and religious or spiritual capacity. Individual differences are thus understood as manifestations of internal differences; reasoning from this, a Confucian would not be surprised that some choose atheism, others agnosticism, and still others various schools of religion and numerous forms of devotional practices. Furthermore, it would make no sense to a Confucian to try to homogenize religious beliefs and practices either by education or persecution. People, as history has shown, will revert eventually to folk practices and/or choose different spiritual paths according to their inclination. For example, there is the resurgence of "religion" or "superstitions" in countries with very different histories, cultures, and civilizations. In Iran and the United States, Islamic and Christian fundamentalisms have taken hold; in the latter, on the other end of the spectrum, are also numerous syncretist New Age groups. In China, the new religious movement Discipline of the Wheel of Dharma or Fa-lun-kung has become popular; and there has been renewed interest in traditional religions such as Islam, Christianity, Buddhism, and Taoism. Contrary to predictions by Western philosophers, religion is very far from dead.

There are profound implications for women in Mencius's skepticism, Hsün Tzu's understanding of innate differences, and the evidence of the persistence of the religious impulse. If all classical writings are not to be adopted uncritically, and if women understand and learn from them in different ways, then there is a huge task ahead for Confucians. Teachings that are unjustifiably hostile to women will have to be trimmed or rooted out; the status and roles of women will have to be reconfigured positively, taking into account assumptions of differences and hierarchy.

In a surprisingly modern understanding of li, Hsün Tzu notes that rites, and by extension various aspects of religions, are a means of satisfaction.[32] It is a way of apportioning resources among people. Not only are there unequal intellectual and spiritual capacities, there are also social differences and economic inequality. After all, Hsün Tzu observes that the "very existence of Heaven and Earth exemplifies the principle of higher and lower."[33] He goes on to say that "Where ranks are all equal, there will not be enough goods to go around; where power is equally distributed, there will be a lack of unity; where there is equality among the masses, it will be impossible to employ them."[34]

In other words, non-differentiation will breed disorder. For example, if we were all managers, there would be nobody to do the clerical work. On the contrary, if we were all clerks, there would be no one to organize the overall process. If all were treated equally, those who are bright may feel no motivation to do their utmost; those who are inclined to indolence would see no reason to work harder. Egalitarianism as an ideal is honorable, but in execution it remains extremely and formidably complex. Given the variety and the many foibles of human personality, equality in the face of arrogance and hatred, for example, will make the masses unemployable. For example, one can imagine that many will want only to be leaders, disbelieving that they are not as good as others, and many will want revenge exacted through just and proportionate means.

In classical Confucianism there is, instead, a humanism that recognizes that "Heaven has its constant way; Earth has its constant dimensions; the chün-tzu has [her][35] constant demeanor."[36] Inconstancy is therefore a part of the human condition: "Order and disorder are not due to [Heaven]";[37] nor by extension to the exemplary person. It is the small-minded and petty person or hsiao-jen[38] who causes chaos; and yet, it is also the hsiao-jen who has the potential which is in every person to bring about harmony by behaving like a chün-tzu.

"NOBLE" AND "MEAN" IN THE CLASSIC ON FILIAL PIETY FOR WOMEN

We encounter here one of the most troublesome ideas for contemporary people who are sympathetic to Confucianism. Expressed in terms of women, the notion of hierarchy, of high and low emphasized by Hsün Tzu has traditionally implied inferiority of the wife to the superiority of the husband. Harvard scholar Tu Wei-ming dismisses this hierarchical structure in the family; he writes that the "authority of the husband over the wife, which resulted from blatantly patriarchal conditioning, has no redeeming feature." Examining the relationship of husband and wife within the three bonds or san-kang, he notes that

> authority here means something different from either authority derived from status as in the ruler-minister relationship, or authority derived from age as in the father-son relationship. The husband-wife relationship is contractual and, therefore, not irrevocable. The Confucians acknowledge divorce as an unhappy eventuality in some marriages . . . (Tu Wei-ming, 132) [T]he value of distinction [between

the husband-wife relationship] is based on a principle of mutuality. The underlying spirit is not dominance but division of labor. (Tu Wei-ming, 127)

Tu then says that some commentators argued for the equality of the wife and the husband by citing linguistic grounds: that the character for "wife," ch'i, which is pronounced in the first tone, is etymologically from the homophone "equal," ch'i, which is pronounced in the second tone. He suggests that the distinction asked of husband and wife probably comes from the concern that "conjugal intimacy may breed nepotism which may, in turn, lead to social irresponsibility if the interests of the nuclear family supersede concerns for other family members and the larger community."[39]

Tu's reaction to the traditional marriage structure is understandable. The husband should not demand absolute obedience from the wife. Tu's position is supported by The Classic on Filial Piety for Women, which while clearly stating that the husband is in the senior or tsün position (as in "The person of husband is Heaven. How can [you] not serve him?") also continues with "Heaven's brilliance exists because of Earth's gain."[40] It also states that when the husband is "not behaving according to the Way," he should be cautioned; and that a wife should obey a husband's command only when he is correct.[41] So the rigid conventional understanding of absolute obedience is not necessarily the textual understanding. It is analogical thinking run amok or familial tyranny gone unchecked. The alignment of women with subservience or p'i in passivity, obedience, and other such so-called feminine characteristics, may be overzealous and misguided, but I believe that the theory of high and low is not altogether wrong when differences in ability and talents are considered.

When Pan Chao tells her readers in The Admonition to Women (Nü Chieh) to place themselves below all the senior members in their husband's family and to serve the junior members with reverence and sincerity, Pan is offering strategic advice. A young wife newly married into an extended family is at the mercy of everyone. She must cultivate her situation in a way that will be beneficial to herself in the long term. In other words, she is literally in a "lower" position because she has very little socio-economic power even if she might in time exercise emotional and psychological power over her husband. If we take self-preservation and protection to be the starting point or the rationale for the power differential in the traditional marriage, the perspective on subordination, obedience, and service must change.[42] Even in today's world, when a young, inexperienced man or woman joins his or her new marital family, humility and deference would be expedient.

To reverse the traditional relationship, a woman in a contemporary family may be the sole breadwinner and the man, by choice, a stay-at-home husband and father. In such a case, he would be in the "lower" socio-economic position[43] that is similar to the one for a traditional Chinese woman. In an ideal situation, the husband and wife would treat each other with mutual respect naturally, according to the Heart of the Way or Tao-hsin. However, should that not be the case, the Confucian parameters would suggest that the husband might, as the "Earth" or lower partner within the relationship, contribute to his Heaven or wife's brilliance. Put another way, the wife must provide for her husband because, as the more economically powerful partner in the relationship, she must be responsible for her husband; moreover, if the husband is more cultivated than she is in exemplary behavior, he is obligated to guide her along the Way as the minister of the inner realm within the relationship, as in the case of the wife in a traditional Confucian spousal relationship.

What I am suggesting here is that tsün and p'i can be construed differently under various situations. Whereas biology used to be the most obvious parameter, we might nowadays use the socio-economic parameter as the standard within one marital circumstance without allowing it to become the absolute standard. In other words, I propose that different measures of tsün and p'i can be used even within one relationship, bringing into consideration the complexity of high and low conceived within categories such as the intellectual, psychological, economic, and spiritual capacities, to name just a few.

Expressed through reciprocity (shu), benevolence (jen)[44] must remain at the heart of the marriage. The core of the marital relationship cannot change. For both husband and wife, their cultivation of themselves as exemplary people (chün-tzu) must remain central. Most importantly they are to be good and responsible toward each other; as chün-tzu they do not compete. The Classic on Filial Piety for Women puts it this way: "When the husband has a hundred tasks, the wife [works along with him] with one will."[45]

And, when a woman serves her husband, "she puts up her hair to greet him; thus she has the dignity of [the interaction between] a lord and his ministers. In pouring water for her husband to wash his hands, and in offering food, there is the respect between father and son. In announcing one's retreat before going, there is the way of older and younger siblings. Being sincere over time, there is the trust between friends. Having no blemish in word or deed, there is thus the capacity for managing the home. Prepare yourself with these five attributes; then you can serve your husband."[46]

Dignity, respect, righteousness, sincerity, and trustworthiness are the characteristics a woman or junior partner serves with. The husband and wife, in assessing their own variants of tsün and p'i, can thus remain complementary and respectful of each other even if their realms of responsibilities are different.[47]

THE CHÜN-TZU IN THE CLASSIC ON FILIAL PIETY FOR WOMEN

The self-cultivation required for such an ideal and harmonious marriage begins with the process of becoming an exemplary person. The Classic on Filial Piety for Women[48] clearly describes the ideal actions and attitudes of the exemplary person. It begins by stating that her focus is hsiao because the "filial person affects [even] the ghosts and spirits,[49] and moves Heaven and Earth. There is nothing that its essence does not reach, and it uses the way of husband and wife as the beginning of all relations."[50] In section seven, Three Beginnings or Talents (San Ts'ai), which include Heaven, Earth, and Human Being, there is a description of what a chün-tzu should do: stand with Heaven and Earth and complete them. Implicit in this is the assumption that the "human being is not something we are; it is something that we do, and become."[51] Jen is, therefore, an achievement; just as

> the love and loyalty of a husband for a wife, however intense it may be at first, is relatively amorphous and impoverished in content as compared to what it may become over the course of many years of married life through crises, good fortune and sheer routine. . . . Suffering . . . and acting are what shape a man. (Fingarette 48)

The cultivation of jen is no different for a woman than for a man. Several parts of the treatise are, in fact, taken from The Classic on Filial Piety or Hsiao Ching. For example, with exactly the same words, "hence the brilliance of Heaven is because of the gain of Earth," the Nü Hsiao Ching is drawn and tied to the male literati culture. The women's Classic marks the consolidation of an integrated, complementary but separate women's Confucian tradition. It is comprehensive in drawing from the available sources, using not only the Hsiao Ching and Mencius but also drawing from classical Confucian texts like the I Ching for the complementary ch'ien and k'un and The Book of Poetry and The Book of History for epigraphic quotes on historical women. Moreover, Lady Ch'eng also draws from Han Confucian texts such as Liu Hsiang's Biographies of Women or Lieh Nü Chuan, Pan Chao's Admonitions to Women, and Tung Chung-shu's Yin-yang Confucianism.

How should a chün-tzu cultivate jen? She is exhorted to avoid laziness, attend to rites, and act with universal love. She does not forget her obligations of filial piety and kindness, manifesting them in virtue and kindness. She is to be deferential, respectfully yielding, and not argumentative. She does not compete, and demonstrates good and bad with ritual and music. Above all, an exemplary person knows what is prohibited.[52] As Cheng I, a prominent Neo-Confucian, reports, his mother refused to take their sides even when he and his brother Ch'eng Hao (1032–1085) were right when they argued with others. She said, "The trouble is that one cannot bend and not that one cannot stretch out."[53] A chün-tzu begins her cultivation in the family, traditionally the woman's sphere. Confucians see the home as the soil from which the exemplary person grows; it is here where a child begins her personal development which is rooted in jen. In a passage attributed to Yu-tzu is this observation:

It is a rare thing for someone who has a sense of filial and fraternal responsibility to have a taste for defying authority. And it is unheard of for those who have no taste for defying authority to be keen on initiating rebellion. [Chün-tzu] concentrate their efforts on the root, for the root having taken hold, the way will grow therefrom. As for filial and fraternal responsibility, it is, I suspect, the root of [jen].[54]

Although the recurring theme here is harmony (he), we should not be lulled into thinking that Confucianism is naïve and believes that harmony should be achieved at all costs. Its earliest advocates lived and developed their philosophies during a war-torn era. Mencius' doctrine of the Mandate of Heaven or T'ien-ming is a sober reminder that rebellion is sanctioned when the conditions demand it.[55] It is stated in the Lün Yu 1:12 that "when things are not going well, to realize harmony just for its own sake without regulating the situation through observing ritual propriety will not work."[56] Nevertheless, the fundamental objective of Confucianism remains clear: harmony.

The expectation of harmony is a broad societal one. The wife, or the junior partner, is said to have failed even if the marriage is "harmonious as the harp and lute" if she fails to do the following: "When in a position of privilege, do not be proud; when in a lowly position, do not be disorderly. When among your own class, do not compete for advantage and become proud and thereby endanger yourself."[57] "He" must be fostered not only within a marriage or a family, but most importantly within the larger community. Harmony is not conceived of as a result of equality or the struggle for equality; rather, according to Hsün Tzu's understanding, it encompasses hierarchy, in the sense of all people doing their own different and unequal acts.

The duties for women within each class are therefore different. The empress and concubines are to be fecund without being lascivious, providing the emperor and the people with many virtuous descendants and potential heirs. The wives of officials are to be impartial in assessing their own achievements. They should also be astute in evaluating what goes on around them. They are to "assume responsibilities calmly and act in an upright way in order not to lose rituals so that descendants can be harmonized and the ancestral temples preserved." The expectations of the wives of the heads of state are less administrative. They are to establish a standard in their behavior, thereby setting the tone of the community.[58] True to the Confucian belief that the chün-tzu is like the wind and the hsiao-jen like grass,[59] upper-class women are enjoined to be leaders, working alongside their husbands to set the standard for the society at large. The private sphere here is thus not understood merely as the family but Families, that is, all families in the empire.

Understood this way, the upper-class woman's reach is wide indeed. As a counterpart to her husband, she is expected to exert influence over the mass of ordinary people of the empire. In contrast, the expectations from a common woman are simpler: "Put others first and yourself last. Look after your parents-in-law by weaving garments, making sacrifices and offerings at the altar." The remark that "women do not participate in public affairs; they rest in the cultivation of silkworms and weaving," quoted from the Shih Ching, is here used only for lower-class women.[60] Upper-class women, women of privilege, are expected to work for the benefit of the state, just as their husbands do, but in the "private" realm of the family. The Nü Hsiao Ching is unequivocal about this. True to form, drawing on "Tradition," it says this:

> During ancient times, a good woman used hsiao to govern the nine degrees of kin. She dared not abandon the wives of the lowly and the young; how much more, then, her younger siblings. . . . She who uses the service of her parents-in-law as family governance would not dare to insult even the chickens and dogs, how much more, then, her avoidance of ridiculing hsiao-jen. That is why they gain the approval of high and low. She who uses the serving of her husband to manage the inner quarters dare not lose the respect of the servants, let alone then, the respect of a chün-tzu. . . . If the distinction between wealth and poverty are not generated, disaster will not be created. That is why a good woman uses hsiao to govern the high and low ranks.[61]

This emphasis and preoccupation with "he" is understandable when one understands classical Confucianism's development in the midst of chaos. Confucius, Mencius, and Hsün-tzu lived during the turbulent Spring and Autumn and Warring States periods from 500 to 300 B.C.E. Their teachings were not adopted as state ideology until some two hundred years later during the Han dynasty. Their works again fell into disfavor as Buddhism and Taoism gained strength from about 250 C.E., only to begin regaining influence during the middle to the late T'ang in the 850s and then more broadly during mid to late Sung period, around 1200, when the northern tribes were threatening the peace and stability of the Chinese empire. This foundational sense of "getting along with each other" is, perhaps, where Confucianism is still relevant in spite of its institutional disintegration. One might hypothesize that the institutions can be rebuilt, as Confucius tried to rebuild them, when one has grappled with and understood how harmony can be achieved. And how is it to be achieved? Confucians would offer that it is fundamentally and initially achieved through the rituals of filial piety (li) within the home. After all, "Achieving harmony is the most valuable function of observing ritual propriety."[62]

In the meantime, Tu Wei-ming has legitimately criticized the traditionally exploitative and patriarchal elements within Confucianism. A revised Confucianism needs to be drawn out—one that will conserve and elaborate on the ideas of tzu-hsiu, ko-wu, "he," the complexity of tsün and p'i, and how women and men in their many roles throughout life can create and maintain a stable and safe community. New emphasis must be placed on the character development of the senior partner, and a careful exposition of a woman in her responsibilities as an older sister, wife, mother, aunt, corporate president, political leader, to mention a few examples, needs to be started.

Finally, there must be a critical look at the foundations of Confucianism. Where are the boundaries to this Confucian remark on hsiao from The Analects 4:19: "In serving your father and mother, remonstrate with them gently. On seeing that they do not heed your suggestions, remain respectful and do not act contrary. Although concerned, voice no resentment"?[63] Is this one root of the traditional tyranny? Or is this one of the first elements in the cultivation of a chün-tzu, a person "who most perfectly having given up self, ego, obstinacy and personal pride," follows the Way rather than profit?[64]

This tension between practicing deference and condoning despotism is taut; and the dilemma is not a new one. Ch'eng I, quoted by Chu Hsi in the Reflections on Things at Hand [Chin Ssu Lu], wrote that "when parents have the nature of an average person and their love and hate do not violate principle, the [child][65] should obey them." As with Confucius' remarks, Ch'eng's pronouncement demonstrates the crucial need for continual and critical inquiry—in this case, to analyze what "principle" might be. Much work needs to be done in resuscitating Confucianism—a Confucianism that maintains but conceives anew community rituals that will encourage the acceptance of differences and recognize the necessity and importance of plurality symbolized by the notions of superior and inferior, forceful and mild, noble and mean. This is important to women especially as an alternative in a world that is enamored mostly by convenience and material success, stresses conformity and allegiance to one group or another, and thrives on the jingoistic "If you're not with us, you're against us." It is also important because at the heart of Confucianism are rituals that acknowledge the work and vitality of women to society; these rituals can be re-choreographed to symbolize the essentially reciprocal and complementary nature of all human relationships. At the beginning and at the end, Heaven and Earth remain mutually brilliant.

4

Taoism

By Eva Wong

THE TRAIN FROM HONG KONG arrived in Beijing on a blustery day in autumn. As I stepped onto the platform, I was met by two blue-robed Taoist priests who welcomed me to White Cloud Monastery, where I would be attending classes on Taoist philosophy, religious ceremonies, and the arts of health and longevity. White Cloud Monastery is the seat of the Chinese Taoist Association. Founded sometime during the thirteenth century, it was closed during the Cultural Revolution of the 1960s. Now it is not only open but is recognized as a Chinese national treasure and is protected by the Beijing municipal government. Today, the monastery is an educational as well as a religious center, and Taoist practitioners from all over the world come here to further their studies of Taoism.

In southeast China, in Kiang-su Province, there is a range of mountains known as Mao-shan. Mao-shan was home to the earliest Taoist mountain retreat communities. These communities date back to the fifth and sixth centuries and were built by the followers of Shang-ch'ing Taoism. This school of mystical Taoism was founded by Lady Wei Hua-ts'un of the Eastern Chin dynasty (317–420 C.E.), who is considered by many to be the most remarkable woman of her generation. Over the years, in my wanderings in Mao-shan, I have met the teachers of Shang-ch'ing Taoism—most of them elusive hermits—and have learned from them the techniques of mystical ecstasy.

In Hong Kong, the festival of Ch'ing-ming occurs in the rainy days of spring. Traditionally, the Chinese honor their ancestors by visiting the graves and making offerings at the family shrines. For many Taoist temples, this is a day of prayer and ceremony. Women and men in Taoist regalia chant and conduct services on behalf of filial sons and daughters who have asked the temples to recite liturgies for their dead ancestors. Many Taoist clergy and devotees who participate in this festival are women. Some are musicians, some are chanters, and some are leaders of the ceremonies. Often, entire ceremonies are conducted by female clergy. On one of these festivals, I asked a woman how she felt about leading the most important ceremony in the festival. She replied that she was only doing what her female predecessors had done for hundreds of years.

My own journey into Taoist spirituality is not the result of an interest in Taoism developed during my adult life but a continuation of spiritual training that started when I was a child. I grew up learning the Taoist wisdom tradition from my family. I first learned about Taoism from my grandmother, who told me stories of Taoist immortals. We would sit on her bed, and while she sewed, she would tell me the lives of Taoist women and men who had attained the highest levels of spiritual cultivation. These stories had a deep effect on me, for in my youthful mind, these realized beings were the kind of people I aspired to be.

After I learned how to read, I discovered, to my delight, numerous novels and newspaper serials on the Taoist immortals. Stories of Taoist immortals are very much a part of Chinese culture. It is impossible to grow up in a Chinese community and not know about the Taoist immortals, for their lives are dramatized not only in books but also in Chinese opera, films, and television.

My interest in Taoism did not wane when I got older. My granduncle was a practitioner of the Taoist arts of health and longevity, and at fourteen I began to learn meditation and ch'i-kung from him. By this time, I was deeply attracted to the Taoist philosophy of living in simplicity and in harmony with the natural world. I read the Taoist classics—the Tao-te-ching, Chuang-tzu, and Lieh-tzu—and decided to follow this wisdom tradition of my ancestors.

Taoist spirituality focuses on cultivating a healthy body and a clear mind. Thus, ch'i-kung, martial arts, calisthenics, and meditation are all integral to the practice of Taoism. Taoism is also a religion, for it believes that a close relationship exists between humanity and the sacred powers. By performing the correct rituals, humanity renews and strengthens its relationship with the deities, and thus ensures peace and harmony in the world. Above all, Taoism is a philosophy of practical living that advocates a lifestyle of simplicity, non-interference, and quietude.

I am a female practitioner of the Taoist spiritual tradition. I believe that as a Taoist practitioner, I can provide non-practitioners with a perspective on Taoism that cannot be obtained from scholars who are not practitioners. Being a woman, I can also give both practitioners and non-practitioners a view of Taoism different from the one that has been traditionally presented by its male practitioners.

In a survey conducted by the Taoist Association of Taiwan in 1961, it was estimated that at that time there were 56 million people who claimed that their preferred religion was Taoism. Over 90 percent of them lived in China (the People's Republic), Taiwan, Hong Kong, and Southeast Asia, and more than half of these devotees and practitioners were female.

For a religion in which the majority of its adherents are women, it seems strange that very little is known about the history of its female practitioners. Were Taoist women rare in the history of China? How accessible is the information about them? What are their contributions to the development of Taoism?

THE PROBLEM OF HISTORY

Anyone who attempts to learn the history of women in Taoism is faced with several problems. First, historical records are not objective. Whether an event is included or excluded from written history will depend on the interest, and some would even say the ideological motivation.

Second, most scholars use The Twenty-four Histories of China (the collection of historical records written through the centuries by imperially sanctioned scholars) and The Taoist Canon (the collection of the scriptures of Taoism) as the authoritative sources for studying the history of Taoism in China. Since the history of China was written by Confucians in a Confucian society, one would suspect that Confucianism, not Taoism, occupied the "center stage" in the "official" history of China. Thus, in a society where Confucian scholars wrote the histories and Confucianism regulated the mode of thinking and social behavior, one would not expect Taoism to be given the same treatment as Confucianism in the history of Chinese thought.

Third, most of the texts collected in The Taoist Canon were written by male practitioners; only a handful were written by female adepts. The relative invisibility of women in this authoritative source of Taoism has led many to believe that female Taoist practitioners have been rare and that their contributions to the development of Taoist thought and practice have been negligible.

Why is there so little information about Taoist women in The Taoist Canon? I think there are two reasons.

First, the Canon was edited by men, without any input from women. In traditional China, women were not allowed to participate in the civil service, and the men who compiled The Taoist Canon saw no reason to consult with any woman, let alone the female practitioners of the Taoist arts.

Second, The Taoist Canon is the "written tradition" of Taoism. Therefore it contains only the teachings of those who are literate. In view of the nature of education in traditional China, this meant that women did not have much chance to contribute to the "written tradition" of Taoism. The education system was closely tied to the civil service, and since women did not participate in the civil service, they rarely received formal education. Thus, in traditional China, the educated woman is an exception, not the norm. Even in the early twentieth century, given the same socioeconomic level, men were more likely to receive formal education than women. My grandfather and my granduncles were all trained in the Confucian classics whereas my grandmother and my grandaunts could barely read the newspapers.

Because literacy in traditional China was the privilege of men, it is unlikely that women would have had much opportunity to write about their training and their spiritual experiences. In the biographies of the immortals, we find that many Taoist women were illiterate, and many lived their lives in the shadows of their husbands and fathers. The few who were educated all came from the nobility and the wealthy families. Given these problems, how can we study women in the history of Taoism? There are various sources of information that we can use.

The first is the biographies of the immortals. There are many sketches of Taoist women in the biographies of the immortals written between the second and the seventeenth centuries. Although short, these sketches are important: they tell us that in the history of Taoism, female practitioners are not rare, and that many women attained levels of spirituality that are comparable to their male counterparts.

Our second source of information about Taoist women is the biographies of important male Taoist adepts (advanced practitioners) who learned from female teachers. The Yellow Emperor was said to have acquired his knowledge of divination, military strategy, and the compass from the Lady of the Nine Heavens, who was a female deity. The Emperor Shun was taught by the daughter of his predecessor. Fei Hang, a highly respected alchemist and magician of the first century, was taught by a woman. Li Ch'üan, a Taoist magician and a provincial governor of the T'ang dynasty (618–906 C.E.), was the student of Li-shan Lao-mu (the old wise woman of Li Mountain). The spiritual mentor of Ma Tan-yang, one of the Seven Masters of the Northern Complete Reality School of the Sung dynasty (960–1279 C.E.), was his wife Sun Pu-erh. From these records, we know that women were not only practitioners but also teachers of the Taoist arts.

The third source of information about Taoist women comes from novels, folklore, and the yeh-shih (literally, wild history), chronicles that are not recognized by the Chinese scholars as "legitimate" historical records. The folk novel *Seven Taoist Masters,* which describes the life and times of Sun Pu-erh, the best-known female Taoist practitioner of the Sung dynasty, is an example.

The fourth source of information about Taoist women is the writings of the female adepts themselves. These include Sun Pu-erh's poems and treatises on meditation and internal alchemy, Lady Wei Hua-ts'un's famous Shang-ch'ing classics on meditation and mystical union with the deities, and the collected poems of female adepts Sun Pu-erh and T'ang Kuang-chen. The writings of female practitioners are an invaluable source of information about Taoist women and their level of spiritual development. Unfortunately, female authors are rare. The female adepts who did not leave records of their lives or their training are forever lost in the shadows of the past.

Using these sources of information mentioned above, it is possible to recover the hidden history of women in Taoism. This history is best viewed in the context of three landmark events in the development of Taoist thought and practice:

- The Mother Empress of the West becomes a Taoist deity circa second century C.E.
- Lady Wei Hua-ts'un and the founding of the Shang-ch'ing School of Taoism in the fourth century
- Sun Pu-erh and the emergence of female internal alchemy in the thirteenth century

The acceptance of the Mother Empress of the West into the Taoist pantheon of deities was a landmark in the development of Devotional Taoism. Today, over 60 percent of Taoists are followers of Devotional Taoism. The devotees express their devotion by chanting the names of the deities, by participating in the rituals, by making offerings, and by asking the deities for guidance and protection. The strength of a devotional religion is built on the faith of its devotees, and the overwhelming majority of the followers of Devotional Taoism are female. These female devotees would make the Mother Empress one of the most popular deities in Taoism, elevating her to the highest echelon of the Taoist pantheon.

The founding of the Shang-ch'ing School of Taoism by Lady Wei Hua-ts'un in the fourth century led to the emergence of Mystical Taoism. Although Shang-ch'ing Taoism ceased to be a distinct lineage during the Ming dynasty (1368–1644 C.E.), its influence on the development of Taoist thought and practice is not lost. Today, many Shang-ch'ing rituals are practiced in Taoist temples and monasteries. Moreover, the Shang-ch'ing techniques of swallowing saliva, breath control, and directing the flow of energy in the body have been incorporated into many forms of ch'i-kung and Taoist calisthenics that are practiced today.

It is not far-fetched to say that Sun Pu-erh's innovations in female internal alchemy have changed Taoist spiritual training forever. For the first time in the history of Taoist practice, gender differences in the internal energetic structures are acknowledged and separate training methods are designed to address these differences. It is to the credit of Sun Pu-erh and her successors that there are now separate programs of training for women and men in Taoist sects that practice the alchemy of internal transformation.

THE MOTHER EMPRESS OF THE WEST

The Mother Empress of the West (Hsi-wang-mu) is one of the most important deities in Taoism today. She is the highest female deity in the Taoist pantheon and is subordinate only to the T'ai-shang Lao-chun (the incarnation of Lao-tzu), who is the highest deity in the Taoist religion. In Taoist religious literature, the Mother Empress of the West is described as the original breath of the Great Yin and the counterpart of the Lord of the East, who is the original breath of the Great Yang. Although the Mother Empress of the West is the ward of all female practitioners of the arts of longevity and immortality, both male and female adepts need to obtain her permission before they can enter the immortal realm. This is a plane of existence inhabited by deities and mortals who have earned the privilege of living forever. In ancient China, immortality literally means "eternal life" in both body and spirit. Later, immortality came to mean the liberation of the spirit to a higher plane of existence after the bodily shell has run its course.

In the religious icons, the Mother Empress of the West is accompanied by female attendants who carry trays of Peaches of Immortality. She herself carries two treasures—a peach and a pill that resembles a round pearl. Each treasure, if eaten, can turn a mortal into an immortal.

The Mother Empress of the West was an ancient folk deity before she became a Taoist deity. She was known as the Golden Mother or the Mother Empress and was the custodian of the immortal lands that were believed to be nestled in the K'un-lun Mountains in western China.

If the Mother Empress of the West was not originally a Taoist deity, how did she come to occupy such a high position in the Taoist pantheon? To answer this question, we must first understand the nature of Chinese religion.

In China, the belief in deities and immortals existed long before Taoism became a religion during the second century. There are two kinds of deities: pre-creation and post-creation. The difference between an immortal and a deity is in their power and status in the Taoist pantheon. An immortal can be thought of as a lesser deity. Some immortals were spirits of nature who became sentient and attained immortality by absorbing the energy of the land; others were mortals who became immortal by practicing the arts of longevity and immortality. It is possible, however, for immortals to be "elevated" to deity status if they performed miracles or were responsible for leading mortals to the Tao. In fact, after the immortals Lady Ho Hsien-ku and Lady Wei got deified, they occupied a higher rank in the echelon of deities than some of the pre-creation deities like the gods of thunder and wind.

The Mother Empress is a pre-creation deity. Legends tell us that she is the incarnation of the primordial vapor of the West and the counterpart of the Emperor of the East, who is the incarnation of the primordial vapor of the East. These two deities constitute the two primordial energies of West and East, that nourish and protect all things. The Mother Empress and the Emperor of the East are also the teachers of humanity. Many legendary shaman-rulers of ancient China were said to have journeyed to the immortal realms to learn from them. These included the emperors Yao, Shun, and Yü of the legendary times.

Even before the Mother Empress became a Taoist deity, she was associated with the western immortal realm of K'un-lun. Two Chinese emperors—King Mu of the Chou dynasty (1122–221 B.C.E.) and Wu-ti (the Martial Emperor) of the Han (206 B.C.E.–219 C.E.)—were said to have met her and to have asked her for the gift of immortality; however, she did not permit either of them to enter the immortal lands.

It is in the story of Wu-ti's encounter with the Mother Empress that we find important clues about female deities before the rise of Taoism as a religion. The story tells us that the Mother Empress visited Wu-ti in his palace on the emperor's birthday, gave him seven peaches, and told him that the peaches came from a tree that yielded fruits only once every three thousand years. When Wu-ti asked that he be taught the arts of immortality, he was rebuffed by Lady Shang-yüan, a subordinate of the Mother Empress, who told him that he could not be given the secrets of immortality because he was greedy and cruel.

From the story, we can first surmise that by the second century B.C.E. (during Wu-ti's reign), the Mother Empress was already a popular and powerful deity: both women and men needed her permission to enter the immortal realm. Second, we can surmise that at least by the end of the reign of Wu-ti, Lady Shang-yüan was also perceived as a powerful deity: she scolded the "martial emperor" as if he were a wayward child.

Like the Mother Empress, Lady Shang-yüan was an ancient deity. Her name Shang-yüan means "early season." In ancient China, the year was divided into three segments—an early season (shang-yüan), a middle season (chung-yüan), and a late season (hsia-yüan). Today, these three seasonal divisions are still observed within Taoist communities. The early season refers to the period between the fifteenth day of the first lunar month and the fifteenth day of the seventh lunar month. Within this season is the important festival of spring planting. As the ruler of the early season, Lady Shang-yüan controls the success of the spring planting and therefore the prosperity of the nation. A common citizen who has offended her or has lost her favor would lose his fortunes that year. However, an emperor who lost her favor would lose his mandate to rule, and this loss of mandate would be reflected in untimely rains and poor harvest.

Thus, the Mother Empress and Lady Shang-yüan were already popular folk deities even before Taoism became a religion. However, after they became Taoist deities, their power and status increased, and they became rulers of the celestial realm with thousands of subordinates, clerks, and messengers. This happened around the third to fourth centuries. By the end of the fourth century, the Mother Empress was considered as the source of inspiration of many Taoist scriptures, suggesting that she had become an important and authoritative high deity in the Taoist religion.

Four hundred years later, in the T'ang dynasty (618–906 C.E.), the Mother Empress's status as a Taoist deity would grow even more: she was the deity responsible for gathering the sages of the world into the immortal realms, supervising all the covenants made between humanity and the deities, evaluating the faith and devotion of believers, presiding over audiences and banquets in the celestial realm, and transmitting the sacred scriptures to worthy mortals. She was also the teacher of sagely emperors, devoted believers, and the patron of all those who practiced the arts of longevity and immortality.

Before becoming a Taoist deity, the Mother Empress had a modest palace and retinue of female attendants. After becoming a powerful Taoist deity, she not only had a group of daughters who were powerful deities themselves, but was also in command of thousands of celestial messengers and clerks.

After the incorporation of the Mother Empress into the highest levels of the Taoist pantheon, many other prominent Taoist women were added to the roster of deities and immortals. The following are biographical sketches of some of the most renowned female Taoist deities and immortals in the history of Taoism.

Ho Hsien-ku (Lady Immortal Ho) is probably the most famous woman immortal and deity. We know much about her from the biographical sketch in The Complete Biographies of the Immortals:

> Her name is Ch'in. She is the daughter of Ho T'ai, a county magistrate in Kuang-tung Province. She lived in the T'ang dynasty during the reign of the Empress in a village near a stream named Cloud Mother. . . . She was seen often running along the mountain paths. Her gait was fast and light. She left home in the morning and returned in the evening, bringing back mountain fruits for her mother. . . . The T'ang Queen Mother (Wu-hou) invited her for an audience but she disappeared on the way to the capital. Later she ascended to the sky in broad daylight. . . . She also appeared to a local judge in Kuang-tung Province; the judge later reported this incident to the emperor.

From this biographical sketch, we know that Lady Immortal Ho was a significant female Taoist adept during her time: she was famous enough to be invited by an empress of the T'ang dynasty. The Empress Wu-hou was no ordinary queen mother: she dominated the politics of the court and was even more powerful than the ruling emperor. So, her invitation was no trivial matter. The biography also states that she appeared to a local judge. This again was something unusual given the political and social climate of the T'ang dynasty. In a Confucian society, women were rarely allowed to voice their opinions, let alone meet with government officials. For Lady Immortal Ho to have met with a local judge and for the judge to consider the incident important enough to report to the emperor, she must have been an immortal of high stature. This proved to be true: she holds the title "Supervisor of the Female Path—the Primal Ruler of the Azure Vapor." Finally, we are told that like many Chinese women, she was a filial daughter: even after she had acquired her magical powers, she did not neglect to bring food to her mother.

Another important Taoist female deity is Chiu-t'ien Hsüan-nü (The Mysterious Lady of Nine Heavens), who was teacher to the Yellow Emperor, one of the most revered sage rulers of ancient China. A student of the Mother Empress, she was instructed by the deities to help the Yellow Emperor unite the tribes of China into a nation. It was her gifts to the Yellow Emperor—magical objects that included the compass, books on divination and military strategy, pearls that glowed like lights, flags of power, feathers of power, and magical swords—that allowed the Yellow Emperor to defeat evil bandits, unite the tribes, and restore peace to his country.

Tung-ling Sheng-mu (Sacred Mother of Tung-ling) was another prominent Taoist female deity. A mortal who became a local deity, she became famous enough to be included in The Complete Biographies of the Immortals. Her biographical sketch reads:

> Native of Hai-ning. She learned from Liu Kang and attained the Tao. She can change into any shape and can sometimes be invisible. She encountered a man named Tu who ridiculed her abilities. The sacred mother was always helping the poor and the needy. Tu complained to the local magistrate. He said that the sacred mother spent too much time fighting evil spirits and neglected to tend her household. The magistrate arrested the sacred mother and threw her in prison. Later, she flew out of her cell, leaving only a shoe on the window sill. The people of the village built her a shrine and prayed to her for help. A green raven is often seen hovering around the shrine. If you were robbed and prayed for help, the bird will lead you to the thief's home. Thus, in that area, people are not greedy and do not take things that are not theirs. Even today, in the region of Hai-ning, there are few thieves and robbers. This is because many robbers have been found either drowned or killed by wild animals, and petty thieves have been plagued with misfortunes.

The first thing we learn about the Sacred Mother of Tung-ling from this biographical sketch is that she was a magician-vigilante. She started out as a local hero and later became the local protector. The biography also gives us valuable information about the kind of society she lived in. We are told that she was taken to the court and accused of not "spending enough time to tend her household." Today, we would find it hard to believe that such accusations could be directed at a woman in a court, but in traditional China, this was not unusual. These social values lasted well into the Republican years.

Mah Ku is probably the most popular female immortal among the Chinese. Her biographical sketch in The Complete Biographies of the Immortals reads:

> The daughter Mah Chiu. There was a drought in autumn. Ma Chiu made the people work all night to build the city wall, allowing them to rest only when the cock crowed. Mah Ku, seeing the suffering of the people, imitated rooster calls. Soon, all the roosters in the village were crowing as well, and the people were allowed to rest. When her father learned what she had done, he tried to beat her. Mah Ku ran away and entered a cave to cultivate the Tao. Later she ascended to the sky near the stone bridge in the outskirts of the town. The bridge was later named Bridge of the Immortal.

There are several female immortals by the name of Mah Ku. However, the Mah Ku of this story is my favorite. She is extremely popular with the Chinese and has been a central figure in Chinese opera, movies, and television dramas. I first heard of Mah Ku's story from my grandmother, who learned it from her mother.

Mah Ku was an unusual woman. In a society where fathers demanded absolute obedience from their daughters, she opposed her father to help people who were suffering from her father's cruelty. Moreover, she was not intimidated by her father. When he tried to beat her into submission, she escaped and ran off to cultivate the Tao by herself. It is likely that the bridge in her hometown was renamed by the people in honor of her courage and integrity.

Cheng Wei's wife was also an unusual woman. In The Complete Biographies of Immortals, she is described as

> The wife of Han dynasty official Cheng Wei. Cheng loved the Taoist arts of alchemy. He married a woman with the family name of Fang. When Cheng did not have a robe for his audience with the emperor,

his wife conjured up two bolts of satin. When Cheng tried to refine gold from base metals, he was unsuccessful. When his wife put mercury into the cauldron, gold appeared. Cheng was astonished and exclaimed, "You have the secrets of the Tao. Why didn't you tell me?" His wife replied, "To succeed in this, it must be in your destiny." Cheng tried to bribe his wife with money and land but she did not disclose anything. Then Cheng plotted to force her to succumb to his wishes. His wife found out and said to him, "The secrets of the Tao are transmitted only to the right person, even if you had only met him casually on the street. If the person is unsuitable, the Tao is not transmitted, even if refusal means being torn apart limb by limb." Smearing her face with mud, she feigned madness and ran away from home naked. Eventually, she shed her bodily shell and vanished.

In this biographical sketch, we learn that Cheng Wei's wife compounded minerals to manufacture pills of immortality. She had her own laboratory and experimented with alchemical techniques of turning mercury into gold as well. As the wife of a government official, she was not poor. Moreover, the family needed to have disposable income to support the alchemical laboratories of both husband and wife. It is also likely that Chang Wei's wife was literate, because she needed to understand the formulas for compounding mercury and to keep track of the minerals used in alchemical experiments. The biography does not hide the fact that she, not her husband, was the one destined to succeed in attaining immortality. However, despite her achievements, Cheng Wei's wife, whose maiden name was Fang, was not addressed as Madame Fang, but was simply referred to as "Cheng Wei's wife." This shows that in traditional China, even women with remarkable abilities often lived in the shadows of their husbands.

The biographies of female deities and immortals reveal important information about women in the history of Taoism: the female deities and immortals occupy just as important positions in the Taoist pantheon as the male deities, and women were as adept as men in all aspects of Taoist spirituality.

From the middle T'ang onward, a new and different kind of female immortal emerged: women who attained immortality by meditation and by ecstatic union with the deities. This change was brought about by the rise of Shang-ch'ing Taoism in the fourth century. The incorporation of Shang-ch'ing practices into mainstream Taoism in the next seven hundred years would make Shang-ch'ing Taoism one of the most powerful influences in the history of Taoist thought.

MYSTICAL TAOISM

Lady Wei Hua-ts'un of the Chin dynasty (265–420 C.E.) is recognized as the founder of the Shang-ch'ing School of Taoism. We are told that Lady Wei Hua-ts'un was born into a wealthy family in Kiang-su Province (in southeast China). From an early age, she studied the Taoist classics, practiced breath control, experimented with various diets, and was adept at yogic techniques of cultivating longevity. When she announced that she wanted to leave the family to learn the arts of immortality, her parents forbade her. At the age of twenty-four, she was married to a nobleman at the orders of her father. After her marriage, Lady Wei gave birth to two sons. When they were able to start families of their own, she built herself a retreat and devoted the rest of her life to studying and practicing the Taoist arts. For a brief period of time, she served as a teacher of religious ceremony in the Celestial Teachers' School (a form of organized Taoist religion founded by Chang Tao-ling and his descendants in the second and third centuries).

Not too long after becoming a recluse, Lady Wei was visited by the immortal Wang Pao, who transmitted to her the technique of attaining immortality by merging with the deities in mystical ecstasy. It was said that Lady Wei eventually mastered Wang Pao's techniques and, at the age of eighty-three, ascended to the sky in broad daylight. In addition, the Taoist legends tell us that after she became an immortal, Lady Wei continued to study with the Mother Empress of the West, and was finally deified and awarded the title Lady Wei, Guardian of the Southern Mountains.

In her biographies, Lady Wei Hua-ts'un is identified by her maiden name Wei, not Liu, her husband's family name. The scriptures that are attributed to her all bear the name Lady Wei. This suggests that Wei Hua-ts'un was well-known in the Taoist community of her time. It also suggests that in the latter part of the Chin dynasty, women's status within Taoism had improved. This was also evidenced by Lady Wei's high rank within the clerical echelon of the Celestial Teachers' School.

In the history of women in Taoism, the most important influence of Wei Hua-ts'un is seen in the change of methods used by female Taoist practitioners to cultivate longevity and immortality. Consider the following biographical sketches of these female immortals.

> Immortal Hua-ku (the Flower Lady) lived during the T'ang dynasty and was a follower of Shang-ch'ing Taoism. It was said that when she heard that there was a shrine dedicated to Immortal Lady Wei Hua-ts'un in the area where Lady Wei ascended to the celestial realm, she journeyed there to seek inspiration. While meditating at Lady Wei's shrine, she saw the immortal appear, telling her that south of the shrine was a lake fed by nine winding rivers. The Flower Lady found the site and ordered the local Taoist priest to gather flowers and prepare a ceremony. After the site was consecrated, she and seven other · female practitioners continued to conduct ceremonies there. The music, chanting, and the fragrance of the flowers were said to travel far beyond the shrine. The community of female devotees of Lady Wei grew, until there were twenty-seven members who lived there permanently to tend the shrine.

This biography contains important information about Taoist women who followed the spiritual path of Shang-ch'ing Taoism. First, we learn that by the time of the T'ang (618–906 C.E.) and the Sung (960–1127 C.E..), Lady Wei Hua-ts'un was acknowledged as a deity and there were shrines dedicated to her. Second, the Flower Lady's pilgrimage to Lady Wei's shrine suggests that Wei Hua-ts'un had become a role model and a patron of female Taoist practitioners during the T'ang. Third, the Flower Lady, a woman adept, "ordered" a male practitioner to gather objects for a ceremony that she, not he, conducted. This shows that by the time of the T'ang dynasty, there were Taoist religious communities led by women, with men serving as assistants. Finally, out of the Flower Lady's devotion, a community of female Taoist recluses was founded. Although this community was not as organized as the Taoist nunneries founded several hundred years later, it nonetheless tells us that there were enough independent and motivated women who could and would leave their families to live in a religious community.

Fei Yüan-ching was also a follower of Shang-ch'ing Taoism. The legends tell us that she was a daughter of a county magistrate and was very intelligent. As a child, she learned the classics and wrote poetry. Moreover, unlike many young women of her age, she was not interested in jewels and beautiful clothes and wanted to study the Taoist arts instead. When she asked her father to build her a meditation retreat, her parents built her a small hut in the garden and supplied her with incense and a female assistant. At the age of twenty, Fei Yüan-ching's father wanted her to marry a man named Li Yen. When she told them that she would rather spend her life studying the Tao, her parents said, "It is your duty to be married. After your marriage, you can continue to study the Tao. Even Lady Wei Hua-ts'un was married before she ascended to immortality."

After her marriage, Fei Yüan-ching continued to meditate in her retreat. One night, her husband heard several female voices coming from his wife's meditation room. He looked through the window and saw his wife talking with two young women. When he asked who these women were, he was told that they were immortals. The women had told Fei Yüan-ching that she was not destined to spend her life with her husband in the earthly realm. The next evening, another female immortal visited the couple's home and promised to give them a son. A year later, three days after Fei Yüan-ching gave Li Yen a son, she was carried to the West on a cloud in the company of a group of female immortals.

The biography of Fei Yüan-ching contains several important clues about Lady Wei's influence on the Taoist women of the T'ang and Sung dynasties. First, it establishes that Lady Wei was a famous figure in the Taoist communities of the time. She was a role model for Fei Yüan-ching, who, like Lady Wei, wanted to build a retreat and practice meditation. Second, Fei Yüan-ching's parents cited Lady Wei as an example of a filial daughter who fulfilled her duty as a wife before immersing herself in Taoist cultivation. However, Fei Yüan-ching's parents were more understanding than Lady Wei's father, who did not consult with his daughter before he married her off. Third, Fei Yüan-ching's husband appeared to be an understanding man who did not oppose his wife's spiritual interests. This is a far cry from Cheng Wei, who was jealous of his wife's talent.

It is interesting that in the biographies of Taoist women, many mortal men were depicted as "villains": Cheng Wei tried to force his wife into giving him the alchemical formulas; Ma Ku was beaten by her father for disobedience; and the Sacred Mother of Tung-ling was the victim of a vengeful man. Moreover, in the stories, the women were portrayed as independent, courageous, strong, and superior to the men in both skill and character. This is interesting because the biographies were written by men. If there was a patriarchal bias in documenting the lives of female immortals (which I think there was), we would expect the men to have been presented more positively in the stories. A closer examination of the stories reveals, however, that the male characters in the biographies would have been condemned as "villains" in mainstream Confucian society as well: Confucianism does not endorse the beating of women, or treachery, or rape, or vengeance. Thus the "villains" in the stories were not "male villains," but simply "villains." Even a patriarchal society would have no trouble presenting them in a negative light.

Another thing that is obvious from the biographies of Taoist women is that the women of the early times (pre-T'ang) had authoritative fathers (Ma Ku's father) and husbands (Cheng Wei) who did not care about their feelings and their interests. By the T'ang dynasty, we begin to see more understanding husbands and supportive parents. This suggests that the social and cultural view of women in general and of women who pursue spiritual interests were changing in the Sui (589–618 C.E.) and T'ang (618–906 C.E.) dynasties. Although women specifically did not enjoy equal status with men in politics and public life, they were beginning to have more freedom in spiritual cultivation. By Sun Pu-erh's time four hundred years later, women's status in the spiritual community had improved even more: Taoist nunneries were established, and many of them received endowments from the imperial coffer.

Thus, while Taoist women are outnumbered by men in the biographies of the deities and immortals, they are not as "invisible" as we have been led to believe. The biographies are a valuable source of information about the lives and times of Taoist women from the Han to the Sung dynasties. However, the last biography of immortals was written in the Ming

(1368–1644 C.E.). Therefore, to learn about Taoist women in more recent times, we would need to turn to a different source of information—the manuals of female internal alchemy and the writings of the female practitioners of internal-alchemical Taoism.

FEMALE TAOIST INTERNAL ALCHEMY

Sun Pu-erh is probably the most famous female Taoist practitioner of recent history. She lived during the early part of the Sung dynasty (960–1279) and was one of the Seven Taoist Masters of the Complete Reality School. A student of Wang Ch'ung-yang (the founder of the school), Sun Pu-erh was said to have attained the highest level of enlightenment among the seven chosen students of the master.

Sun Pu-erh's life has been dramatized in the famous folk novel *Seven Taoist Masters*. We are told that she was married to a wealthy merchant named Ma Yü. Intelligent and compassionate, she developed an interest in the Taoist spiritual arts at an early age. Both she and her husband became students of the Taoist master Wang Ch'ung-yang, and later each established their own Taoist sect. Sun Pu-erh is considered the founder of female internal alchemy. Recognizing that the energetic structures and the internal transformational processes are different for women and men, she developed special techniques to help women cultivate body and mind and attain longevity.

Internal alchemy is concerned with transforming three kinds of internal energies in the human body: procreative/generative (ching), nourishing/vital (ch'i), and consciousness/spirit (shen). To cultivate and refine these energies, the practitioner must understand the properties of these energies and know how to produce and transform them inside the body. Thus, the internal alchemist must be knowledgeable and sensitive to gender differences in anatomy, physiology, and energetic structures.

Sun Pu-erh's contribution to female internal alchemy lies in her understanding that women need a separate program of internal-alchemical training and that they need encouragement and support to overcome the social stigmas that hinder their spiritual training. She asserted that women have a natural disposition toward the Tao because they embody the essence of tranquility and softness. Today, about 20 percent of those who claim to be Taoist are practitioners of internal alchemy. Less than a quarter of them are female. Of the female practitioners, the majority live in China.

As a female practitioner of the internal alchemical arts, I would like to make this Taoist practice more well-known in the West. I would also like to describe the nature of that training from the perspective of a practitioner, so that women who are interested in pursuing this form of Taoist training will know what to expect. Training in female internal alchemy can be divided into four stages.

1. Building the Foundation— Cultivating Stillness and Tranquility

Women should begin their training by cultivating their natural disposition and intrinsic nature, which is stillness and tranquility. This is especially important for young women.

The Mother Empress of the West's Ten Precepts on the True Path of Women's Practices (believed to be written by Sun Pu-erh) advises the female practitioner:

> In her youth she should be quiet and not wild. . . . If she is peaceful and tranquil in her life, if she can follow the rules of womanly behavior and be natural in her stillness, then this substance (generative energy) will remain close to its prenatal nature and return to its primal unity. . . . But unfortunately, the common girl is ignorant, childish, and attracted to action. She engages in games and wild careening. Her spirit becomes confused and her true energy becomes unstable.

Second, women need to free themselves from social pressure and be focused in their spiritual training. The Answers to Questions Concerning Cultivation says:

> Men are yang in nature. Their energy is difficult to control. For example, if it takes a man three years to control the flow of the energy, the woman will accomplish it in one. . . . Moreover, she can do it

with less effort. . . . However, women need to be especially strong, motivated, and disciplined. . . . Then they will be able to accomplish the task.

Third, women need to free themselves from sexual desire and mood fluctuations. The text Cultivating Stillness for Women—also written by Sun Pu-erh—says: "If women realize the value of their health and life and do not succumb to the wishes of the opposite sex, then it will be easy for them to attain health and longevity. . . . They must first sever their attachment to sexual desire before sitting down to meditate."

Fourth, women need to have supportive families and understanding teachers. The Mother Empress of the West's Ten Precepts on the True Path of Women's Practices states: "There is no lack of gifted women. Unfortunately they do not have wise parents, or teachers, or supportive friends. Thus, their thousand gifts are wasted."

These excerpts from the classics of female internal alchemy assert that women, because of their natural disposition toward stillness, actually have fewer obstacles in building the foundation for training in internal alchemy. Men, on the other hand, need to develop the "feminine" qualities of tranquility and receptivity before they can begin their training. This is probably why many Taoist monasteries use art and poetry to help their male novices develop inner calm and reflectivity. Modern women in Western society may not have the kind of social pressure the women of traditional China had, but in many contemporary households, it is still uncommon for women to leave the spouse on evenings or weekends to attend meditation or martial arts classes. Thus, compared to men, women may still have more obstacles to overcome before they can train seriously.

2. External Strengthening— Transforming the Skeletal Structure

Once the foundation of inner peace is built, the next stage is to strengthen the body. This stage of training in particular needs to take into account sexual differences in muscular-skeletal physiology. The goal of external strengthening is to prepare the body for cultivating and circulating internal energy. This entails changing the skeletal structure. Almost nothing is written about this stage of training, so I shall discuss these processes from my own experiences.

First, compared to men, women in general have smaller bones and weaker muscles. Therefore, in external strengthening, the initial focus for women is to build larger bones and stronger muscles. Typically, women will need to work harder than men in this aspect of training. Taoist calisthenics, postures, and the internal martial arts (such as T'ai-chi ch'uan) are used for this purpose.

Second, women's tendons are more elastic than men's. Thus, in general, women are more flexible. This means that women will find it easier to increase, maintain, or even regain flexibility. Men, on the other hand, must not reduce the amount of stretching after they have achieved the desired level of flexibility, or their tendons will lose the elasticity.

Third, women tend to have a stronger and more flexible spine because structural skeletal strength is required to carry a fetus. Spinal flexibility and strength are important for later stages of internal alchemy because a major channel of energy circulation (the tu meridian) is aligned with the spinal column. However, the programs of training are different for men and women. While both women and men need to develop spinal flexibility, women will achieve the goal faster. Moreover, once women attain the desired balance of spinal strength and flexibility, they should reduce the amount of spinal stretching, or spinal strength will decrease. Men, on the other hand, need to maintain their regimen of training to maintain spinal flexibility.

Fourth, women and men have different pelvic structures. Women have a wider pelvic bowl compared to men because the female pelvis is built to carry a fetus. Therefore, it is easier for women to widen the pelvic bowl further and open up the pelvic joints to prepare for meditation in the higher stages of internal alchemy.

Thus, in general, it is easier for women to achieve external strengthening than men. Given the same motivation and amount of training, women will complete the stage of external strengthening faster than men.

3. Internal Strengthening—"Slaying the Dragon" and Circulating Energy in the Breast and the Womb

The goal of internal strengthening for both females and males is to culti-vate the three internal energies—procreative/generative (ch'ing), nourish-ing/vital (ch'i), and consciousness/spirit (shen).

Generative energy is the primordial energy of creation; in the body it is manifested as procreative energy. In females, the mundane form of this energy is the menstrual blood; in males it is the seminal fluid. Vital energy is the primordial energy of nourishment. In the body it is manifested as breath, and it is the same for females and males. Spirit energy is the pri-mordial energy of consciousness. In the body it is manifested as original (the empty) mind, and it is the same for males and females.

Because generative/procreative and vital/nourishing energy are both linked to female and male physiology, the process of internal strengthen-ing is extremely sensitive to gender differences in physiology (manifested in the physical body) and energetic structure (manifested in the subtle body).

Both men and women begin the process of internal strengthening by preserving, refining, and transforming procreative energy. The woman's method of preserving and refining generative energy is called "slaying the dragon."

"Slaying the dragon" refers to stopping the flow of menstrual blood; it is, however, not equivalent to menopause. The menstrual flow is the "mundane" form of female generative energy. When a woman reaches pu-berty, the primordial generative energy that she was endowed with at birth is transformed into energy for procreation. If the energy is not used for reproduction or the nourishment of the fetus, it will flow out as men-strual blood.

The Mother Empress of the West's Ten Precepts on the True Path of Women's Practices tells us that

> At age thirteen, fourteen, or fifteen, the woman's primordial energy is plentiful and her "true blood" is full. She has the one yang embod-ied in the yin. This is when the light of the full moon is resplendent. When the menses descends, her primordial energy is broken and the

"true blood" will leak out. After marriage and the birth of children, her primordial energy continues to weaken and the "true blood" is gradually destroyed. Although every month the menstrual blood continues to flow, in reality, it is re-injured every time the menses occur. This is why it is difficult for a woman to cultivate life. . . . The key to a woman's life is tied to her menses. If the menses is not transformed, how can she preserve her life?

If a woman does not practice internal alchemy to conserve and preserve the generative energy, the energy will continue to flow out of the body. When this energy is gone, the aging process will speed up, and the woman's health will decline rapidly. This is remarkably consistent with contemporary medical theories about women's aging process and the loss of estrogen after menopause.

All internal alchemists agree that it is best for a woman to begin internal cultivation before puberty. If this is not possible, then she should begin her cultivation before menopause. Finally, those who begin their training after menopause will have to work the hardest.

After the "red dragon" is "slain," the female practitioner can begin the next stage of internal strengthening. The procreative energy, which has been transformed into primordial generative energy, is channeled to the area of the breasts. At the same time, the energy of nourishment is stimulated in the breast and transformed into the primordial vital energy. In female internal alchemy, this process is referred to as "cultivating the breast." The Essentials of the Golden Elixir Method for Women says, "The woman's life energy is in the breast. In the breasts is the essence of the mother's ch'i."

When the energy of nourishment is transformed into the primordial vital energy, the woman's breasts become firm, resembling those of a young woman before puberty.

With the completion of the transformation of procreative and nourishing energy into their respective primordial forms, the distinction between generative and vital energies no longer exists. The two have coagulated to become an undifferentiated energy called the primordial vapor, which is then circulated through the body. For women, the breast is the starting point for the circulation, whereas for men, the area between the kidneys (ming-men or Life Gate) is the starting point.

With time and practice, the primordial vapor is refined and cultivated and is stored in the abdominal area. For women, the vapor is stored in the womb; for men, it is stored in the area of the kidneys.

When females and males complete the processes of external strengthening, differences in their muscular-skeletal systems—bone mass, muscular strength, tendon elasticity, spinal strength, and spinal flexibility—begin to disappear. When they complete the process of internal strengthening, the subtle body, which is not gender-specific, directs the functions of internal physiology. From here onward, female and male practitioners undergo the same program of spiritual training.

4. Merging with the Tao

This is the highest level of internal alchemy. The distinction between female and male is dissolved as one sheds personality and aggregates to merge with the Tao. Here, sexual, social, or physiological differences no longer matter. In fact, one needs to shed attitudes and perspectives of gender before the mind can be emptied. When the thought processes stop, the original mind of emptiness will emerge.

Although Sun Pu-erh is considered the founder of female internal alchemy, many techniques have been refined by her successors. Today, the spiritual successors of Sun Pu-erh can be found in China, Taiwan, and Hong Kong. They have survived wars, political changes, and even the Cultural Revolution. Some are hermits living in small temples in remote regions of China and Taiwan; some have returned to the Taoist temples and nunneries after the People's Republic of China lifted its ban on organized religion; some always lived in Hong Kong, hiding as "urban hermits." I have been fortunate to have met and learned from some of these remarkable women.

CONCLUSIONS

In this chapter I have tried to uncover the hidden history of women in Taoism. I have reconstructed a history of Taoist women from biographies of deities and immortals, unorthodox histories, treatises on female internal alchemy, and my personal experiences in spiritual training. This reconstructed history shows us that female practitioners are not rare in the history of Taoism. It also shows that women have played important roles in the development of Taoist thought and practice.

The goal of this chapter is not to discredit or belittle the contributions of the men of Taoism; any great religious tradition must be built and maintained by both its female and male practitioners. However, I hope that in making the history of women more visible in the history of Taoism, I have given practitioners and non-practitioners, women and men, a more balanced view of the religious and spiritual tradition of my ancestral culture.

5

Judaism

By Susannah Heschel

I WAS A STUDENT when my father died, suddenly and unexpectedly in his sleep one night. The shock and horror felt overwhelming, and I was grateful for the family and friends who came to our home, brought us food, and led us through the intricate mourning observances of traditional Judaism. Since my father's family is Hasidic, a very devout branch of Judaism, our religious observances were numerous, and I was glad for that; I felt I wanted more and more ways to express my grief. My mother and I spent the first week at home, receiving visitors and praying three times each day the special prayer for the dead, the kaddish (literally, the prayer sanctifying God's name). Gradually, we emerged, tentatively, and returned to some of our normal activities. After a month, I returned to school, but carried my pain with me. My friends felt awkward, and I understood that they just didn't know what to say to me. Still, I needed some way to express my grieving, and I thought of my religion as a great source of comfort and support, even more reliable to me than my friends.

According to Jewish tradition, the mourner's kaddish (prayer for the dead) is recited daily in the synagogue for eleven months by sons, not daughters, and I was frequently told to leave or be treated with contempt at synagogues I attended. My experiences are not unique, but very much shared by numerous other Jewish women during the past few decades. Indeed, just as we were mourning our fathers, we came to realize that we were also mourning certain aspects of our Jewish identity that we had taken for granted—our acceptance by the community and by the tradition, both of which, we suddenly realized, failed to understand and support us at a time of deep anguish. Just as we were attempting to reconstruct our lives without a father, we also had to reconstruct our lives as Jews.

Most Conservative and Orthodox synagogues maintain daily services, gathering a minyan, a quorum of ten men that constitutes communal worship. These gatherings are usually composed of elderly men who are themselves saying kaddish for family members. The daily attendance at services offers them a social meeting, with breakfast following the early morning services. This was my first encounter with such groups, as I woke up at 6 and rushed to the early morning services at synagogues near my mother's home or my school. I liked the idea of being in the company of elderly men; they reminded me of my father. I expected they would welcome me, a young woman affirming her religious commitment. I had no idea of the hostility I would evoke.

In some congregations, I was simply tolerated. Placed in the back of the room, or off to one side, I was ignored. Often, one of the men announced to me the page number in the prayerbook, despite the fact that I followed the Hebrew prayers fluently and joined everyone else for the recitation of the kaddish. The assumption seemed to be that I knew nothing, although my education in Hebrew and Jewish religious texts was quite extensive. Sometimes, I seemed to be an irritant, as if my presence disrupted the community.

At other synagogues, my presence was not tolerated at all. Once, while driving to New York through Connecticut, I stopped in New Haven for the afternoon service. I arrived a little early in the Sunday School classroom where daily services were held, and when the elderly men arrived they informed me that they had no place for me and that I would have to leave. I tried to explain that I was saying kaddish, that there was no time to get to another synagogue for services. I even offered to stand in the back of the room, unseen. That was not good enough. I was told in plain, blunt words: "If you don't leave, we can't pray."

Not only in New Haven, but in New York, Boston, and Israel, where I happened to visit during that year of mourning, I had similar experiences. Indeed, in Israel, dominated by Orthodox synagogues, there was simply no opportunity whatsoever for me to say kaddish. I was banned from the daily services of Orthodox synagogues, and the Conservative synagogues only held services on the Sabbath. Being treated with contempt is painful enough; experiencing a banishment from the synagogue during a period of emotional fragility was devastating. My experience in Israel, which is supposed to be a place of homecoming for all Jews, taught me that I would have to abandon my Judaism to live there. Not only had I lost my father; I had lost my sense of being a full member of my religion. Death and institutionalized sexism hit me simultaneously.

The recitation of kaddish is a custom, not a commandment, and it has traditionally been carried out by men. A son is traditionally called his father's "kaddish," the guarantor that someone will recite the prayer for the father. And for a father who has only daughters? Customarily, a male relative or religious student would recite kaddish in such a case. Daughters were not part of the custom. And kaddish for a mother? Somehow her kaddish has been less important in the tradition.

In recent generations women have become increasingly vocal about their desire to say kaddish for a parent, spouse, or child. In a famous letter from the early part of this century, Henrietta Szold, the founder of the international women's Zionist organization Hadassah, thanked a male friend for offering to say kaddish for her father, but insisted that she would do so, pointing out that the love she felt for her father was the crucial element of the prayer. In the past twenty years, the difficulty of trying to recite kaddish for a father has become a common moment of awakening for many Jewish feminists. Quite a few have written about their own experiences, which have been much like my own. Encountering the sexism of Judaism as a full blast during a period of mourning, when a supportive community is so important, has caused many Jewish women to look more deeply at the roots of Judaism's attitudes toward women, and at their own commitment to their Jewish faith. According to many Jewish women, myself included, the sexism they experience from the community is unusual because their own fathers did not treat them in a discriminatory fashion. My father, for example, believed strongly in women's equality and always included me equally in prayers and other aspects of Jewish life. Indeed, he even suggested to me that I apply to rabbinical school, long before 1983, when women were finally ordained rabbis by the Conservative movement. The contrast between his views of women's inclusion in Judaism and the views I encountered in many synagogues made his death all the more painful, and my awareness of the sexism all the more striking.

During the year I said kaddish, I read Mary Daly's remarkable book, *Beyond God the Father*, which had been published in 1973.[1] Reading that book was an extraordinary experience for me. I was both devastated and exhilarated. Daly explained that the sexism of religion is not rooted in individual teachings, which might be modified or eliminated, but in the central symbols of religious faith—most importantly in the symbol of God as male. Her book explained to me why I had been feeling so devastated, which was a great relief, but it also made it clear to me that there were no easy solutions. If anything, I felt that an abyss had opened with the revelation of the depth of sexism and misogyny intrinsic to religion, including Judaism.

The feminist movement has brought remarkable changes to the religious life of Jewish women. For the first time in Jewish history, women are now being ordained rabbis, and have equality in most non-Orthodox synagogues. Within the field of Jewish Studies, too, feminist theory has had an impact. For the first time, questions about the role and status of women in Jewish history and in Jewish texts are being asked. Recovery of women's history has been a dominant concern, as well as analysis of misogynous traditions embedded within Judaism's texts.

The results of Jewish feminist studies have been mixed. Some historians have enthusiastically brought to light evidence that women participated actively in Jewish societies through the centuries, that many were educated leaders of their communities, and that women were engaged in religious practice as actively as men—even if their engagement was undertaken in separate locations. Texts that ignore or forbid women's involvement in Judaism's religious life have sometimes been contradicted by historical and archeological evidence. For example, despite the patriarchy and sexism of the Hebrew Bible, Susan Ackerman has demonstrated that women functioned as ritual musicians and singers in the religious life of ancient Israel.[2]

On the other hand, Judaism is also a religion of law and theology, and feminist studies of those spheres have been less promising. The legal and theological literature of Judaism produced through the centuries has been composed exclusively by men, and reveals negative stereotypes and, frequently, harsh biases toward women. The central concern of those texts is the religious life of Jewish men; women enter into the discussions insofar as they may enhance or disturb men, but their own religious needs are not taken into consideration. For example, although there are Jewish prayers for all sorts of bodily experiences, there is no prayer for giving birth. A man marries or divorces a woman; she may not take the initiative. As Rachel Adler has pointed out, Jewish law is rooted in a "methodolatry," an idolatry of method that not only favors men's interests, but often does not even have the intellectual rubrics for considering women's concerns.[3]

The dilemma for most Jewish women is that if they could simply re-gard Judaism in a detached manner as a sexist institution, they could walk away and not think twice about it. The difficulty is that Jewish identity is as fundamental as gender identity; it cannot easily be abandoned without losing a sense of oneself. Luckily, Jews are shaped by a host of loyalties, not only to the written texts, but also to Jewish history and community; to re-ligious beliefs and practices, but also to ethnicity, even to special foods, jokes, and languages. Jewishness is constructed not only by the written word, but by cultural attitudes. Thus, the basis of Judaism may begin with the Bible and the Talmud, the collection of rabbinic law and teachings compiled from the first to the sixth centuries, but it includes commen-taries, analyses, sermons, philosophical and mystical treatises, and extends to Jewish cultural memory from antiquity to the present day. That cultural memory is recapitulated in the prayerbook and in holiday celebrations such as Hanukkah, which celebrates the victory of the Hasmoneans over the Syrians in 165 B.C.E., and continues, as a contemporary Jew sees her-self or himself not only as a survivor of Hitler's genocide, but as one of the slaves who left Egypt under Moses' leadership in 1600 B.C.E.

Yet the pride in such identifications is mitigated for Jewish women by the realization that our specific experiences as women have been ignored by our tradition, or even denigrated by it. To enter the prayerbook, with its references to God as male, is to join the community on condition that our femaleness is left at the door. The mitzvot, commandments of the Bible and Talmud, considered divinely revealed law, place women in a cat-egory strictly separated from men. Even contemporary historical surveys of Jewish experience, including textbooks used in the college courses, such as *Jewish People, Jewish Thought*, rarely mention a single woman when covering several thousand years of Jewish history.[4] It is as if Jewish women are erased from the community, as if to be a Jew is to be a Jewish man.

As Jewish feminists began their efforts to recognize and overcome the sexism of Judaism, one of their first efforts was that of recovering women's own experiences. Attention was paid to the few women mentioned in the Bible as prophets, as well as to those whose lives were marked by the horror of rape and murder. New investigations of Jewish law were undertaken, to question whether the limitations on women's participation in Jewish religious life were truly mandated by the Talmud, or were the result of biased interpretations of the law. Historians attempted to uncover the traces of women's lives in documents and archeological artifacts, to see how women experienced their own sense of Jewish identity, despite patriarchal constraints. All of these efforts involved overcoming obstacles. How, for example, could the history of Jewish women be found when all the major extant texts of the premodern period had been composed by men? How could rabbinic literature be analyzed by women when the schools for studying those texts, yeshivot, were limited to male students?

Enormous changes have occurred during the past thirty years in the opportunities afforded Jewish women to express themselves spiritually and intellectually. Schools for training Jewish women in traditional rabbinic texts have been opened, with the result that some women have become authorities on matters of Jewish law. The academic study of Judaism at universities has also created a new generation of women scholars, many of whom bring feminist concerns to bear on their study of history, literature, and religious thought. Most dramatically, women participate equally with men in the public worship at most non-Orthodox synagogues. Even within certain spheres of Orthodox Judaism, women have created their own prayer and study groups, abiding by Jewish law yet taking advantage of the opportunities permitted under the law for women-only gatherings. Indeed, the transformation of Jewish public life to include women may be one of the most dramatic changes in Judaism of the modern era.

The question for Jewish feminists is whether the changes they are bringing about are entirely new in the history of Judaism, or whether they have some basis in Jewish history.

Many have described Judaism as among the world's most sexist religions, yet others have discovered teachings that support women's empowerment. One of the great difficulties has been locating appropriate sources that reflect the reality of women's lives. Most extant Jewish texts were written by men, and little survives to indicate the actual experience Jewish women have had of their religion.

Ancient Israel emerged around 1200 B.C.E. within a larger Canaanite society and was influenced by features of Canaanite religion, including its worship of goddess figures.[5] Both the prophetic expressions and more direct archeological evidence indicate that some goddess worship existed alongside male monotheism in ancient Israel and Judah.[6] The Israelite effort, described in the Bible, to shift from polytheistic to monotheistic worship meant the elimination of goddess figures in favor of a single male deity, Yahweh. Despite that effort, some of the characteristics of Canaanite goddesses can be found among the attributes of Yahweh. In addition, some of the women leaders who appear in the Bible, such as Deborah and Yael, assume the style of the warrior goddesses of Canaan. Archeologists, moreover, have challenged conventional assumptions that monotheism was widely accepted by the eighth century B.C.E. with evidence that heterogeneous-style worship continued long after, including worship of goddess figures and pagan deities alongside Yahweh.

The worship of goddesses, however, does not necessarily mean an elevation of women's social status, as the feminist biblical scholar Tikvah Frymer-Kensky has pointed out.[7] Cross-cultural studies clearly reveal that patriarchy often produces goddesses. The presence of powerful women within the biblical narrative more likely arises from the fact that ancient Israelite society was not formally structured in its institutions, allowing women a greater role to play not only in military exploits but also, perhaps, in religious life. Biblical texts indicate that women were active both as prophets and as ritual musicians, at least prior to the emergence of the monarchy, around 1050 B.C.E.[8] Both Miriam and Deborah, as well as several other women, were designated prophets, and their activities are related in some detail by the biblical texts of Exodus and Judges. The advent of the monarchy shifted the role of women as ritual musicians from the public sphere to the private. In early Israelite history, women led the community in song to celebrate military victory; later, they became ritual mourners and probably focused their religious activity in their homes.

The lack of female leadership, especially in the priesthood, contributed to women being blamed for failures in Israel's loyalty to Yahweh. Several prophets use female imagery to describe what they condemn as sinful behavior. Isaiah, for example, uses metaphors of jewelry and women's clothing when condemning religious corruption. Although condemning both women and men for their religious failings, Isaiah creates associations between femininity and evil, with inevitable consequences for the position of women within society. Biblical literature is full of these associations.[9]

Some have argued for a further decline in women's religious status during the period of the Babylonian exile after 586 B.C.E., as Judaism came under the increasing control of both the male priestly and scribal leadership. Others disagree, noting that Jewish women living under Persian administration, which extended to Judah, enjoyed broad legal powers, despite male control of religious life. Sixth-century papyri found at Elephantine (an island in the Nile River in Upper Egypt), for example, reveal that women had the power to divorce their husbands, despite the biblical law that only a man could divorce his wife.[10]

During the Second Temple period, from 536 B.C.E. to 70 C.E., in Palestine a variety of Jewish religious groups flourished, while the Jewish Diaspora expanded, spreading through much of the Greco-Roman empire and Babylonia. Within Palestine, women were excluded from the leadership of the Sadducees, the hereditary priesthood that ran the Jerusalem Temple, and from membership in the Essenes at Qumran, a group of monastic men living near the Dead Sea who denounced the corruption of the priesthood and believed in the imminent messianic era. Yet, as Ross Kraemer has shown, women did play an active and sometimes prominent role among the Pharisees, scribes who interpreted biblical Judaism for application to everyday religious practices, and who constituted the vast majority of Jews during the period.[11] Women's teachings are recorded in the Pharisees' texts, the Mishnah and Talmud. In addition, women formed their own monastic community in Egypt, known as the Therapeutae, and were active as guerrilla warriors against Roman rule in Palestine. Women were also prominent within the many messianic movements that flourished during the era, including the movement around Jesus. Indeed, the many female followers of Jesus indicates Judaism's openness to women and may be one reason why Judaism began to acquire female converts, the most famous of whom is Queen Helena of Adiabene, who converted to Judaism in the early years of the first century C.E., together with her son, who later became King Kzates.

The destruction of the Jerusalem Temple by the Romans in the year 70 C.E. was a major catastrophe in the history of Judaism. The sacrificial system of worship, conducted by the priests, came to an end, and Jews had to create liturgies and religious practices to replace the Temple. Their religion was no longer practiced at a central national shrine, but at home and in communal institutions, particularly synagogues, rabbinical academies, and ritual baths (mikvah). The purity laws of the Bible and Talmud, which mandated immersion in water as a cleansing of sin prior to entry into the Jerusalem Temple, were no longer applicable. Instead, categories of purity were limited to sexuality.[12] Women were required to immerse themselves in a ritual bath, containing collected rain water, seven days after the cessation of menstrual bleeding, with abstention from sexual relations during menstruation and the week following. Both women and men attended communal religious worship service, particularly on the Sabbath and holidays, but women were not under obligation to pray three times a day. Instead, their religious influence increasingly revolved around the home, the site of holiday celebrations over festive meals. Study of religious texts and their commentaries became the nearly exclusive domain of men. Starting in antiquity and continuing until the modern era, Jewish men composed a vast literature of biblical commentaries, interpretations of Jewish law, and works of philosophy and mysticism. If women also wrote learned texts, they were not preserved.

The Talmud, a collection of Jewish laws and religious teachings compiled over several generations and written down in the sixth century, set forth both restrictions on women's participation in public religious life and protections against the exploitation of women. Some feminist scholars, such as Judith Hauptman, interpret the Talmud's rulings concerning women as advancing the status of women over what was common in Greco-Roman society.[13] Other scholars see a more complex situation, in which women are accorded freedom in some circumstances, while restricted in others. Judith Wegner, for example, points out that the Mishnah, the earlier stratum of the Talmud, generally excludes women from the study of Torah and public worship, yet permits unmarried women wide freedom in carrying out independent business transactions.[14] Hauptman points out that although the Talmud allows only men to dissolve a marriage, it mandates a husband's obligations to his wife in the marriage contract. The Talmud is also relatively lenient regarding the use of contraception, and even permits abortion in certain circumstances.[15] Others, such as Howard Eilberg-Schwartz, Daniel Boyarin, and Miriam Peskowitz, have turned attention away from the laws and looked instead at the literary rhetoric of the Talmud, especially the role of gender. Some of the Talmud's more informal religious teachings, known as aggada, contain negative or even hostile images concerning women, such as the warning against men listening to a woman's voice. Although those aggadic teachings do not carry the force of law, they exerted an influence over the imagination of the Jewish community, creating stereotypes regarding women and men that often were translated into customs or taboos.[16]

While women were generally excluded from leadership within the synagogue in the Middle Ages, it is not clear when that exclusion began. Bernadette Brooten has discovered inscriptions from antiquity that describe Jewish women as synagogue leaders, and she has also pointed out that no evidence exists that women sat separately from men in the ancient synagogue.[17] Her evidence contradicts the legal prescriptions of rabbinic law, indicating that the law may not have always reflected the reality of religious practice. For example, the Talmud prohibits women from reading the Torah in the synagogue, stating, "a woman should not read from the Torah because of the honor of the congregation."[18] The very existence of the prohibitions within Jewish law may actually give evidence that women did read from the Torah, or the prohibition would not be necessary. The women's section of the synagogue may have originated in the early Middle Ages, under Muslim influence. Once they were relegated to a separate section, however, women frequently were led in their prayers by a designated female leader, who also translated and explicated the weekly Torah reading.

Both in antiquity and the Middle Ages, some women achieved positions of great economic success, accruing wealth and property. Some became benefactors of their communities and held positions of leadership. Most, however, lived in poverty, with all the constraints that poverty imposes.

In the Middle Ages, for the most part, Jewish women took leadership roles in the domestic sphere of communal life. They were generally in charge of collecting and distributing charity, and were regarded highly as midwives and healers, serving both Jews and Christians. Because Jewish law permits contraception, in contrast to Catholic canon law, Jewish women often had smaller families and hence greater independence than their Christian neighbors, which occasionally stimulated anti-Jewish resentments. The tendency of Jews to assimilate to the culture in which they lived, however, meant that women were confined by the surrounding social norms of non-Jewish society. Within Christian Europe, Jewish women were able to travel and engage independently in business, but within North Africa and other Muslim lands Jewish women lived most often within a demarcated domestic or even cloistered sphere until the modern era. Although polygyny was banned for European Jews at the end of the eleventh century, it remained common among Jews living in Muslim areas until the twentieth century.[19] Yet among Jews in Egypt, for example, marriage contracts preserved from the tenth and eleventh centuries indicate a partnership that also granted the wife the right to divorce her husband.[20] At the same time, Jewish women were rarely literate, and those who were literate were almost never taught the Talmud and its commentaries. Since the practice of Judaism entailed the interpretation of intricate laws that governed social and business relations, as well as religious observance, women were not empowered to interpret and regulate their lives.

Describing sinful behavior with metaphors of femininity, the tradition of Isaiah was continued in the Talmud and in medieval Jewish texts. Women were regarded as fountains of sexual temptation seducing even the most pious man if he were momentarily distracted from his study and prayer. Gatherings of women came under suspicion; they might be practicing sorcery, and men were warned not to walk between two women or to speak unnecessarily with any woman outside his family. Menstrual taboos increased, especially in Christian Europe, and customs developed that a menstruating woman should not enter the synagogue, pray, recite God's name, or touch a sacred book, even though rabbinic law does not require it and some rabbis insisted that women should attend the synagogue regardless of their menstrual status.[21]

The two major medieval movements within Jewish thought, philosophy and mysticism (Kabbalah), excluded women from participating in their composition and generated further negative images of the female. The greatest Jewish legal authority and philosopher, Moses Maimonides (1335–1204), permitted husbands to beat their wives, although other rabbis in his day did not. Further, Maimonides did not believe women possessed the faculty of reason, necessary to the attainment of divine inspiration.[22] In Jewish mysticism, feminine imagery involving God abounds yet plays only a secondary role within the God. The female aspect of God is passive and receptive, while the male is active, and the female must remain under the control of the male or she will be taken over by the demonic forces that supposedly lurk about her. Despite these sorts of unfortunate details, Kabbalah provided the greatest attention to female imagery of any Jewish literature. Central to the Kabbalistic understanding of Jewish religious life was the requirement to reunite the separated male and female aspects of the divinity, and that reunion should be the goal of all religious devotions.[23] Divine immanence, called the Shekhinah, is central to Kabbalah and elaborates freely on the feminine aspects of God. Some Jewish feminists today attempt to reclaim the Shekhinah as a female divinity, while others find the Shekhinah's associations with passivity and receptivity typical of patriarchal values and unacceptable for feminist reclamation. Also, the Kabbalah's stress on reuniting the female and male aspects of God reinforces heterosexism—often encouraging the oppression of women.

Spiritual devotion within Judaism was directed almost exclusively toward Jewish men. Cultivating an inner religious life was bound up with the study of Torah and regular worship, activities limited to men. Yet Jewish women developed their own spiritual traditions, enhancing the domestic activities to which they were limited. For example, books of women's devotional prayers contained meditations for kindling the Sabbath lights, baking the challah (special bread for holidays), and immersion in the mikvah—an observance that entails a ritual bath following menstruation and childbirth.[24] Some women adopted stringent ascetic practices, such as staying away from the synagogue while menstruating, daily fasting, frequent prayer, placing ashes on their heads, and wearing sackcloth. Although such practices were not forbidden, increasingly in the early modern period, some rabbis sought to limit them by declaring that they interfered with women's obligations toward their husbands and children.

Women's religious devotion, however, remained strong. During the Inquisition in Spain and Portugal, for example, many Jews who had converted to Christianity still practiced Judaism in secret. Renee Levine Melammed has demonstrated that records of the Inquisition indicate that women more than men were maintaining secretive Jewish religious observances at home, and women were disproportionately victims of the Inquisition's torture.[25] Within other parts of Europe and the Ottoman Empire, Jewish and crypto-Jewish women (Jews who practiced faith in secret to avoid the brunt of the Inquisition) engaged in widespread business dealings, often involving successful political and commercial connections. Increasingly, women from wealthier families were given secular educations in languages, mathematics, and sometimes even music and the arts, in order to enhance their abilities to engage in trade within the non-Jewish world.[26] Study of Hebrew and Jewish texts, however, was rare and limited to women from elite families. Women unfortunately did not contribute to the vast body of religious literature composed by Jewish men during the Middle Ages.

Independence among women was not always regarded favorably by rabbis. Howard Adelman has demonstrated that leading rabbinic figures, such as Joseph Caro (b. 1448–1575), author of the most important code of Jewish law, sought to limit women's rights within Jewish law. Caro placed limits on women's right to demand a divorce from an abusive husband, and Moses Isserles (1530–1572) viewed wife-beating as a simple domestic dispute, rather than a sin. Increasingly, sexual intercourse was presented as an act that should be carried out with ascetic religious devotion, rather than pleasure and delight.[27]

The eighteenth century brought important changes in Jewish life. Within Eastern Europe a new pious movement arose, Hasidism, that significantly altered the religious values as well as communal structures of the Jews. In Central and Western Europe, political and intellectual upheavals introduced notions of citizenship and began the process of Jewish political emancipation.[28]

Hasidism, which began in the late eighteenth century as a spiritual movement around Israel ben Eliezer, known as the Baal Shem Tov (Master of the Good Name), developed over the next two centuries throughout most of Eastern Europe into communities of adherents of a particular rebbe, or Zaddik, who advised and inspired his followers. The Zaddik held court for his male disciples, who would leave their families to spend Jewish holidays with their Zaddick. Hasidism increased the stringency of gender separation, requiring head coverings for married women, and urging men to combat any sexual thoughts that might distract them from their prayers and study. Women were not participants in the creation of Hasidic literature, nor were they taught the doctrines of the new movement. Although one nineteenth-century woman, Hannah Rachel Verbermacher, known as the Maid of Ludmir, managed to gain a few adherents through her reputation as a miracle worker and woman of great piety, her marriage brought an end to her leadership role.

Within Western Europe, major political changes were occurring. The French Revolution of 1789 brought an end to the communal status of social groups and introduced the notion of individual citizenship. The modern state demanded abolition of legal privileges as well as disabilities for all groups, whether aristocracy, clergy, peasantry, or Jews. As a result, emancipation of the Jews became essential for the modern state to take shape. Jews were granted civic status as citizens of the state, marking a crucial transition. In Western Europe this process occurred gradually from 1789 to 1871, while in Eastern Europe it took longer, starting only with the Bolshevik Revolution in 1917. During the course of the nineteenth century, Jews were increasingly able to enter a secular realm, free from coercive efforts to convert them to Christianity, free from laws that had long barred their admission to schools, universities, guilds, armed services, civil service, or other professions. Secular freedom ironically led to religious freedom: Jews were no longer bound by the authority of rabbis, who for centuries had been able to use the threat of excommunication to enforce their will. Religious observance of Judaism or any other religion became a matter of free choice. Being Jewish could be an expression of religious faith, or simply of ethnicity.

With that freedom, being Jewish in the modern period has entailed a wide variety of options for religious and ethnic identities. Jews choose the extent of their religious observances, marry non-Jews, or even convert to other religions, and growing numbers of Jews have. The authority of Jewish law and of the rabbis is now a matter of choice. The modern era shattered the "sacred canopy" of religious belief and practice that had characterized premodern Jewish religious life. Both extreme piety and assimilation into Christian culture are matters of free choice, rather than an imposition or, as had been believed, the will of God.

Although modernity brought a decline in Jewish religious observance, it presented new denominations within Judaism that offered a range of religious observances and beliefs. Reform Judaism began in the early nineteenth century when individual families, dissatisfied with synagogue services, initiated their own worship services in private homes. Prayers were recited in the European vernacular instead of Hebrew, music was played on the organ, and edifying sermons were delivered weekly, instead of the traditional twice-yearly sermon. Those reforms eventually entered the synagogues, particularly in urban areas, beginning in Western Europe and the United States, and became and continue to be the predominant forms of Jewish religious expression. They were complemented by a rapid decline in Jewish observance of private religious commandments, such as daily prayer and dietary regulations.

Despite the radical changes in Jewish observance that were initiated in the early nineteenth century, equality for women was not part of the reforms. By the mid-nineteenth century, teenage girls were given ceremonies of confirmation along with boys, but women still sat separately from men in the Reform synagogues. Mixed seating was introduced in the United States in 1851 in Albany, New York, and in 1854 at Temple Emanu-El in New York City; it only became common in the United States after 1869, when many new post–Civil War synagogues opened, and did not spread to European Reform synagogues until much later. Within Orthodox synagogues, separate seating still prevails today, although a range of styles can be found, with women seated on a balcony, or behind a curtain, or in a separate room.

An offshoot of Reform Judaism emerged toward the end of the nineteenth century among Eastern European immigrants to the United States. Known as Conservative Judaism, it situated itself as a moderate force between Orthodox and Reform Judaism, and soon became the largest of the American denominations. The Conservative movement was the slowest to grant women some rights in the synagogue services, and even today its seminary refuses to ordain lesbians and gay men as rabbis. On the other hand, Reconstructionist Judaism, an offshoot of the Conservative movement, began in the United States during the 1930s, with a distinct religious philosophy based on the writings of Mordecai Kaplan. It quickly became a pioneer in granting equality to women in matters of Jewish law, permitting, for example, women to give a Jewish divorce to their husbands. The Reconstructionist Rabbinical College, located in Philadelphia, was the first to welcome gay and lesbian students for the rabbinate.

Within Orthodox Judaism, which adheres strictly to rabbinic law, women suffer the greatest disadvantages. Men have control over marriage and divorce, women sit separately at synagogue services and are not counted in the quorum for communal prayer, and heterosexual marriage is the required norm. Homosexuality is condemned as a sin. Still, modernity has brought some changes in women's status even within Orthodox communities. In part, fear of secular influences motivated the creation of schools for Orthodox girls, both in Europe and the United States, to inculcate traditional learning as well as secular subjects within a pious framework. Orthodox women also formed organizations to promote Zionist and social-service causes through fund-raising and volunteer work. Within the ultra-Orthodox communities, women's studies of biblical texts are encouraged not for the sake of educating and empowering women, but for maintaining their ignorance and dependence on men.

Although the modern era is conventionally assumed to have seen the decline in Jewish religiosity and the growth in assimilation, intermarriage, and conversion to Christianity, its impact on women has also had the effect of opening new religious opportunities for education, careers, and religious leadership. Pressure from the changes in secular society that encouraged women and men to take advantage of equal opportunities in education and careers affected the Jewish world, too. Classical Jewish texts, particularly the Talmud, which had been the exclusive domain of men, were increasingly taught to women as well, and reforms undertaken by the synagogues began to open some avenues for women's participation. The emergence of secular Jewish literature also brought opportunities for women's Jewish self-expression through what's known as Les belles lettres. The secular feminist movement made the exclusion of women from professions such as the rabbinate seem inappropriate, and pressure from Jewish feminists, starting in the 1970s, resulted in a new openness to women in Jewish religious life.

Secularization actually brought about new possibilities for Jewish women to become involved, often for the first time in Jewish history, in central modes of Jewish religious expression. Thanks to non-Orthodox institutions of Jewish learning, as well as university programs in Jewish Studies, women were able to study the Talmud and its commentaries, Kabbalistic and Hasidic texts, codes of Jewish law, and other religious documents that had previously been accessible only to men. Pressures on Jews to assimilate into Western norms also meant that women were given the right to lead public worship services in synagogues, eventually becoming ordained rabbis and cantors.

Of course, however, older forms of discrimination were not entirely erased. In the name of equality, for example, distinct spheres of women's traditional expression of Judaism were minimized or eliminated by non-Orthodox Jews, such as mikveh observance (immersion in the ritual bath following menstruation and childbirth), which declined radically in the modern era. Certain secular movements, including Zionism, while proclaiming adherence to the equality of men and women, nevertheless kept positions of leadership firmly in men's hands.

The United States, which became the center of Jewish feminism after World War II, had a small and relatively uneducated Jewish community prior to the 1880s. Women received only minimal Jewish education and were not voting members of the Jewish community. The demography quickly shifted at the turn of the twentieth century, as over two million Jews from Eastern Europe immigrated to the United States between 1881 and 1924. They included women exposed to political organizing and analysis, and they quickly became major forces in the labor, socialist, anarchist, and communist movements in New York and other cities in the early years of the twentieth century. Rose Schneiderman, for example, was a leader of the Women's Trade Union League, the campaign for women's suffrage, and the International Ladies Garment Workers Union. However, once those movements were institutionalized—as labor unions and political parties—women were unfortunately removed from these leadership positions.[29]

During the early years of the Zionist movement, there was similar ambivalence toward women. Zionism presented itself as a movement that would revive the masculinity of Jewish men; it was thought that centuries of study and piety and lack of physical exertion had weakened their manhood.[30] During the early waves of immigration to Palestine prior to statehood, women worked alongside men in the cultivation of farmland.[31] Yet with the establishment of the State of Israel, women were not granted proportional roles of power within the government. Instead a myth of gender equality within the state was promoted, which covered up the reality of women's subservience. For example, although women are drafted into the Israeli army, they are assigned subordinate tasks and kept from combat duty.

After the Enlightenment era when Jews began experiencing political, social, and economic emancipation, women managed to retain some influence in social-service charities within the Jewish communities of the United States and Europe, collecting and distributing funds and goods, and running schools and vocational training programs. Those activities, a central feature of maintaining Jewish communal cohesion, became the basis for modern women's organizations, such as Hadassah, the National Council of Jewish Women, and Women's American Organization for Rehabilitation and Training (ORT), which became wealthy and powerful institutions during the course of the twentieth century. With the growth of assimilation, women are generally more reluctant than men to abandon religious traditions and Jewish identification.[32] Paula Hyman's description of a strike in 1902 by New York immigrant women against a sudden rise in the cost of kosher meat captures both the commitment of these housewives to maintaining Jewish traditions and the power they were able to exert in subverting the price rise.[33]

Despite the increased opportunities for women in modern Jewish life, Jewish identity is still defined by the male Jewish experience. Few women writing modern Hebrew or Yiddish literature were accorded the same recognition for their work as their male colleagues by the male-dominated literary establishment. Women's writings were not included in the canon.[34] Denigrated as a diaspora language by the Zionist movement, Yiddish was also viewed derogatorily as the language of women.[35] From the writings of noted American Jews, such as Saul Bellow and Philip Roth, to Israelis, such as Amos Oz and Aharon Appelfeld, Jewish literature in all languages remains overwhelmingly preoccupied with male experience as the vehicle for exploring Jewish identity. Increasingly, however, women writers are giving voice to their Jewish identity, and the works of earlier generations of Jewish women writers are being discovered. Grace Paley, one of the most influential stylists, Tillie Olsen, Jo Sinclair, Mary Antin, and Anzia Yezierska are among the most highly recognized writers of American Jewish experience, and new translations are giving attention to the work of Hebrew women writers, such as Devora Baron.

Modern Jewish theology defined Jewish experience in male terms. Often written in apologetic terms for a wider Christian readership, Jewish theology defends the traditional role of women as an expression of respect for femininity, Jewish theologians from Moritz Lazarus to Emanuel Levinas proclaimed the moral superiority of Jewish law, but disregarded the ethical significance of the inferior status of women in Jewish law.[36] Likewise, Jewish history has been almost exclusively about men's experiences. The standard surveys of Jewish history barely mention any Jewish women.

The Jewish Women's Organization in Germany, founded in 1904, was the first organizational effort to promote women's rights within the Jewish community in Europe.[37] Among its achievements was winning women's right to vote in Jewish communal elections and establishing alliances with the wider German feminist movement. Its fight against white slavery within the Jewish community was less successful, and its ties to German Christian feminists were broken with Hitler's rise to power in 1933.[38]

Anti-Semitism became a central feature of Jewish life in the modern era, affecting religious as well as political decisions. Although Jews expected the tolerance of modernity to overcome the Christian anti-Judaism that had led to periods of religious persecution during the Middle Ages, the rise of racial theory in the nineteenth century transformed theological prejudice into a secular Judeophobia. Heightened during periods of economic or social unrest, anti-Semitism became a central element within the political and social landscapes of Europe, the Soviet Union, and the United States, reaching its culmination with the rise of National Socialism and the Nazi genocide of the Jews during the Second World War.

Some might ask what ideas led to such strong anti-Semitism. Modern anti-Semitism often drew on gendered stereotypes that marked Jewish men either as emasculated or as potential sexual aggressors.[39] Jews were considered abnormal for a variety of reasons, ranging from their lack of an independent state to their alleged sexual degeneracy. Anti-Semites sometimes pointed to the inequality accorded Jewish women under Jewish religious law as a sign of Jewish sexual perversity. At the outset of Emancipation, anti-Semites called for the thorough assimilation of Jews into Christian society, but by the 1870s they feared the alleged threat of assimilated Jews whose identity could not be readily distinguished from non-Jews. Anti-Semites then revealed the supposed threat posed by Jews to Christian society, complaining that Europe was in danger of being "Judaized." By the early twentieth century, Jews were compared to bacilli, vermin, and rodents and calls for their extermination were expressed even before the Nazis began their murdering of European Jews. This all brought a virtual end to European Judaism.

The Holocaust—the murder of approximately six million European Jews by Nazi Germans and their collaborators during World War II—affected Jewish women in some ways different from men. Although Jewish men were more likely to be killed in labor camps in Poland from 1939 to 1941, more women were among those deported from East European ghettos to death camps from 1942 to 1943.[40] At the camps themselves, women were more likely upon arrival to be sent immediately to the gas chambers, while men had a better chance of being selected for slave labor. Any woman who arrived at a camp with a small child, or who was visibly pregnant, was automatically sent to her death. Because younger Jews emigrated from Germany prior to the outbreak of the war, the remaining German Jews, who were less likely to survive, were primarily elderly and female. Still, women participated in resistance and partisan groups alongside men and made significant contributions. Women were responsible for an important revolt at the death camp Birkenau that resulted in the destruction of a crematorium.

Jews responded to this anti-Semitism in various ways. There were calls for more assimilation, efforts to prosecute authors of anti-Semitic literature, and published defenses of Judaism. Anti-Semitism, particularly in Russia, spurred the emigration of about two million Jews to the United States and also inspired many Jews to become active in political movements, particularly socialism and communism, that promised to end the social and economic conditions allegedly responsible for anti-Semitic sentiments. Early Zionism was also motivated in large part by anti-Semitic movements in Europe, with the belief that anti-Semitism could never be overcome in Europe, so that Jews would simply have to leave and establish their own state. Zionists called for the renewal of Jewish culture by establishing a homeland, and for a Jewish state that would meet other nations on equal footing.

Even as Zionism sought to overcome anti-Semitism and inaugurate a new era in Jewish history, it mimicked aspects of the gender stereotyping found in anti-Semitic writings. For example, Zionism sought the creation of a new, "muscular" Jewish man, escaping an image of traditional Judaism and diaspora Jewish history as effeminate and emasculating. Equating the

Jew with the male and with masculinity left no apparent place for Jewish women, as Jewish feminists have pointed out.[41]

Efforts by women to win ordination as rabbis within the Reform movement were initiated in the United States and in Germany in the early twentieth century. Henrietta Szold was granted permission in 1903 to study at the Conservative Jewish Theological Seminary in New York City, but only on condition that she not request ordination. Martha Neumark was permitted to study at Reform Judaism's Hebrew Union College, but its Board of Governors decided in 1922 that women should not be ordained rabbis.[42] Regina Jonas, who completed her studies and examinations at the liberal seminary in Berlin in 1930, was denied ordination by the institution. Ultimately, Jonas became the first woman rabbi by receiving private ordination, in Germany in December 1935. After serving the dwindling Jewish community in Berlin, she was deported by the Nazis to Theresienstadt in 1942, where she continued to preach to the inmates until her deportation and murder in Auschwitz in 1945.

Only with the rise of the Jewish feminist movement in the 1970s did ordination of women rabbis and the equality of women in non-Orthodox synagogues become the norm. Sally Priesand was ordained at Hebrew Union College in 1972, the Reconstructionist Rabbinical College ordained Sandy Sasso a rabbi in 1974, and the Jewish Theological Seminary ordained its first woman rabbi, Amy Eilberg, in 1984. At present, each of the denominations is experimenting with revised liturgies that attempt to use inclusive gender language.

Within the Orthodox community rabbinical ordination of women continues to be rejected, although some liberal Orthodox congregations have appointed women in official pastoral and teaching positions. Orthodox women have also begun to form women's prayer groups, which meet regularly to expand women's engagement in public worship within the constraints of Jewish law. These, in turn, have been condemned by some Orthodox rabbis as contrary to women's duties under Jewish law. Orthodox women who have gained fluency with rabbinic texts have also challenged those interpretations of Jewish law that leave women in an inferior position, particularly in relation to marriage and divorce laws. Some are now becoming official advisors to women who are petitioning Orthodox rabbinic courts in regard to marriage and divorce. Even among ultra-Orthodox women, education of girls and women is respected, although a recent study by anthropologist Tamar El-Or suggests that ultra-Orthodox women are taught just enough to distract them from a serious education and maintain their general ignorance of central features of rabbinic law.[43] Despite what appears to be a greater degree of sexism within Orthodox Judaism, however, significant numbers of non-religious Jewish women have been attracted to the Orthodox community during the past several decades.[44] According to sociological studies by Lynn Davidman and Debra Kaufman, most women report that they are attracted by the strong sense of community and family that they find within the Orthodoxy.

Within the State of Israel, women's religious rights are much more limited. The Orthodox rabbinate, which controls all Jewish marriages and divorces, has condemned non-Orthodox forms of Judaism as illegitimate. Indeed, efforts by women to pray as a group at the Western Wall have been rejected, not only by the rabbinate, but also by the secular Israeli courts. Groups of women, and groups of women and men, who have sought to hold prayer services at the Wall have been subjected to serious verbal and physical abuse. The inequality of women and men within the Israeli military service, combined with the centrality of the military in Israeli life, has also contributed to a social position of women's inferiority within the state. However, a growing number of institutions in Israel have trained women in the study of traditional Jewish texts, particularly Talmudic law. Many have been serving as advocates within the religious courts on behalf of women fighting for marriage and divorce rights.

The equality of Jewish women taken for granted in the United States is rarely found in contemporary Europe. Great Britain's small Reform movement, which ordained a woman rabbi for the first time in 1975, has endorsed the principle of gender equality. Elsewhere in Europe, however, Jewish worship exists almost exclusively in its Orthodox forms. Only one woman rabbi serves a congregation in Germany, and one in France, and many who have sought to obtain pulpits have been rejected. The legacy of the Holocaust is often invoked by Jews opposed to women's rights, on the grounds that respect for Hitler's victims requires that pre-Nazi Judaism be preserved intact.

As the Jewish feminist movement flourishes in the United States, its products are numerous, and its positions are not unified. There are many texts of feminist commentaries on the Bible, as well as feminist liturgies and rituals. Feminist Passover Haggadahs, for example, abound, interpreting the Exodus from Egypt as a model for women's liberation. Marcia Falk, who seeks to eliminate all personal attributes associated with God, on the grounds that any attribution of personality will reify divine masculinity, has published an alternative, feminist prayerbook in which God is addressed using inclusive language that attributes neither gender nor personality to the deity.[45]

Jewish feminism has also brought into being a tremendous body of work on women and Judaism. While historians are primarily concerned with discovering forgotten aspects of women's history, feminist scholars are also reconsidering the nature of Judaism in light of women's experience. As women increasingly take active roles in all facets of Jewish life, from secular political involvement to leadership as rabbis, Judaism will undergo the most radical transformation it has faced since the Roman destruction of the Temple in Jerusalem in the year 70 C.E. Given the ability of Jewish identity to survive such radical challenges in the past, there is no doubt that Judaism will emerge strengthened by feminism. Indeed, it is precisely the creative tension between feminism and Judaism that has enriched contemporary Jewish religious life and thought. What is perhaps most remarkable is how rapidly changes have occurred for women in Judaism. When I said kaddish for my father in 1973, few synagogue congregations would tolerate me. Now it is clear that no woman will ever again be denied the possibility of saying kaddish, or of participating fully in synagogue life, or find the books of classical Judaism closed to her. For Jewish women, feminism has come as a great promise and an enormous relief. Feminism has infused women with a new sense of opportunity, and has brought the talents and insights of women to positions of leadership. Most important, feminism signals the intense engagement of women in Jewish creativity. A revolution has occurred in the practice of Judaism, one that was unimaginable until recent generations, and one that will remain a permanent feature of Jewish life. The kaddish that I recited was not only for the death of my father, but also for the death of Judaism's exclusion of women.

6

Christianity

By Mary Gerhart

VALERIE SAIVING GOLDSTEIN (1921–
1992), while a student at the University of Chicago Divinity School, wrote
an article on the concepts *love* and *sin* by male theologians. She began the
article with two assertions:

> I am a student of theology. I am also a woman. Perhaps it strikes you
> as curious that I put these two assertions beside each other, as if to
> imply that one's sexual identity has some bearing on his theological
> views. I myself would have rejected such an idea when I first began
> my theological studies. But now, thirteen years later, I am no longer
> as certain as I . . . was then, [that] when theologians speak of *man*,
> they are using the word in its generic sense. It is, after all, a well-
> known fact that theology has been written almost exclusively by
> men. . . .[1]

Saiving suggested that male theologians, unconfident that they could
practice selfless love, thought of love as a woman's rather than a man's
ideal; correlatively, they understood the sin of pride as a temptation for
men, since they thought women were not expected to have achieved anything in a man's world to be proud about. Saiving's 1960 publication began a new wave of feminist studies, outside as well as within religious
studies, in the United States. Her article was more influential than Eliza-

beth Cady Stanton's *The Woman's Bible*,[3] a compilation of Old and New Testament texts with a scathing and often witty feminist commentary on their denial of equal rights and respect to women published six decades earlier. Saiving provided the impetus for systematic investigations based on gender differences and quickly spread to other fields as well.

Stanton's *The Woman's Bible* and Saiving's "The Human Situation: A Feminine View" were both interpretations different from men's interpretations before or since. My own interpretation springs from my belief that women, as well as men, have had some sense of alternative horizons and held a range of beliefs at any given time during the almost two millennia of Christian history.[4] Changes do not take place without the preexistence of some kind of diversity. Women's relationship to Christianity does not reveal a linear progression: rather, a couple of steps away from old constraints, a couple of steps backward, then a strong step forward again. Just as the women who had elected Stanton president of the Women's Convention refused to endorse *The Woman's Bible* and then voted to remove her from office in 1898, some Christian women today think that they have enough of a voice in the church and oppose moves such as the ordination of women. On the whole, however, there has been a steadily growing recognition that gender should be neither a privilege nor an obstacle for admission to ministry and that women's voices need to be heard in liturgical and policy-making events, despite the reticence of some church leaders to change ecclesiastical structures sufficiently to include women's voices as full participants.

Writing four decades after Saiving, whom I was privileged to know as a colleague, I will foreground the voices and work of Christian women. I am most interested in specific women's lives and their own responses to major religious events of their times. Did they notice the events without questioning? Were they able to use events productively? What legacy did these women leave? My view does not assume that a majority or even a predominant view tells the entire story. Indeed, the knowledge that voices have been lost can be a dangerous memory. The study of Christian women has passed through at least three stages: heightening awareness of the extent of women's oppression and the need for gender equality; retrieving texts by and about women; and re-understanding the texts as providing information about women—creative, courageous, tragic, and witty—as well as providing a paradigm for understanding oppression. It has been said that the root of all oppression is sexual oppression—meaning that if it is permissible to oppress women, then the oppression of other groups is easy to justify because anyone can be treated as a women. At the same time, Christianity is the story of repeated attempts to live out a vision of new possibilities. Failures, even repeated failures, have not dimmed the original vision.

Apart from the midrash presenting both the specialness and commonality of Jesus' birth and childhood, the first momentous description of Jesus occurs early in the Gospel of Luke. It shows him coming to the synagogue to pray as he usually did. This time, in his first public appearance, he reads a passage from Isaiah from the scroll given to him:

> The Spirit of the Lord is upon me, because God has anointed me to preach glad tidings to the poor . . . to proclaim release to captives, and recovery of sight to the blind, to let the oppressed go free, and to proclaim a year acceptable to the Lord. (Luke 4: 16–21)

What happens in the subsequent three years of his life is encapsulated in this announcement and expanded in the gospel (the "good news") narratives. The fact that Christianity grew out of the intensification of meanings that surrounded the event of Jesus Christ and the women and men who were his followers has meant that those meanings have been re-expressed for better and for worse for 2000 years. Today it is impossible to represent all of those meanings. The contemporary world is highly differentiated, and what is "Christian" must be compared and contrasted with the alternative visions (secularism, liberalism, other religions, and individualism). This difficulty could be partially set aside if it were not for a second difficulty—what is "Christian" is itself plural both at its origin and today—not to mention that each contemporary form of Christian tradition has a history. What follows are both fragments and interpretations of the fragments that I find most provocative.

Jesus radicalized what was newly emerging—the spirit-dimension of religion—by both his behavior and his language. At an early age he was "lost" to his family while he spoke with rabbis in the temple and astounded them with his wisdom. At a wedding party he agreed to his mother's request to replenish drinks but after he asserted that he didn't care if the wine ran dry. He left his acquaintances at the beginning of his public life to live in the desert for over a month where he survived only on what was available.

Shortly before he was taken captive, he left his close friends to pray alone in a garden. He advised people not to strain after possessions or even the basic necessities of food, drink, and clothing—but rather to trust that these things would be given if people attended to the life of the spirit.

In the same vein, he inspired the principle that one's nationality, particular gender, and social status should not make a difference in the new community of the spirit. People experienced Jesus as model or index of how to live. It is interesting to speculate whether Jesus would have been emulated had he been a woman. If part of the attention drawn by Jesus had to do with his breaking gender stereotypes, would a woman's breaking her gender stereotypes have been noticed?

Jesus offered one alternative among other reform movements within Judaism. His lifestyle within a non-familial community also ran counter to Greco-Roman and traditional Jewish culture. Non-traditional gender assumptions in the Gospels are in tension with patriarchal structures in both worlds. Jesus is criticized for keeping company with women, tax collectors, sinners, and prostitutes: Doesn't he know who she is? asks the crowd of his relationship with Mary of Bethany. Mary of Magdala is portrayed in apocryphal literature as someone he praised publicly for understanding him and as a leader among the apostles, especially after Jesus died.[5] In the Gospels he announces that these social outcasts will participate in the reign of God before those who see themselves as righteous. He not only announces that the reign of God belongs to the poor in spirit—among whom have always been great numbers of women and the children they care for—but he predicts that the rich will find it extraordinarily difficult to enter this realm and that someday the poor in spirit will inherit the Earth. For sick and crippled women and men, Jesus restored humanity by vanquishing dehumanizing powers, demonizing forces, and destructive spirits.

What were the reasons for Jesus' death in his early 30s? The Gospel accounts of his death emphasize that he taught truth and righteousness and that his miracles were done out of compassion rather than from self-aggrandizement. Jesus apparently made religious observances subordinate to the practice of truth and justice. He disappointed those who wanted him to lead an uprising of Jews against Roman occupation, and he was perceived as a threat by religious leaders to their continued collaboration with Roman power. References to curious, cowardly, and faithful women and men abound in accounts of his trial and passion. After his ignominious crucifixion as a common criminal between two thieves, only women came to visit his tomb the third day after his death. According to the text the women were charged with the responsibility of telling the other disciples that his body was no longer in the tomb. (Peter, in the apocryphal Gospel named after him, questions why Jesus' message had been transmitted by women—indicating Peter's assumption of a male prerogative.) In the narrative accounts of his mysterious appearances, two results are clear.

His frightened followers became courageous proclaimers of his life and message, and from being a local figure Jesus became present and accessible to all people in all times. The vision of Jesus was accompanied by his presence—his promise to be with those who lived in his way until the end of their days, his presence as the living, dying, and resurrected Christ in the Eucharist celebrated weekly by the growing communities, and the identification by Christians of Jesus with other people, especially the poor ("Whosoever does this to the least of my brethren does it to me").

During the founding years, noble and landed women used their houses and their status to create new Christian communities. A strong case can be made that women exercised many kinds of leadership in the earliest Jesus movement and the missionary efforts of the first and second century while the earliest communities were organizing themselves within and beyond house churches. Some have regarded Paul as the founder of Christianity in the sense that, unlike Jesus, who wrote nothing, Paul composed the first texts, the Epistles, that were to become canonical in the new religion. In this view Paul founded the churches addressed in his letters and chose companions to help minister to them. In fact, several house churches were in existence before Paul was shocked into changing his life from one of persecuting Christians to one of proclaiming Christ. We now know that some of Paul's companions on his missionary journeys were women. Christian women, either alone or with their spouses, provided the houses that served as Christian gathering places. Many women are named prophetesses in the early church and accorded special privileges.[6] In addition, the earliest practice of drawing lots to determine roles from meeting to meeting gave women equal eligibility. Because they went unmentioned in traditional interpretations of the texts, however, these crucial roles played by women have been diminished or entirely overlooked.

A dominant patriarchy was not an immediate development within Christianity. It came about slowly and with difficulty. Specific women, like Prisca (or Priscilla), went on missionary journeys and, like Aphia of Colossae, Nympha of Laodicea, and Lydia (from Thyatria) in Philippi, led the early house church communities.[7] At the same time the young Christian communities were urged by Paul to choose conservative practices with respect to women in general. Women should not speak in church assemblies, their heads should be covered. The single reason given for these gender-differentiated rules was that it was against nature for women to have authority over men, an argument supported by quotations from Genesis. However, in some communities, notably in Greece, women were ordained to the deaconate to instruct women catechumens and to assist with the baptism of women. Deaconesses also carried the sacrament of the Eucharist to women shut-ins and had special privileges in handling and transferring sacred vessels. However, only male priests could administer ecclesiastically scheduled rituals. Even in the early church, when the order of widows (constituted by enrollment) and deaconesses (who were ordained) was active in the early church, the restrictions placed on them were much more onerous and the privileges and honor less generous than those prescribed for male bishops.

The new Christian communities were more likely to be diversified with respect to class, race, and gender than were their religious contemporaries (the Roman state religion, Judaism, Mithraism). The revolutionary text reflecting and encouraging this diversity was Paul's Letter to the Galatians:

> For as many of you as were baptized into Christ have put on Christ. There is neither Jew nor Greek, there is neither slave nor free, there is neither male nor female for you are all one in Christ Jesus. And if you are Christ's, then you are Abraham's offspring, heirs according to promise. (3:27–29)

This passage from Galatians is thought by many to be a fragment of an early baptismal formula. For the early Christians, gender equality was not a goal in itself. This passage encouraged many to challenge the prescriptions of both state and church on what women were permitted to do and led to different positions for women, because of Christian views. Written texts, such as Galatians, were of less importance in their culture than they are for ours. In their culture, 96–98 percent of the general populace were not literate nor would they have considered themselves deprived because they could not read or write.

For today's readers, Galatians carries a liberationist mandate. For the early Christians, however, it probably meant that any individuals having fulfilled the requirements of the catechumenate can be accepted within the community and that none will be excluded because of their race, their social status, or their sex. This openness stood in contrast to Judaism for which racial identity was primary (even though conversion was also important in this period), to Mithraism for which occupation and gender were primary, and to Roman state religion for which hierarchy and family were primary (in spite of its tolerance of other religions). This attempted openness to all distinguished the Christian religion as one of the first "universal" religions and accounts for its having had "global" appeal right from the beginning. It is also notable that the earliest Christian communities came from different parts of the economic spectrum as well as from different lands—present-day Israel, Italy, Greece, Syria, and northern Africa.

Greece, for example, today sees itself as the true birthplace of Christianity. Its national history is intertwined with religious feast days. The Greek national holiday is celebrated on the day of the annunciation of Mary's pregnancy, and religious images such as resurrection appear in pop songs as well as on church walls.

Although they contributed disproportionately to what became the Christian mainstream, Syriac Christians have been a minority throughout history. In the first century they spoke a dialect of Aramaic, the language of Palestine, and lived in southeast Turkey. Syriac Christian culture and language spread throughout the Mediterranean Christian communities in the first and second centuries. By the fifth century, Syriac Christians in the East existed within Zoroastrian, and later within Persian, Byzantine, and Muslim majorities. In western Syria, Roman rule was replaced by that of Muslim Turks. Many splinter Christian groups originated in Syria— the Marcionites, Valentinians, Messalians, and Manichaeans. The biggest crisis within Syriac Christianity came in 451 C.E. over the question of how to understand the divine and the human "natures" of Christ so that neither was diminished. Most Syriac Christians rejected the Chalcedonian outcome of the debate, backed by the Orthodox, and only recently have the Oriental-Orthodox Syriac churches begun dialogues with Greek and Russian Orthodox.

The written canonical texts about Jesus and the lives of his followers, the earliest of which existed side by side with the oral tradition and other, non-canonical, texts, are likely to have been composed between the year 50 C.E. (the approximate date of Paul's letter to the Thessalonians in northern Greece, believed to be his earliest letter) and 90 C.E. (the date suggested for the Gospel of John). Of all the texts written during and after that time—including the Qumran Scrolls and apocryphal texts such as the Gospel of Thomas and the Gospel of Mary—those ultimately included in the canon of the New Testament were the four gospels (by Matthew, Mark, Luke, and John), 21 Letters (13 by Paul or his followers, others by James, Peter, John, and Jude), the Acts of the Apostles, and the visionary Book of Revelation (by John). After centuries of assuming that all of these texts were authored by men, some scholars have entertained the possibility that Acts may have been authored by a woman rather than by Luke. What was known of Jesus and his followers initially was primarily through the modes of communication common at the time—eyewitnesses, word of mouth, memory by and of witnesses—although some references are to be found in the work of Jewish and Roman historians, such as Josephus and Pliny the Younger. But by the mid-second century and from then on to the present, what was known of Jesus was primarily through the interpretation of written texts. Christians decided by the middle of the second century to keep both the Hebrew Testament and the New Testament (about 3.5 times shorter) as canonical scriptures and continued to interpret the New in relation to the Old and vice versa. The shift to written texts was more significant for women than has been traditionally understood.

One of the current issues in the study of Christianity is that of "voice." Most people are surprised to learn that almost 250 Christian women (that is, women who regarded themselves as Christian) authored texts or remnants of texts over the first 15 centuries—authors whose writings have been available in editions accessible to the general public since 1800.[8] This evidence is remarkable in light of the fact that, before Gutenberg's invention of the printing press in 1437, only a small fraction of the population was literate. Some males were educated because of their status in society. Other males were trained as scribes for business and legal transactions and for correspondence. Scribes taken into captivity usually continued to work as scribes. Some females were educated, usually along with males in particular families. If instead of marrying they entered a female monastery, they had a better chance, up to the time of the founding of universities, of becoming literate. Even though this number of texts by Christian women is small compared to the number of those by men, it is far greater than one might expect when compared with the number of texts by women in the general population before or during that time.

Some have found evidence that women's voices have been diminished or lost in the first- and second-century transition from orality to writing in the canonized written texts. In the Synoptic Gospels, for example, the ratio of miracle stories that involve men to those that involve women is 33:10.

These stories involving men are also two to three times longer than those about women, and in them men converse back and forth with Jesus much more than do women. And although the sex ratio in brief action stories is four to three in favor of women, even in them women act but do not speak. They are portrayed as examples for men who observe and talk with Jesus about them.[9]

Besides public announcements by town criers, culture and tradition were communicated largely by male and female story-tellers. Nursemaids and mothers educated and entertained children with stories. Street performers and story-tellers were hired by temples and synagogues to bring people in to worship. I used to wonder why the early church kept all four Gospels with all their overlaps, differences, even contradictions. One explanation has to do with this story-culture, which habitually celebrates and retains different versions of its cherished stories. Christians were proclaimers of as well as listeners to the stories that became the tradition. Several of these stories were most likely introduced in the repertoire by women. A radical shift happened when the tradition of orality changed into text.

What we glimpse is a tradition changing from a predominantly "oral subculture, with full participation and leadership open to all regardless of status and gender"[10] during its first century to a culture in which writing became authoritative in its second century.

One of the burning questions for Paul and other leaders was raised by the fact that both Jews and Gentiles were joining the Jesus-movement. Henry Chadwick summarizes the problem as follows:

> Faith that Jesus was God's anointed prophet and king [Messiah] was basic to self-definition for the first church. The Christians did not initially think of themselves as separate from the Jewish people. . . . God's call was to the Jew first. The call to Gentiles was a disputed matter for a time. To the earliest Christian communities Jesus was not the founder or originator of the community of God's people, but the climax of an already long story of a divine education of humanity through the special illumination given to the prophets of Israel. To interpret his significance they turned to the Hebrew sacred books, the Mosaic law as well as the prophetic writings. . . . Like some Greek-speaking liberal Jews, the early Christians read the prophets as foretelling a universal mission of the Jews to illuminate all peoples. Yet the law imposed prescriptions apparently designed to mark off the Jews from other nations. The Christians believed that by the death of Jesus, the suffering servant of Isaiah, God had formed a new covenant not only with the Jews but with all peoples of the earth.[11]

The requirements of being Christian were in continuity with what Jewish followers of Christ did as Jews. Jews attended the synagogue and celebrated the breaking of bread and drinking of wine with those who were identified as being faithful to Jesus' vision. But issues of diet and of ritual circumcision gradually became contentious and divided the community. Who determined whether or not the communal meals were to be kosher? And did non-circumcised males wishing to join those communities of former Jews, now also Christians, have to be circumcised as part of the initiation ritual?

In retrospect, it was probably more a question of ritual than of doctrine that eventually divided those Jews and Christians into meeting separately. What we have in the texts is a story of this dispute, not between Christians and Jews, but among those who were recognized as the leaders of the Christians—namely, Paul, James, and Peter. Yet it is reasonable to think that the leaders of the house churches—both women and men—

successfully accommodated diverse practices of members in the house churches before the dispute gained momentum and sides were taken. Perhaps some of the dissension can be related to the demise of the house churches and the use of larger buildings, such as basilicas, for Eucharist and worship.

MARTYRS, ASCETICS, EMPERORS, PATRIARCHS, 150–325 C.E.

The most significant opportunity for women's liberation from compulsory marriage and child-bearing came about with their embrace, equal to that of Christian men beginning in the first century, of martyrdom and later of the ascetic life. The religious rituals of both Roman and Jewish women were centered in the home or in the synagogue. Funerary inscriptions name some Jewish women as officers of first-century synagogues, but it is not known whether they officiated in ritual services or, as is more likely, administered some aspect of synagogue organization, such as finances. In early Christianity, we see Jewish and Roman women breaking away from traditional roles—in defiance of Roman state religious mandates and Roman and Jewish family expectations.

In the earliest church "virgin" was a central symbol of single-minded dedication of women and men to depending on Christ rather than on ordinary domestic structures. The term "monk," dating to 324 C.E., seems to have emphasized the geopolitical dimensions of that orientation. Nevertheless, Christian women very early in the tradition created spaces for themselves to pursue lives of prayer, contemplation, and good works. There are stories of wives and husbands reallocating their wealth and occasionally changing the form of their relationship to each other. There are letters of Paul negotiating the situation of women and men who wish to lead a Christian life with or without the consent of their spouses. We find women turning their houses into convents and women living in their own family houses as if in a convent. The virgins of the early church were largely independent in the sense that they established their own range of ascetic practices and seem to have been corrected by the church authorities only when they appeared to exceed what was healthy.

In the past three decades, our understanding of early Christianity has grown tremendously. As Gillian Cloke writes:

For this has long been the problem with this period [the patristic, 350–450 C.E.] and this topic of study: for years, even centuries, the thought, decisions and writings of the churchmen of the patristic age have been influential entirely in self-referential terms. . . . But no thought arises out of a vacuum. All ideas are the product of an environment and in this case, the fathers' thought-processes were the product of a female environment. . . . These great men of their age were bought and sold by women . . . . For this is the crux of what I discovered when I was researching for this study: the absolute ubiquity of these "holy" women—once one starts to look for them. It is not possible—or it should not be possible—to separate them from a study of the patristic age, for they are everywhere: humble women from the lowest levels of the social strata adopting harsh lives as hermits with such frequency that priests and monks tripped over them at every turn; middle class Hausfraus planting ideological trip-wires in the consciences of their children and turning out priests, monks and bishops by the seminary-load; on up to the elite women of the very top-drawer who gave up on secular life and their worldly possessions to such an extent that they precipitated economic crises at the heart of the empire.[12]

Cloke finds women questioning, challenging, taking initiative in both their domestic and public arrangements. That women not only got Jesus' message but acted upon it is amply evident in the texts of the Fathers and in texts and stories by women and men who were informed by the new vision (New Testament). They believed that they would have life and have it abundantly, that it was worthwhile to sell everything they owned, give it to the poor, and accept his invitation to "Come, follow me." Stories abound about men and women   adopting either an hermetic or a communal life. Indeed, in many instances women's monasteries were less regulated than men's, especially if the women were convented in their own or some other woman's house.

For the first three centuries, renunciation and celibacy were among the major spiritual models for all Christians—spiritual values that are reflected in the stories that model lives of the faithful either literally or symbolically. Perpetua, a contemporary of the Stoic philosopher Justin, gave a first-person account of her trial before martyrdom.

Justin, Irenaeus, Clement, Tertullian, and Origen laid the foundation for doing theology in a way that was tolerated and usually enriched by the best philosophical thought of the time. But the early theological debates are punctuated by the accounts of persecutions.

Before Christianity became legal (313 C.E.), Christians were in danger of suffering martyrdom if they refused to give obeisance to the state gods, including the emperor. In the Acts of the Apostles 8:1–3, Paul, before his conversion, is reported to have "laid waste the Church, and entering house after house, dragged off the men and women and committed them to prison."

Tacitus, the Roman historian, reports that in the gardens of Nero at night, the bonfire-lit spectacle of Christian men and women torn to death by dogs was open to the public. Clement of Rome marvels that women, as well as men, among the Christian elect "suffered terrible and impious indignities and thereby safely completed the race of faith and, though weak in body, received a noble reward of honour." According to a recent tabulation of 950 Christian martyrs and confessors mentioned by name or anonymously in ancient texts, 177 are women, 170 clergymen, 70 soldiers, and 540 ordinary men. Some women and men were unable to stand the torture, but stories of stunning courage are emerging.[13]

Two stories are of special interest—the first because of characteristics that make it highly probable that it was written as well as narrated by a woman. It is the story of Febronia, a 22-year-old woman, raised in a convent, who because of her extraordinary beauty and holiness was hidden from all visitors unless ordered by the abbess to speak with a visitor. Febronia was taken captive by persecuting soldiers, and the account of her resistance to an arranged marriage is as gruesome as her courage. The details of physical labor and education in the convent, the portrayal of women's friendships as sincere, intellectual, fervent, and philosophical, and the bonding between laywomen and religious, married and unmarried as they recognize what they had in common make it an extraordinary text. A second story is about Pelagia of Antioch, a prostitute who becomes Christian after meeting a bishop notable more for his humanity than his ecclesiastical authority. In this story the bishop is also extraordinary for his defense, in the company of his fellow bishops, of Pelagia's candidacy for conversion. Several features of this story are remarkable: one is that Pelagia's waiting period for baptism is waived because of her fervor; and a deaconess is summoned to stand witness for her before her initiation as a Christian. On the night before she leaves the community that has received her, Pelagia goes to the holy bishop, strips before him, and asks to be clothed in some of his garments. From that time she lives an ascetic life, disguised as a man until her death in the city.

On the whole, the stories show that during times of peace the life of Christ in the Gospels was the model for the stories of extraordinary Christians whereas during times of persecution, the death of Christ became the model. The striking feature of these martyr stories is that adversity appears in the form of something that is insurmountable. The best of these differ from stories in which adversity occurs but is either decisively overcome only as a result of one's own or another's personal heroism or in which adversity is victorious only at the expense of personal defeat. These stories of good tidings, whether they end in victory or defeat, have—in addition to detailing the utmost in personal effort—the extra element of recognition of "extra power," "fellow traveler," "graceful assistance," and "angelic uncanniness."

The story of Olympias, granddaughter of Ablabius, who had served as consul and prefect in Constantine's first senate, is a good example of another kind of story. After her husband died, Olympias rejected the Emperor Theodosius I's attempt, for political reasons, to have her marry into his family, opting instead to give her property away and to become an ascetic. She was punished by having her property removed from her control and put into a guardianship so that she could not give it away. She eventually was able to give much of it (the rough equivalent of $900 million) to the church.

Becoming ordained a deaconess, she went on to "maintain" Nectarius, the bishop of Constantinople. Elizabeth Clark sees Olympias' withdrawal of her fortune from the state—as later that of Melania the Younger— as symbolic withdrawal of the female body from "the breeding of future aristocrats."[14] She had, as one writer put it, a different goalpost in mind. From these texts, it is clear that basic standards were based on the performance of men as these exceptional women were often labeled as "men."

The surprise and wonder at women's victory over the physical challenges of martyrdom reveal a culture that depended primarily on physical assets to survive travel, warfare, and political intrigue. During this time, one's very being was identified with one's sex and the horizons of possibility determined by it. What the Christian stories show are multiple attempts to break this barrier by women and sometimes by men—a father, a lover, even a bishop. And many of these stories are exceptional and unique. But the survival and popularity of these stories suggests otherwise. Other stories reveal the solidarity of women in this quest to wrest for themselves what was in the Christian view the most perfect form of human life—that of giving one's life for others in the new dispensation, as God had in Jesus Christ. In her remarkable book, *Church Fathers, Independent Virgins* (1991), Joyce Salisbury shows not only how certain women ignored patristic gender prescriptions but how they actively created alternative ones. Salisbury finds these alternative ideals in four kinds of stories: women gaining freedom from social expectations, freedom of thought, freedom of movement, and freedom from gender identification.

Another way to know if Christians brought about change for women can be learned by studying Christian women's earliest extant writings. Records on women in the fourth century show that they abandoned many of the classical models of womanhood for the increasing appeal of a life concentrated on the holiness ideal of Christianity.[15] There are, of course, inconsistencies and ambiguities to be found among these records. We find an aristocratic Roman woman plotting to kill her husband for some slight offense then suddenly diverted from this plan when she was seduced by another man. She then accuses her husband of treason. We find other women awaiting trial for fornication and adultery, taken naked to their deaths if convicted, or often committing suicide while imprisoned. We find Christian women described as heads of convents, passing the nights in prayer (for example, Lea), neglectful of their appearance (Asella), abstemious in appetite, and profligate in giving away their possessions. The same woman might have been in both groups at one or another time. And women from the bottom to the top of the social classes left the first group to join the second in the later fourth and early fifth centuries. Married women were primarily the subjects of Roman histories, and their actions were primarily against others. Christian women were willing and able to devote themselves to improving their spiritual lives, and their activity was primarily for the good of others. The best-known Christian male leaders—Jerome, Basil, Origen—wrote panegyrics about many of the women they knew and treatises on the behavior of women in general. Oddly there was a gap between the ignorance and fear of sexual differences and their magnanimous admiration of women's spiritual and physical achievements.[16]

There are those who belittle the orders of widows or deaconesses. They see in it little more than parish assistants or ministers by accommodation for reasons of sexual propriety whereas others present them as significant as full-fledged formal positions defined in the church hierarchy. The second-century church father Origen comments that Paul, in Romans, teaches with authority that even women are instituted deacons in the Church. . . ."[17] and the several Eastern (including the Syrian) bishops considered the Apostolic Constitutions (Book 8) to order them to "ordain also a woman deacon who is faithful and holy." Although ordination to the deaconate might have been an accommodation on the part of men, the very existence of deaconesses challenged the social and political assumptions of the day and precluded women's absolute exclusion from formal positions of leadership within the church.[18]

Virgins and martyrs were neither feminists, enjoying a golden age of liberty, nor oppressed victims of patriarchy. In Roman Catholic, Eastern Orthodox, and some Protestant churches, they have been and continue to be an intrinsic part of monastic life. When Antony (251–356) withdrew from society into the desert to follow the Christian way, he helped his sister enter a women's community in Alexandria. This detail, which has traditionally highlighted Antony's founding the hermetic way of life, also suggests that women's communities predated this event. When Pachomius (286–346) founded what is regarded as the first "full-scale" religious community, he founded it as a mixed community for both women and men who wished to devote themselves to lives of poverty, chastity, and obedience. Nevertheless, the desert hermit tradition is permeated by its denigration of women—possibly as an expression related to the hermits' fear of not being able to live chastely.

The genius of early Christianity was to perceive that spirit, heart, enthusiasm, and hope, even in the face of obstacles, are the sine qua nons of human beings at their best and that people are inspired to the extent that they have a vision that graciously surpasses the status quo. The accumulated power of the Roman state was replaced with the imminence of Christian apocalypse ("you know not the day nor the hour") and of eschatology ("then I shall know even as I am known" [1 Cor 13:12]).

FROM ROME, OUTWARD BOUND: 325–700 C.E.

According to Paul, love—of God and of human beings—was the key characteristic of Christians. "Love one another as I have loved you."

Saying one loves God is not enough. If you do not love your neighbor whom you can see, how can you claim to love God whom you cannot see? Even though all others will know you are Christian by your love for one another, the experience of loving is frequently one of self-correction and purification of desire. This tension between the seen and the unseen, the mandate and its fulfillment, gave rise in the fourth century to new questions along with new practices. Christmas, for example, came to be celebrated as a liturgical feast in the Roman church in addition to that of Epiphany (which is still the major feast day in the Eastern church), with increased attention on children as a result.

The first major event after Constantine became sole emperor of the West in 313 C.E., was the Council of Nicaea held near his palace in 325 C.E., twelve years before his baptism. The gradual change in the status of Christians, after Constantine's accession, from that of a persecuted minority to a fast-growing majority became a source of worry to thoughtful people who saw that it could now be profitable for a person to be a Christian. But consolidation of doctrines was just as much a problem. Both problems can be seen in the gathering at Nicaea of representatives of the Greek Eastern churches, Alexandria and Antioch, and two legates of the Roman church. The major question, arising from the need to clarify references to Father, Son, and Spirit found in the Hebrew Bible and Christian Testaments, was that of the status of the Word, as Jesus is called in the Hellenistic Gospel of John, in relation to the meaning of godhead. Dissension had arisen regarding the way "Son of God" was to be understood. The council adopted the ambiguous phrase "identical in being" and denounced those who thought that the phrase opened the door to other misunderstandings as heretical. These were the questions asked: Is

Jesus fully divine and co-eternal with the Father? Is he really kin to the Father? And the formal answers were yes, Jesus is fully divine, he exists from the beginning of time with the Father, and he is the Son of the Father. Encouraged by his mother after the council to identify the holy places of Jesus' life in Palestine, Constantine began to endow Christian churches rather than pagan temples: the Church of the Resurrection (today called the Holy Sepulcher) in Jerusalem, and the Church of the Nativity in Bethlehem. He also built St. John Lateran and St. Peter's basilicas in Rome and a new Eastern capital, Constantinople, at Byzantium, to be the "new Rome." (From the fifteenth century, Moscow has been thought of in Russian Orthodoxy as the "Third Rome.") Constantine's mother, St. Helena, is remembered for her finding the True Cross while the Church of the Resurrection was under construction. The cross was understood to have been made by Adam and Eve's son Seth from wood of the Tree of Life in the Garden of Paradise. Constantine is more honored in the Eastern than in the Western church, but his influence on Christianity is undisputed.

But dissension continued after Nicaea, and it was necessary to call another council, this time at Chalcedon in 451 C.E., to answer another set of questions, which complemented those addressed at Nicaea: Is Christ fully human and like us? Does he really exist as a human being? And again formal answers were given: Yes, Christ possessed a human body. Yes, he is equally of human and of divine natures. It was between the two councils that Augustine of Africa (354–430) wrote his detailed reflections on the Trinity. Not insignificantly Augustine credited his mother Monica's prayers and active piety for his conversion to Christianity.

The theology in these two council meetings, which were decisive for how many Christians understood themselves up through the present, reflects a growing differentiation of genres among Christian writers. Christian understanding was from the beginning informed by Roman and, increasingly, Greek intellectual traditions. Several genres were used by the church fathers when they referred to women: sermons, homilies on women; inspirational works, commentaries, exegeses, histories, Vitae, and letters.[19] Although the genres that contain the most references to women are to be found in kinds of literature called the "lower" genres—letters, homilies, pilgrimage accounts, martyrologies, hagiographies, and the apocryphal acts—the industry that the church fathers took in their writings about gender showed how much they depended on women. These men were, after all, following in the Roman tradition of philosophers, great men of letters—"part of the Christian expression of the ratio bene vivendi, the Roman preoccupation with the good life translated into terms of Christian duty."[20] Why did they perceive their women friends as exceptions if not because they were exceptional? This time proves crucial to the development of norms of what it means to be Christian. Oddly, some women were astonishingly literal in their imitation of Christ. And leaders issued correctives that were often clumsy and partial. The same woman was sometimes praised and condemned by different leaders and, occasionally, by the same leader. The church fathers' frequently quoted misogynist reflections on gender do not inspire confidence today; but judging from the number and intensity of their letters, they did not seem to have been the last word for their time either. Records show that the early Christians coped with this tension in many different ways. Some Christians continued on without much change from their ancestors. No longer in danger of persecution, they continued to strive for the Pax Romana as law-abiding citizens—the major difference being that they participated in the Christian Eucharist instead of state-mandated rituals.

Before 313, Christianity had been called a pagan religion because it did not conform to the state religion. A reversal gradually took place as Christianity became the religion of the majority. Others, especially women, took advantage of the new possibilities either by refusing to marry at all or if married or constrained to marry, persuading her partner to have a celibate relationship. Melania the Younger and Pinianus at Melania's urging after she had one stillbirth and one miscarriage, had such a relationship.

This couple wanted to liquidate their estate and to distribute the money to the poor. Rome, however, was in dire need of money for military defense and even engaged in legal battles for their wealth. Others took a more radical stance and renounced family to live a life completely devoted to self-reform and renunciation. One extreme case was Paula, who borrowed money to give it away, which not only deprived her daughter of subsistence money but left substantial unpaid debts at her death. Some fashioned a life of contemplating and loving God completely apart from human company except for colleagues who provided for their minimal needs. Others led a communal life devoted to the care of poor and underprivileged Christian leaders. As long as lifestyles were in considerable flux, some women and men entered into "spiritual" marriages, dependent on each other for everything except conjugal sex, which both had renounced under vow. The leaders of later Christian communities continued the senator's and philosopher's roles of giving advice to individuals, giving sermons to communities whose conflicts were well known, and setting down principles for the achievement of holiness.

Holiness meant perfection: control over one's appetites, both physical (desire for food, drink, comfort, material goods, sexual pleasure) and spiritual (desire for esteem, recognition, power, others' gifts). Perfection involved abstaining not only from all sinful fulfillment of desire, but like the rules that formed the "hedge" of Torah, even from legitimate fulfillment that was not strictly necessary for one's life. Sexual relations, for example, were considered by the fourth-century preacher John Chrysostom as "a waste of time." Understandably, the leaders' praising of holiness led to excesses by some individuals who emulated the rules. The exaltation of virginity over marriage resulted in a problematic, if unintentional, denigration of the state of marriage. And the praise of some women for "manly" achievements divided them from other women. The traditional Greek and Roman assumption that women were inferior in general continued to dominate the social context despite many obvious exceptions. Nevertheless, it seems to those who understood the meaning of being "in Christ," the call to dismantle gender inequality was clear.

Less is said about married women even though the majority of Christian women were probably married. We do have the advice of John Chrysostom to a woman who, in a spiritual marriage, found herself in charge of the business affairs so that her husband could give his attention to spiritual matters. Chrysostom said that, undertaken for the love of God, attention to business matters was just as worthy a pursuit as explicitly religious pursuits.

Christians made two innovations in the area of sexual ethics. One was the insistence on sexual fidelity on the part of both men and women—something recommended by Roman philosophers but not supported by the Roman state, which punished women but not men for adultery. The other was first a disapproval, then an increasing condemnation of divorce and remarriage, even if permitted by law. Regarding the public activity of women, when women supported Christian leaders, they were praised. When they opposed leaders of the church, they were reviled.

Women's actual activities can be glimpsed in "official sources" such as church histories, canons of church councils, and church orders—especially regarding expectations of women's behavior in the household and in the church. The so-called higher genre of theological treatises, however, contain the least information about women although it does reveal the writers' general views of women in normative and exegetical passages. Jerome, Augustine, Basil, Clement, Chrysostom, and Tertullian reveal that they had love for their "sisters" and that they had close spiritual friendships with several women. However, none revised the ontological definition of femaleness as passive and carnal and in opposition to the definition of maleness as active and governed by the mind and the spirit. Ambrose, for example, wrote that "a woman can't be blamed for being as she was born."[21]

A tension developed between those who saw the possibility of transcending gender differences and those who saw this transcendence as impossible in the present world. Unlike the crisis precipitated by the rituals involving circumcision and food that resulted in the separation of Judaism from Christianity, the fourth-century crisis was precipitated by rituals involving the anointing of leaders and labor practices. The leaders of the Christian communities condemned Eustathius' followers (340/41) and the Messalians (c. 390) for violating certain ascetic principles: the two groups claimed that they had reached a state of apatheia that allowed them to ignore the difficulty of controlling the passions. In this new freedom, they rejected work as a worldly concern, lived by receiving alms, and invented new feasts and models to celebrate other than the martyrs and canonized saints. Perhaps the heretics' most grievous departure from established practice was their criticism of hierarchical structure as preventing those advancing in it from "truly leaving the world," as contrasted with their own lifestyle that, they claimed, was in accord with the original principles of the Christian movement.[22] This claim was at best ambiguous because as soon as the initial founding phase of fringe groups—such as the Montanists, Encratites, Apotactics, Eistathians, Messalians, or Euchitai—had passed, the breakaway groups were forced to adapt themselves to the constraints of nature and society. The extremes of the climate forced them to settle; settlement required rudimentary organization, and a process of institutionalization set in, mirroring more or less precisely that of the "great Church"—which had after all undergone a similar transformation.

The very people who thought they could develop a communal resistance to hierarchization initially included women as leaders but later, for various reasons, reverted to the tradition of male leadership. Another recurring surprise is the discovery that frequently the leaders of what became fringe heretical groups were individuals who had previously had long-standing friendships within the great Church. The failed friendship of Basil of Caesarea and Eustathius, in 373, is an example of the adage that internal enemies are more dangerous than external ones. Nevertheless, what is very clear is that the ascetic movements in the early church had immense influence on the development of doctrine.

From the beginning, after the first generation of his companions, attempts to follow the example of Jesus were of three basic types of ascetic life: men and women who practiced harsh asceticism and who, rejecting society, took up wandering; men and women who practiced asceticism in their own homes in the midst of a family life; and those who led settled lives in communities of men and women. The latter—including some bishops and clergy—were located in urban areas and were engaged in practical and useful service to others. They were vocal in matters of doctrine and ecclesiastical appointment matters and were described by the fourth century theologian, Gregory of Nazianzus, as *megas bios* (which has been translated as "prone to turbulence") as compared with *eremikos bios* (translated as "solitary").

It has been suggested, however, that "megas bios" could as well have been translated as "mixed" rather than "turbulent": that is, as mixed communities of men and women who participated actively in society as compared with ascetics who were solitary.[23] There are several textual references to mixed communities from the beginning. In the *Life of Theodotus and the Seven Virgins*, male and female Montanists refer to themselves as martyrs, apostles, and catechists. They wrote "catholic letters," and had female bishops and female presbyters in their community. Another community in Seleucia, the parqenwn of the blessed virgin Thecla, is identified as the "retreat of a female saint" in the account of Gregory of Nazianzus who stayed there for four years after the death of his father and after the dissension over his appointment as bishop. In her famous account of her pilgrimage to the Holy Land, Egeria records a large enclosure surrounded by a thick wall with "monasteries beyond measure of men and women."[24] At the same time, it does not run contrary to the records to think that women were in the forefront of many of the groups who became troublesome.

The record of women's influence on males who were leaders in the "great Church" is becoming ever more clear. Similarly, there is no good reason to ignore the charges made by these "fathers" against the fact of women's prominence in the break-away groups. Some scholars think that the attraction of so many women to heretical and schismatic sects in the third and fourth centuries may have been a backlash against the second century churchmen's attempt, as recorded in the Letter of Timothy I, to increase "eligibility" requirements on widows and deaconesses, thus reducing the number of women who could have public roles in the "mainstream church."

In traditional studies of early Christianity, the line between heretical and orthodox is clear. The reasons given by the orthodox for pronouncing certain positions heretical in both the East and the West—for example, the Gnostics for their dualism on the origin of good and evil, the Manicheans for their denial of the physical suffering of Jesus, the Marcionites for their rejection of the Old Testament and three of the Gospels, the Montanists for their claim to continuing revelation—all seem to validate the Orthodox church's decision to reject these competing alternatives. But recent studies have shown that an additional reason was operative in many of the declarations of heresy: namely, the sects' willingness to give positions of authority and leadership to women. Particular groups of Christians attempted to assert the dominance of their own theological and social models in situations of profound religious pluralism and ambiguity."[25] To join these groups, men had to renounce participation in public secular life. Because women rarely expected to have a public secular role, they gained a voice in the ascetic community. To the extent that women resisted subordination and privatization, they were seen as usurping the role of men and therefore as destabilizing male/female and public/private distinctions, and to the extent that men did not resist women's participation in the ascetic community, they were seen as feminized.

Monastic life was the model for spiritual life, with solitaries appending themselves to a particular monastery. In the East, Pachomius' Rule was the first and together with Basil's Rule has provided the basis for all other monastic orders. Basil was the grandson of Macrina the Elder, who with her prominent and wealthy family lost all her possessions during the persecution of Maximus. Basil's sister, Macrina the Younger, founded the monastery that became the model for his own in Cappadocia. The first monastic rule in the West to gain widespread acceptance was that of St. Benedict of Nursia (480–527). A contemporary of his, Cesarius of Arles (c. 470–542), wrote a rule for nuns at the request of his sister (Cesaria), but his and other attempts to write a rule for women failed. When the Anglo Saxons first converted, there are accounts of many solitaries with varied backgrounds: Drythhelm left wife and children; Columba became a prince in exile; Aiden was an activist with retreats into solitude; and Christina of Markyate fled a betrothal that was against her wishes. Although the first solitaries learned from other solitaries, "sayings" came to be written when, after invasions by barbarians, the solitaries' need for a spiritual father could no longer be fulfilled by a person. The early lives of the Fathers, rewritten by the author of Ancrene Wisse, for example, were read with different presuppositions and concerns by the solitaries and with different results.

The vision kept alive by the Christian community from beyond the Roman empire to Frankish territory was, at its best, varied, large, and productively imaginative surely because it included women as significant figures from the beginning and through its history. That women's inclusion was problematic should not be used to detract from their importance.

CONVERSION AND CONFLICT: 700–1054 C.E.

In traditional histories of this period, Christianity becomes inextricable from its relationship to Islam or from the drifting apart of the Eastern and Western churches. Four other developments also caused a sea-change within Christianity. The fall of Rome to the barbarians in 410 C.E. left much work to be done to reconstruct the territory of the former Roman empire. The absence of a strong central political structure made the situation in the West significantly different from that in the East where the emperor and the patriarch were accepted, up to the middle of the sixteenth century, as counterparts with interlocking responsibilities. The Jews in the West, for example, found themselves without the protection of a consistent policy and instead were subject to the vagaries of local governments. The rapidly expanding missionary activity and the established centers of Christian identity had reciprocal effects on each other. The eighth through the eleventh centuries saw invasions of these centers by Magyars, Saracens, and Vikings.

So we must ask what was the effect on Christianity of missionary work like that of the famous Boniface and Anskar as they learned to accommodate the military threats posed by the variously warlike and aggressive Franks, Saxons, Gauls, Frisians, Danes, Swedes, Bohemians, Hungarians, and Slavs in western, northern, and eastern Europe. Besides the monasteries organized and built in this period, the formation of numerous parishes also gives evidence of vibrant local Christian communities. The growth and subsequent defeat of the iconoclastic movement in the Eastern church at the beginning of this period decisively shaped the future of Christianity and quite possibly that of Christian women. The apparent contradiction between fear of women as temptations to men's chastity and commonality between women and men with respect to spiritual ideals continued from before. The threat to eliminate human images of the sacred from the Christian tradition was also a threat to one of the few existing public representations of women on an equal scale (even if not frequency) with men.

There was a change in spirituality from the time of early Christianity to the eleventh century—a focusing on the ritual consumption and voluntary restriction of food. In early Christianity the Eucharist was at the center of a communal meal. For Christians from the beginning, eating the bread and drinking the wine was "not only to be mystically and individually fed with the bread of heaven, it was also to be present at sacrifice . . . a death that was simultaneously glory and resurrection."[26] Concomitantly, fasting was a weekly act of preparation for this weekly meal, a 40-day preparation for the feast of the resurrection, a seasonal coming back to life after death by winter. When Christians voluntarily experienced hunger to recognize the threat of famine to all living things and to offer to God the tithe of the harvest, they thereby expressed thanks and prayed for continued bounty and fertility. Food, however, is culturally located more in women's than in men's domains of control. Because women's space was traditionally the home—also the space where food is prepared—it was less disruptive for women to enter communal monastic life than for men. Men's space was traditionally the public square; to renounce a life lived in the public sphere for one lived within a monastery was more different and less continuous than was a woman's decision to take vows. Food became a likely candidate for a woman's renunciation as a manifestation of difference from her former life in the world. Stories of women's self-denial with respect to food (men's stories were fewer and on the whole less excessive) stretch from the early anchoresses through the High Middle Ages. The greater number, however, are from the eleventh through the fourteenth centuries.[27]

In Bede's *Ecclesiastical History*, written in the early eighth century, Hilda of Whitby appears, along with 19 other women—fewer than the number of men included but not less respected and emulated by later readers. Hilda was 66 when she died, having spent her first 33 years as fully secular, and the ensuing 33 as abbess of Hartlepool and then Whitby, which she also built.

Many men came to be instructed by her. She taught them to love to study the Scriptures, and several decided to be ordained because of her guidance and example. Hilda and her company were among those who participated in the Synod of Whitby, which was called to settle the questions of the date of the celebration of Easter, the tonsure, and other matters. Bede summarizes several of the arguments but does not record whether women spoke during the proceedings.

The relationship between Islam and Christianity was preceded by a history of Arab-Christian relations. Originally, Arabs controlled the desert between Rome and Persia with efficient military organizations. After Rome and Persia suppressed the Arab caravan cities, Arabs were readily absorbed into the Eastern Roman empire, and large numbers of Aramaic-speaking Arabs who became Christian during the third to fifth centuries were included in the Syriac church. The old Arab military aristocracy and the Christian Byzantine church influenced each other mutually. In the fifth century, however, Nestorianism (Persian-Syriacs who held Jesus to be two separate natures and Mary to be mother only of one) and Monophysitism (Byzantines who, in reaction to Nestorianism, held Jesus to have only divine nature) complicated Arab-Byzantine relations.

After the founding of Islam among Arabs in a part of Arabia, the first Muslim expansion, in the seventh century, was an expedition into the rest of Arabian territory and its borders for the purpose of establishing unity among the Arabs. On the borders the Byzantines and Persians counter-attacked to protect the territories that they ruled, but they were decisively defeated more because of their own internal weaknesses than Muslim military strength. With this unexpected victory over the Byzantines and Persians, the Muslims invaded Spain, France, Africa, and Byzantium. The campaign in Byzantium ultimately failed, but by that time the Muslims were positioned to advance in the ninth century into Sicily, from which they invaded Italy and Constantinople for a second time. The West rallied in the eleventh century to regain Spain, but the Byzantines were defeated by the Seljuks in 1071. The Crusades, thought by many scholars to have been overrated in terms of Christian-Muslim conflict, began 25 years later.

While the Western church was expanding in the ninth century to the north and west, missionaries of the Byzantine church went to the Slav people outside the empire. Cyril and Methodius translated the Greek Bible, which was used exclusively within the Byzantine, into Slavonic—the first known instance of the Bible in the vernacular. Christian churches were built in Bulgaria, Serbia, and Russia, but in Moravia, Latin missionaries succeeded in drawing converts to the Western church. To understand the division that occurred between Eastern and Western Christians, we must go back to 330, when Constantine built Constantinople as "New Rome"—the center of the Byzantine Church—except for a disastrous 57-year occupation by Western Crusaders in the thirteenth century—until it was captured by the Ottoman Turks in 1453. The effects of this occupation—during which those who thought of themselves as responding to the Eastern church's request for help in defending the holy land themselves turned into marauders—are still evident among many Greeks, for example. When I visited women's monasteries in Greece and in conversation let it be known that I was Roman Catholic, one of the interviewees responded that she did not see how I could possibly understand their lives as Orthodox Christians. Nuns in other monasteries, on the other hand, welcomed my questions and regarded that part of the history of the relationship between the two churches as terrible and sad, but over.

The seventh council had to choose whether the Christian tradition would be iconic (using images) or aniconic (renouncing use of images). The iconoclastic controversy raged from 726 until 780 and resulted in the vicious destruction of many valuable icons. Two women played crucial roles in bringing the controversy to an end. Empress Irene called the Council of Nicaea (787), which ratified the iconic tradition in Christianity by defining the difference between worship (latreia) given to God alone and the appropriate veneration of icons. Empress Theodora put an end to the second, lesser spate of violence from 815 to 842 by her restoration of damaged icons in 843. Her settlement of the conflict came to be known as the "triumph of Orthodoxy" in the East. The precedent that these two women rulers set for taking active roles in reconciling decisions has unfortunately been virtually ignored in both the Western and the Eastern churches.

Relations between the Eastern and Western churches continued to deteriorate and, following an initial clash between Pope Nicolas I and Patriarch Photius, the papal legate to Constantinople and the patriarch Michael Cerularius issued anathemas against each other in 1054. These condemnations were taken as evidence of a formal break between the two churches until they mutually revoked them in 1965 during Vatican II.

EARLY MEDIEVAL PERIOD: 1054–1400

This period manifests amazing ambiguity with intentions and results. Three general features characterize the period. Because Western Europe was almost entirely Christian, leaders began to consolidate Christian practices and beliefs that before had been administered locally or regionally. For example, Benedictines began to hold general chapters and to establish "daughter" houses, that is, new religious houses, founded by monks and nuns of an established monastery, which maintained administrative ties with the older house. The administration of parishes, chapters, and collection of tithes, which until then had been restricted to religious houses, were now put under the direction of laypeople. Church leaders undertook reform of clergy with respect to patronage and cohabitation with women. In the twelfth to thirteenth centuries, the rise of the universities corresponded to other "internationalization" movements. Before the founding of universities, the level of learning was relatively high in men's and women's monasteries.

However, only men's orders sent their most gifted members to be educated at universities. The effect of this difference grew such that in 200 years the level of learning within women's communities was low for the first time in the Christian tradition. In spite of the benefits of the shift to theory from earlier symbolic and metaphysical expression, laypeople too were affected by the potential split among philosophy, theology, and spirituality. Unlike Orthodoxy in the East, which was thought to have triumphed with the restoration of icons by Empress Theodora, the European church was ambivalent in its response to Reform movements within— sometimes supporting their efforts (e.g., the Beguines, Franciscans, and Dominicans), at other times treating them as heretics (for example, the Waldensians, the Beguines, and Cathars or Albigensians)—often depending on the reformers' attitudes toward the authority of the church as well as on their beliefs. Nevertheless, what happened in the early Medieval period was a microcosm of what was to come in the next.

There were three major reforms of monastic life between 909 and 1226, the first having occurred in France when Cluny was founded in 909. The second was led by Bernard of Clairvaux, and the third—a major structural change—was inaugurated by Francis of Assisi and Dominic of Padua. Women participated in all three reforms, especially by founding their own orders.

Clare and her sisters, for example, founded several houses but maintained a special relationship with Francis and his brothers. In Germany, Hildegard moved the women's Benedictine community away from the monastery at Disibodenberg—although not without opposition—to a new women's monastery at Rupertsberg in 1150. The categories "monasteri aperti" (open monasteries) and "clausura" (closed) included a broad range of types of communities (mulieres religiosae, mulieres de penitentia, sorores, pinzochere, bizoke, mantellate, terziarie, monache do casa, monacelle, sante, and santarelle) even after Boniface VIII's decree in 1298 that "all nuns . . . shall henceforth remain in their monasteries in perpetual enclosure"—exceptions were permitted—and until Pius XI's Counter-Reformation bull imposed "clausura" on all women's communities in the sixteenth century. The great influx of women into religious life can be seen in England, for example, during the twelfth and thirteenth centuries when the number of nunneries burgeoned: 10 abbeys continued from before the Norman Conquest and 132 nunneries were founded or newly reorganized after the Conquest, mainly from 1100 to 1250. This number is comparable to the Cistercian Order, which grew from 344 to 530 abbeys from 1153 to 1200.[28] It is assumed that, with few exceptions, nunneries in Western Europe established before the Conquest followed Benedict's Rule. In 980, for example, Jutta took up the life of hermitess on a hill near a hermitage at Disibodenberg in Rhineland.

One of the women who came to study with her was the ten-year-old Hildegard of Bingen. When Jutta died, Hildegard was elected abbess, and the community of men and women, electing to follow the Rule of Benedict, built a new monastery, the ruins of which still exist today. Hildegard preached in parish churches up and down the Rhine, and her writings (among others, a theological compendium, three books of visions, a book of physical things, a book of medicine, a book of songs, and numerous letters to popes, kings, and lay men and women) are becoming widely known today. The most important theologian of this period was Thomas Aquinas, a Dominican, who taught at the University of Paris.

Many monasteries were "double monasteries" (a community of monks and a community of nuns, established on the same site but usually within different boundaries, observing the same rule, and together forming a single legal and religious body)[29]: sometimes for reasons of proximity, sometimes for helping with physical labor needed in maintaining the buildings and land, and because of the lay status of the religious women in need of ordained men for celebrating the liturgy and administering the sacraments. Women also needed the patronage of men to found communities, as can be seen in *The Life of Christina of Markyate,* where support from hermits, bishops, archbishops, and an abbot was solicited to stabilize the small group of women who formed around Christina of Markyate. Church law, however, has most often discouraged men and women religious living together or in proximity.

The Council of Agde in 506 forbade men to place nunneries "in the neighborhood of men's cloisters for fear of Satan's cunning and people's gossip."[30] Nevertheless, allusions to a community of women linked with a monastery, or to brothers, monks, or canons have been found throughout the history of religious orders up through the Middle Ages.

At first gender symmetry prevailed between women's and men's religious communities. Then backlash against equality occurred in the twelfth century. Augustinian canonesses continued to resemble cloistered nuns while Augustinian canons became quite different from monks. Dominican and Franciscan nuns were also cloistered. That is, their lives were not much like the itinerant friars even though both Clare and Francis, her friend and spiritual brother, are equally lauded for their practice of poverty. Besides the women in convents who were associated with the new praxis, other women in the twelfth century became renowned for their charitable service: they took no vows, followed no traditional rule, and made a life together in small houses called béguinages. Others, called beatas, were religious women who did not have enough money for dowries for convents. They wore the habit and followed the rule of a particular community and lived either at home or with other beatas. The domain of their piety was the parish church and the streets where they counseled prostitutes, visited women's prisons, and did other charitable work. Some became hermits or religious leaders of small congregations; all were watched carefully for disorderly tendencies.

We know about lives of women from documents such as hortatory sermons, prescriptive treatises, theological tracts, charters of monasteries (including deeds and titles of lands), and especially the detailed visitation records of Archbishop Eudes Rigaud in Normandy in the thirteenth century. Monks and nuns apparently shifted their allegiance to individual monasteries quite often. Their activities, the sex of the monastic populations, and their geographic location did as well. Many of the new movements required imitation of the apostles, which meant basically being poor and preaching while wandering.

With all that was going on in this period, one might wonder why so little change took place on the issue of gender. Some clarification can be found in Héloïse's argument against Abelard's offer of marriage after he, an abbot, and she, an abbess, had been disciplined for their violation of the vows of chastity: in Abelard's account she argues that having children makes a career in philosophy improbable:

> What possible concord could there be between scholars and domestics, between authors and cradles, between books or tablets and distaffs, between the stylus or the pen and the spindle? What man,

intent on his religious or philosophical meditations, can possibly endure the whining of children, the lullabies of the nurse seeking to
quiet them, or the noisy confusion of family life? Who can endure
the continual untidiness of children? The rich, you may reply, can do
this, because . . . their wealth takes no thought of expense and protects them from daily worries. But to this the answer is that the condition of philosophers is by no means that of the wealthy, nor can
those whose minds are occupied with riches and worldly cares find
time for religious or philosophical study. For this reason the
renowned philosophers of old utterly despised the world . . . and denied themselves all its delights in order that they might repose in the
embraces of philosophy alone.[31]

Héloïse cannot think of any way that Abelard's marrying her would
make his life better. Of course, the passage may also be read as implicitly
revealing her own realization of the cost to herself of having already had a
child and that marriage would go contrary as well to the demands of her
own intellectual life. Further on, Héloïse observes that at the time virginity for both women and men was still considered to be the ideal religious
way of life even though perfection was also deemed possible for those
who had chosen the married state.

LATE MEDIEVAL CHURCH, REFORMATION,
AND ENLIGHTENMENT: 1400–1800

What has been called the Reformation, or Reformations, is more accurately understood as one of several reform movements within Christianity.
Until recently, histories of European religion in the fifteenth and sixteenth
centuries were written as though women were invisible, except for the
two English queens, Mary of Scotland and Elizabeth, who as women leaders, were respectively reviled by Protestants and Catholics. Today we know
that women were actively involved on both sides of the debate. In the
1530s women defended St. Nicholas Priory with pitchforks against the
king's messengers who had come to destroy it. In the changing of royal
heads, women on both sides suffered martyrdom although more men than

women died because those who held public office and exercised power were most likely to be visible to the opposing regency. But in the gradually changing doctrinal and ritual requirements of the English church, for example, women were among those who suffered martyrdom because of their personal beliefs.

The leaders of the three major Protestant reform movements in the sixteenth century acted primarily as individuals. Luther, a former Augustinian monk, in 1517 nailed his 95 theses of dissent on the door of the church in Wittenberg, where he taught at the university. Although Henry VIII wrote a refutation of Luther's theses in 1521, the conflict with the papacy over his divorce and remarriage prompted him to reject the authority of the pope and, in 1534, to declare himself head of the English church. In 1536, Calvin finished writing his Institutes, a systematic unification of Luther's points of dissent into a Protestant theological vision. Of the three, Calvin has the most innovative position on women in the church. Calvin held that the Pauline command for women's silence in church and the ban on women's teaching are indifferent with respect to salvation even though they are not morally indifferent. This means that if women violate the command or the ban, they do not risk their salvation; nevertheless, because the command and the ban are in Scripture, they do violate decorum and therefore their acts are not matters of indifference.

The two major Reformation changes brought about within Protestantism were, first, the rejection of an intermediary between God and human beings, that is, rejection of clergy as dispensers of the sacraments and as vehicles of grace, and second, an increase in men's authority within the home. Both changes were detrimental to women. In the first, women lost access to an external mediator when their domestic well-being was threatened. In the second, the loss of women's monasteries diminished the crucial control—if only relative to men's—of many 'women over their persons, property, company, and lives. The growth of individualism attributed to Protestantism hardly applied to women. With respect to church governance, however, the question of women's role was repeatedly discussed, and reports of local solutions indicate some accommodations—although in the Church of England the only lay position open to women or men was that of church warden and in the Presbyterian church the position of elder was open only to men. In the Independent churches and sectarian congregations where gifted people were called to ministry by gathered congregations, there was no rule against women's filling the same role as men; nevertheless, the Pauline injunctions against women speaking in church continued. In John Rogers's Dublin Independent Church women had a voice and a vote so long as they did not exercise power over men. Women could give testimony when seeking admission, vote on the appointment of deacons, and serve as church officers, that is, minister to the poor, the sick, and strangers. Prophetesses (daughters were preferred to wives) in the new congregations enjoyed certain liberties of speech but only so long as they did nothing to challenge the male authority in the church. Reports of some all-women preachers' meetings gave rise to suspicion and mockery, and shortly after, in 1645, Parliament passed an ordinance forbidding lay preaching. Anne Laurence concludes that the seventeenth-century English fear of women exercising authority over men was more restrictive for women than were the attitudes of the Roman church toward pre-Reformation heretics, such as the Lollards (who had women preachers), Wyclif (who stipulated that any layperson, including any woman, could celebrate Mass), the Waldensians, and Cathars. Although Reformation theologians wanted to raise the status of marriage as an ideal, they did not think of it as spiritual or religious. Their teachings on marriage and virginity differed from those of the early church fathers, and the divines were just as contradictory when applied to women. Patricia Crawford thinks that "the Protestant emphasis on the value of marriage for women was based on misunderstanding of the Catholic doctrine of virginity"[32] since by this time virginity in Catholicism was understood more as spiritual than physiological, and married women and widows were thought to have the same capacity for holiness as virgins.

Two reasons account for the narrowing of what was possible for women in English Reformation churches: there was general agreement, based on a precise reading of Pauline epistles, that women could not exercise authority over men, and a distinction was made between ministry and jurisdiction. In the pre-Reformation church, anyone could baptize and everyone could receive Communion, so it was conceivable that women could administer the sacraments (even if they were permitted to administer only one sacrament). In the Church of Reformation, however, the administration of sacraments became part of church jurisdiction (as distinct from ministry) because their reception was restricted to certain people, so it was inconceivable that women could exercise this kind of authority over men. To curb women's expectations that they could be part of general church governance, women-only religious meetings were forbidden in the New England synod of 1637. To the extent that there were networks of refuge among women, they had to go underground. Dorothy Hazard, for example, made it possible for a woman to bear her children in her husband's parish so that she did not have to undergo the impositions of churching and the like laid upon them by other parsons.

Nevertheless, beginning with the testimony of their conversion experience, middle-class Quaker women who could afford child-care regularly acted as itinerant preachers as well as within their own meetings. In addition, Reformed churches increasingly thought of their clergy as communicating the scriptures and the words of God rather than as administering the sacraments.

Teresa of Avila (1515–82), named in 1969 the first of now three women "doctors of divinity" in the Roman Church, is a classic example of someone who used the existing structures of religion in her time for an alternative place to live without giving herself over to what she perceived to be the mediocrity of the status quo. During the maelstrom of the Inquisition in Spain initiated by Ferdinand and Isabella and feebly condoned by Pope Sixtus IV, Teresa defended herself by using the gender stereotypes of timidity, ignorance, and weakness, but her ironic view of this strategy often shows through: "In the case of a poor little woman like myself weak and with hardly any fortitude, it seems to me fitting that God lead me with gifts, as he now does, so that I might be able to suffer some trials He has desired me to bear. But servants of God, men of prominence, learning, and high intelligence . . . when they don't have devotion, they shouldn't weary themselves."[33]

Teresa of Avila languished for twenty years in a Carmelite convent before she began to make progress with the help of a friend, Peter of Alcantara. From that point on she traveled all over Spain, reforming and founding new structures for women in which they could reach a saner spirituality than in the old structures. She was outspoken about the unequal opportunities of women and men and made gender equality a principle of divine complexity:

> It seemed to me that, considering what St. Paul says about women keeping at home (Titus, 2:5), (I have already been reminded of this

and I had already heard of it) that this might be God's will. But [God] said to me, "Tell them [Teresa's critics] that they are not to be guided by one part of Scripture alone, but to look at others; ask them if they suppose they will be able to tie my hands."[34]

Teresa grew to be able to discern and transform into strengths the liabilities relating to gender and self-hatred. She advised religious women to abandon trivial behavior and being feeble. She did not hesitate to draw upon gender stereotypes to make her point: "resemble strong men; . . . if you will do what lies in your power, the Lord will make you so virile that you will astonish the menfolk" (II, 70).

In some ways, the sixteenth century was initially one of gain for women. Desiderius Erasmus (c. 1466–1536) urged all Christians to study the Scriptures. Both he and René Descartes (1596–1650) supported translation of the Bible into the vernacular and declared specialized training not necessary to write philosophy and theology. Cardinal Ximénez Cisneros supported bibles for convents and granted women larger roles in the administration of convents. Then groups, calling themselves Illuminists or alumbrados, many with women as leaders, began meeting in homes and emphasized the capacity of individuals to be illuminated. Teresa's lifetime spans that of the misogynist entrenchment against these anti-clerical movements: she saw the meaning of "mulierculae" shift from "unlettered, can read only vernacular" to "silly woman who presumes to read and understand the literal and spiritual meaning of the scriptures." Teresa moved between the orthodox and the heterodox, "holding the explosive theological issues of her day in oxymoronic tension, and came perilously close to losing all."[35] Her autobiography was under investigation for thirteen years, she was ordered to burn another of her manuscripts, and after her death theologians for the Inquisition advised all her books be burned. In 1614, seventeen years after her interrogation, the first step toward her canonization was taken. But personal heroism was found not only among monastic women. Quaker women and Seventh-day Adventist Prophetesses like Ellen White tell how they had to overcome the self-doubt and fear of speaking ecstatically in religious assemblies.

Catholic religious women also faced more severe restrictions during sixteenth-century Reformation Catholicism. Reflecting this loss, the percentage of women saints declined from 27.2 percent in the fifteenth century to 18.1 percent in the sixteenth. The medieval church's tolerance of significant ambiguity in lifestyle, for example, that of the beatas and the béguines, ceased. Religious women were forced after the reforms initiated by the Council of Trent (1545–63) and the prelates of the Spanish Inquisition to subscribe to clear rules for religious enclosures to define their relationships with the world. The Jesuits, a new religious order, was founded by a former soldier, Ignatius Loyola (1491–1556). His initial desire was to go to the Holy Land and, by imitating Christ, to convert the Muslims. Because of the Turkish wars he was diverted to the work of education in Rome instead.

Nevertheless, the Mother of God as ideal woman continued in both the Western and the Eastern Church, and for some generations, men took "Maria" (grammatically unmasculinized) as their second name.

In 1618, only 101 years after Luther's nailing up the 95 theses, The Thirty Years War, the result of an intractable intertwining of territorial, religious, and political motives, broke out and gradually spread throughout Europe. Together with the Spanish Inquisition, acts of anti-Semitism, and the persecution of witches from the fourteenth to the seventeenth centuries (including the Salem witch trials in America), the Thirty Years War is surely one of the most lamentable events in Christian history. Begun in Bohemia by Protestant nobles against the Holy Roman Empire, it resulted in devastating losses of population, religious and personal property, especially in Germany, and in the break-up of the empire into national states. The best result was that the Treaty of Westphalia in 1648 brought about a new age of religious tolerance. By the terms of the treaty each state was to adopt as its established religion the religion of its ruler.

The eighteenth century is known as the Enlightenment—with vast confidence in the power of reason, a new kind of certitude, based on logic and scientific deductions, and belief in progress. From their new confidence in reason, Enlightenment philosophers challenged traditional religious views. The university-trained religious thinkers responded in Enlightenment terms, and the resulting truncated account of religion is still familiar.

Enlightenment thinkers did support women's education and the improvement of women's legal status, but many of the old attitudes toward women prevailed in everyday life. By this time women had been excluded from the universities for 500 years. The relationship between this exclusion and the burgeoning of women mystics has yet to be studied, but it seems no mere coincidence that from the twelfth century onward, female mystics—Catherine of Siena, Julian of Norwich, Agnes of Feligno, Marguerite Porete, Mechthilde of Magdeburg, Gertrude the Great, Margery Kempe, Hadewijch of Antwerp, Jeanne Guyon—outnumbered male mystics, and their writings were influenced by the new religious communities (such as the béguines). The mystics, female and male, articulated a via negativa view of intelligence—a view immortalized in Blaise Pascal's famous statement, "The heart has reasons the mind knows not of." Blaise and his sister Jacqueline both converted to Jansenism, and in 1651 she entered the convent at Port-Royal, which became a center of the movement. It also seems relevant to ask whether that century's vexed relationship between religion and science might have been different had there been a significant number of women scientists.

Meanwhile in America during the founding years, most of the activities of women were subordinated to the needs of home, family, and church. However, the introduction of new strictures for Catholic women in church manuals before the Revolution suggests that many women had begun new practices with respect to marriage, pregnancy, and conception—a defiance of traditional sexual teaching that would increase into the twentieth century. And although many of the colonies were founded in protest over the lack of religious freedom, religious tolerance had to be learned. Maryland, founded by the prominent Catholic Lord Baltimore, at the urging of his wife, was the first to grant religious tolerance to all denominations. Women like Margaret Brent (1602–c.1671), for whom the Catholic woman suffrage society was named in 1918, were prominent in state and church in Maryland and provided administrative and business leadership. But shortly after Brent left office, a Puritan revolution threw the colony into religious confusion with the result that by the end of the seventeenth century, Maryland reverted to being a royal colony, with Anglicanism as the established religion and public Catholic worship proscribed. Chroniclers of that time omitted names of the subversives lest they be discovered, but in the absence of parishes, it was primarily women who provided house churches and religious instruction. Sharing a common enemy, Protestant and Catholic women undertook political and military activities together during the Revolutionary War: women like Sara McCalla, Mary Digges Lee, Catherine Meade FitzSimons, and Mary Waters acted as spies, saboteurs, and sometimes fought with the troops.

After the Revolutionary War, religious liberty gradually became the norm, and lay initiatives grew steadily with the number of immigrants. Numbers of religious communities were founded by women as well as men: religious communities were founded by Catherine Spalding, Mary Rhodes, Elizabeth Bayley Seton, and Mother Alfred Noyes. Bishop Carroll wanted only teaching orders and requested that rules regarding fasting and prayer be revised so that they did not detract from the work of the Sisters.

The expansion of European interests into the Americas and Africa and Asia beginning in the sixteenth century is inextricably bound up with Christian missionaries whose efforts elicited a broad range of responses. Between the two extremes of complete rejection and complete conversion can be found the alternatives of syncretism (a blend of indigenous and Christian religions), nepantilism (external conformity), dissimulation, passive resistance, and rebellion. These missionaries also exhibited a range of efforts, from one extreme of complete rejection of indigenous religions to the other extreme of studying them in order to find cultural concordances. Sometimes missionaries protected native populations from economic exploitation. Other times they were as greedy for spiritual victories as the explorers were for land and goods. Historically the Spanish/Portuguese pattern of conquest, settlement, and evangelization was strongest. Exceptions were the Philippines and Goa (India), where indigenous populations took leadership roles. In the Congo, Angola, and Mozambique in West Africa, for example, Portuguese missionaries supported local leaders and Christian rituals amalgamated with traditional practices and beliefs. In the Philippines, Christian rituals and sacraments provided a language for transcending death, a language that fit well with the fluid world of spirits in Tagalog debt offerings. A Jesuit college in Goa trained young Indians as assistants to missionaries. But racial and political prejudices initially prevented ordained Indians from serving as priests in Goa, and tensions frequently erupted. One of the few women to be named in this colonial history was the Congolese Kimpa Vita, who, because she saw herself as a prophet and had a large following dedicated to the restoration of Congolese greatness, was executed by the Congo king, reportedly at the request of Capuchin missionaries.

In China, Protestant and Catholic missionary efforts vacillated between a policy toward a concordance of faiths and one that was antagonistic toward

Asian classical traditions. Francis Xavier and Matteo Ricci in the sixteenth century took the first option and they and like-minded companions led to forty thousand conversions. A 1724 ban forced Christians to go underground until 1840. Persecution continued and in the Boxer uprising of 1900 approximately 32,200 Christians died in the riots. Indigenous clergy and bishops in China have been ordained since 1922. In Japan, waves of favorable treatment and persecutions oscillated, with Christians being perceived as threats or as facilitators of traditional ideals.

Early Protestant missionary efforts in the seventeenth century included that of the Dutch East India Society in Malaysia, the Puritans and the Society of Friends among the North American Indians, and in the eighteenth century, Anglican, Methodist, Lutheran, and Moravian missionaries worked among the American Indians, the East and West Indies, South Sea islands, India, and every continent except Australia.

Although the evils of missionary activity have been emphasized during the last two decades almost to the exclusion of any redeeming features, Stephen Greenblatt offers an interesting summary of New World missions in the following quotation: "[The] recovery of the critical and humanizing power of the marvelous does not magically make up for its use in the discourse of those who came to the New World to possess and enslave . . . but it does suggest that wonder remains available for decency as well as domination."[36]

END OF THE SECOND
MILLENNIUM: 1800–2000

This period begins in the aftermath of the American and French Revolutions. Women's religious lives as before were increasingly bound up with national political developments. In England, for example, the 200-year-old dissolution of Roman Catholic monasteries ended with their reestablishment in the nineteenth century. In women's communities, the distinction between lay sister and choir nun varied considerably from one monastery to another, but the working-class aspirants were not always relegated to being lay-sisters.

The Church found employment for thousands of women in professional full-time church work. The founder of the Sisters of the Society of the Sacred Heart, Madeleine Sophie Barat, wrote, "In convents all are on an equal footing. Why is the world not like that? It would be better governed and a happier place."[37] Ironically, the Virgin Mary continued as an ideal in art and literature in anti-Catholic England, not as a woman who questioned the will of God in the scriptures by asking "How can this be done because I know not man," but as a shy, modest, gentle girl who elicits respect. This image reflected one of the ideals of the Victorian Age, which sought to replace religion with the new myth of women as non-sexual child-angels.

Condescending treatment of religious women and interference in religious women's lives by the American hierarchy increased during the nineteenth century and contributed to the popular image of nuns as naive children in American films. It was not until 1943 that the first program granting the doctorate in theology to women was founded by Sister Madaleva Wolff at St. Mary's College in Notre Dame, Indiana.

In late nineteenth-century France, the strong anticlericalism in domestic policies can be traced to the 1870s when a rightist government and anti-Semitic military regime brought Alfred Dreyfus, an Alsatian Jew, to trial for treason. After a number of exposés and a retrial as corrupt as the first, Dreyfus was pardoned. But by this time the country was hopelessly divided and a law mandating the separation of church and state was passed in 1905.

This law culminated a stormy history in which the Huguenots (Protestants of the middle class) had been granted religious rights under the Edict of Nantes in 1598 only to have to flee to other countries when the Edict was revoked in 1685. Following the highly contested law of 1905, the movement called Social Catholicism attempted to recognize problems of industrialization, to search for remedies through the study of the problem and theory, and to make a commitment to the working poor through practice.

The 1905 law was subsequently repealed largely because of the efforts of Marc and Renée Sangnier to found Sillon (which had men's and women's sections) to demonstrate its harmful effects on women. But Jeanne Chenu with Baronne Picard founded Action sociale de la femme,

which became an officially registered society after a highly successful lecture series, begun in women's homes, expanded to fill a 1,000-seat lecture
hall. The society's monthly bulletin, *Action sociale de la femme,* contained articles on social issues (such as the lack of legal rights for married women),
on the possibility of a Christian feminism, and on literature. The organization was powerful within the Social Catholic movement and strengthened
the discussion of women's roles in society, especially in support of
women's suffrage.

Several French Catholic upper-class women attempted to build
bridges with the working class. Mule Gahéry, Mime Lye Fer de la Motte,
Mule de Miribel, and Léonie Chaptal independently founded a series of
houses in working-class districts to help poor women with child care,
laundry services, medical care, nursing schools, and popular education.
Mule Marie-Louise and Soeur Milcent, a Vincent de Paul nun, organized
a union for women workers to improve working conditions and to intro-
duce labor reform legislation.

Perhaps the most militant women's organization was the Ligue patriotique des françaises (originally the Ligue patriotique des femme
françaises), founded in 1902 to protest the 1901 state decree banning all
unauthorized religious orders and barring all members of religious orders
from teaching. Although the Ligue was unable to get the law repealed,
they found their own voice and prepared the way for a later generation to
challenge both papal and clerical pronouncements, as well as those of the
secularist state.

Even though some of these efforts, inspired by Pope Leo XIII's Re-
rum Novarum, undoubtedly continued the patriarchal and hierarchical
view of family, religion, and society, these women nevertheless subverted
the restrictive dimensions of Christian social doctrine by engaging in social action. They did things that were novel for women to do and thus
changed the image of women in society as a whole. By encouraging
young women to take up other careers than traditional ones, they were
among the first female trade unionists in France and the first to profes-
sionalize social services. They made Catholic women the most effective
lobby in France for women's suffrage between the two World Wars. They
also maintained a Christian presence during a time when it was unpopu-
lar to speak as Christians, and although they may have been inhibited by
certain kinds of Christian discourse, they changed it by bringing it to bear

on new situations. In addition, they were the forerunners of the priest worker movement and the Taize brothers—individuals and communities that lived among the industrial workers and the poor. Simone Weil, philosopher and mystic, continued the tradition by voluntarily taking a factory job, living among the working poor, and writing penetrating analyses of the problem of dehumanization.

In the United States, both Protestants and Catholics initially had strong European ties or ancestry. By the 1800s most Protestant churches had become independent: the Episcopal Church in 1789; and the Lutheran Church—from approximately 150 distinct groups—formed the Evangelical Lutheran Synodical Conference of North America in 1872, the United Lutheran Church of America in 1914, the American Lutheran Church in 1961, and the Lutheran Church in America in 1962. The Protestant Episcopal Church observes the Scriptures as the ultimate norm of faith and holds as its symbols of doctrine the Apostles Creed, the Nicene Creed, and the 39 articles of the Church of England. By 1970 virtually all Protestant denominations admitted women to ordination, including the United Church of Christ, the American Baptist Convention, the Presbyterians, and the Methodists. In 1971 and 1973, the Anglican bishop of Hong Kong, with the approval of his synod, ordained three women, and in 1974, eleven Anglican women were ordained and prompted the American Episcopal Church later to approve ordination of women. Both Methodists and Episcopalians now have women bishops. Of the Catholic Church, Ann Carr suggested "a new way of thinking about the church as sacrament that might emerge if women were to be included in the future, a model of equality and mutuality that is fully inclusive."[38]

The Adventist Church, founded with William Miller's prediction that the world would end in 1843, reflects the more ambivalent side of the reception of women among Protestant denominations. In 1863, Joseph Bates and James and Ellen White founded the largest branch of Adventists, known as the Seventh Day Adventists. Ordination was forbidden to women on the grounds that they should not lead men; they could, however, act as soloists and directors of congregational singing. In the early years of the Adventist Church, women also contributed many songs in the gospel song tradition; their lyrics were preoccupied with care for children, the needy, home relationships, and the suffering. When gospel singing became commercialized in the twentieth century, however, the number of woman composers declined, and hymn books include only a few, if any, songs by women. In contrast to the Adventist churches, the Shakers believed that the male principle was incarnated in Jesus, the female principle in Mother Ann Lee, the founding mother, and practiced sexual equality, celibacy, and communal ownership of property. Mother Ann, a visionary, used singing, dancing, and marching to move the community to religious feeling and duty.

Gospel song derived originally from African-American spirituals and reflected a "rediscovered matriarchy." For the first century of their existence in North America (from 1619 to the 1740s), blacks were not encouraged by and large to enter Christian churches and continued their own traditions and religions of Africa—which centered on good and evil forces in the universe and included the Christian God, who could free them from slavery. Black women, both free and slave, were more likely than black men to become Christian. During the First Great Awakening (1730s and 1740s) and especially during the Second (early 1900s), many blacks were attracted by the evangelical emphasis on subjective knowledge of God: amalgamating the African cosmology of spirit and body with Jewish and Christian symbols, they founded churches with a theology of liberation, self-determination, and autonomy. Out of these churches grew the traditions of accommodation and protest—traditions immortalized by black women writers such as Sojourner Truth, Phillis Wheatley, Amanda Berr Smith, Ida B. Wells-Barnett, and Anna Julia Cooper, traditions that shaped the Civil Rights movement of the 1960s. Historians have spotlighted the work of Martin Luther King, Jr., a Christian minister, and Malcolm X, a Muslim. But it was Rosa Parks and 15-year-old Claudette Colvin who, in separate incidents, set off the movement by refusing to give up their seats on a bus. In King's own view, they had been "tracked by the Zeitgeist—the spirit of the time."[39] Renata Weems on womanists' use of the Bible, Jacqelyn Grant's distinction between white women's Christ and black women's Jesus, and Delores William's retrieval of Hagar in the Book of Genesis are examples of current developments in black womanist theology.

Christianity in Africa continued through World War II and after as recognizably Protestant or Catholic. Today, however, other church forms, such as the African Independent Church, the Aratai (Spirit-church, or African Orthodox Church), and the Sacred Order of the Cherubim and

Seraphim are new combinations of Christian liturgical, symbolic, or charismatic emphases and indigenous regional religious sensibilities. In all of these denominations, women are trained for and exercise parish leadership roles.

Among Hispanics in South America, Cuba, Mexico, and Puerto Rico, Pentecostalism, Catholic liberation theology, and mujerista (Spanish for "womanist") theology all explicitly include women. For example, mujerista leaders Ada María Isasi-Díaz and Yolanda Tarango emphasize praxis (reflection with action) to make a new human world of ideas, symbols, language, science, religion, art, and materials. A mujerista struggles to liberate herself from the sexism in her own and in the dominant culture, not as an individual but as a member of a community. She aims to understand how racism/ethnic prejudice, economic oppression, and sexism reinforce each other. Mujerista theology attempts to make sexism recognized by men and women, to do critical reflection from a specific place, and to make explicit one's ongoing commitment either to tolerate or to resist sexual oppression. At the same time mestizaje combines three sources— Amerindian, African, and Spanish—in communal expressions of popular religion, such as fairs, processions, and novenas. Since the movement is only twenty years old, mestizajes have a vivid sense that "La vida es la lucha" (life is the struggle).

Today the zeal to restore women's voices at all levels of the Christian church has burgeoned into a global chorus. To recognize this chorus is not to devalue silence whenever it is voluntarily undertaken. But in the words of poet Audre Lorde, whose life was celebrated in the Cathedral of St. John the Divine in New York City on the occasion of her death in 1993, "it is not difference which immobilizes us, but silence."[40] What will be the "place" of women in the church and society? Only women can determine that based on their own experience.

7

Islam

By Riffat Hassan

THE STORY OF my life began in an old house that stood at the end of a galee, or narrow street, adjoining Temple Road in the historic city of Lahore in what is now Pakistan. From an objective standpoint, my siblings and I were privileged children. We were born into an upper-class Saiyyad family, and the Saiyyads, being the descendants of the Holy Prophet Muhammad, are regarded as the highest caste of Muslims, even though Muslims constantly protest against the idea that Islam has any caste system. My father and mother came from among the oldest and most distinguished families in the city. We lived in a spacious kothee (bungalow) and had a glamorous automobile (when only a handful of people had any) and a household full of servants who performed all the domestic chores. We went to the best English-medium schools (which were regarded as a status symbol), where we received a sound British education. However with all of these bounties, I have few happy memories of the house in which I was born, where I spent the first seventeen years of my life. What I remember most distinctly about being a child was how lonely I felt in a house full of people, and how unhappy, scared, and bewildered I was most of the time.

My father was resolutely traditional and conventional. Through most of my life I hated his traditionalism, because I understood it almost exclusively in terms of his belief in gender roles and his conviction that it was best for girls to be married at age sixteen to someone who had been picked out for them by their parents. My mother was equally resolute, but as a non-conformist. What made her very unusual in a traditional society, and in my father's house, was her rejection of the hallowed cult of women's inferiority and submissiveness to men. Pre-Islamic Arabs had buried their daughters alive because they regarded daughters not only as economic liabilities but also as potential hazards to the honor of the men in the tribe. Islam notwithstanding, the attitude of Muslims toward daughters has remained very similar to that of their nomadic forebears. Against this, my mother, a gifted poet with a brilliant mind, believed strongly in women's autonomy and independence. She protected me from being sacrificed on the altar of blind conventionalism and certainly gave me the opportunity to become a "person." Although long before I began to understand the complexities and ambiguities of the Muslim value-system, I knew that my mother would not win any popularity contest vis-à-vis my father. My father, who was admired and loved by so many, seemed to me through most of my early life to be a figure of dread, representing conventional morality in a society that demanded that female children be discriminated against from the moment of birth.

My twelfth year was a landmark year because during it my struggle as an activist feminist began. Until that time I had been a quiet child living for the most part in an inner sanctuary. My second sister, who was sixteen, was married off to a man with a lot of money and very little education. She had tried to resist the arranged marriage but had succumbed, as most girls do, to the multifarious, crude as well as subtle, ways of persuading wavering girls to accept the arrangement in order to safeguard the family's "honor" and her own "happiness." Seeing her fall into the all-too-familiar trap, I experienced total panic. I was the next in line. At twelve I had not yet learned to fight. I had not wanted to learn to fight. I simply wanted to be left alone in my dream world, where I could write my poems and read my books . . . but I knew then, as I know now, that if one is born female in a patriarchal society in which girls are regarded as objects to be given and taken, one has no option but to fight. And so I learned to fight, and the fight continues to this day.

That year my father wanted me to withdraw from the co-educational school where I studied and enroll in an all-girls school. Thinking with the mind of a twelve-year-old, I believed that if I said yes to him once, I would always have to say yes to him. Therefore, I refused and said that if I was forced to leave the school where I had studied for a number of years (and where my brothers still studied), I would not go to another school. Fortunately my father did not force me to leave, but he upbraided my mother constantly for spoiling and misguiding me. From that point on, my mother believed that I had what it took to do what she had wanted to do in her life. Much of what I am today is due to my mother's schooling. But, I could never become the Nietzschean superwoman with a will-to-power she wanted me to be.

My career as a feminist theologian began—almost by accident—in the midst of a very difficult period of my life when I had moved with my very young child to a little-known place called Stillwater, Oklahoma. I had a Ph.D. but very few survival skills when my search for a job that could support me and my child, after the collapse of a marriage in which I had invested a lot, brought me to a small university town in which I knew no one. There, in the fall of 1974, I was asked to be the faculty adviser to the Muslim Students Association (MSA) chapter at Oklahoma State University (OSU), where I had been appointed a visiting assistant professor in Religion and Humanities. The MSA had chapters in many colleges and universities in the United States and Canada.

The membership of the MSA chapter at OSU consisted entirely of Arab men largely from Saudi Arabia and Kuwait. These men were so patriarchal in their mindset that they did not allow women to become members of the MSA. However, there was a rule at OSU whereby every student chapter had to have a faculty adviser, and that year I happened to be the only Muslim faculty member on campus. This is how I came to be the faculty adviser to this group of Arab men who made it clear to me from the outset that they were not too thrilled at the prospect of working with a woman!

The MSA at OSU had a tradition of having an annual seminar in late fall, and it was customary for the faculty adviser to make an introductory presentation on the subject or theme of the seminar. However, in my case, I was asked to read a paper on women in Islam which—incidentally—was not the subject of that year's seminar. Knowing that, in general, faculty advisers were not assigned specific subjects, I resented being asked to address a topic in which I was not much interested at that time. Furthermore, I knew that I had been assigned this particular subject because in the opinion of most of the chapter members, it would have been wholly inappropriate to expect a Muslim woman, even one who taught them Islamic

Studies, to be competent to speak on any other subject pertaining to Islam. Despite my reservations I accepted the invitation for two reasons. First, I knew that being asked to address an all-male, largely Arab Muslim group, which excluded women from being even a part of the audience (though many of the male Arabs had wives who helped them in organizing the event) and which thought that hearing the voice of a woman unrelated to them was haram (forbidden), all this was in itself a breakthrough. Second, I was so tired of hearing Muslim men pontificate upon the position, status, or role of women in Islam, while it was totally inconceivable any woman could presume to talk about the position, status, or role of men in Islam. I thought that it might be worthwhile for a Muslim woman to present her viewpoint on a subject whose immense popularity with Muslim men, scholars and non-scholars alike, could easily be gauged by the ever increasing number of books, booklets, brochures, and articles they published on it. Having accepted the invitation, I began my research, more out of a sense of duty than with any clear awareness that I had set out on the most important journey of my life.

Prior to engaging in any discussion of women's issues in Islam, it is useful to have a clear understanding of what is meant by the source works of Islam or the Islamic tradition, since there is much confusion regarding the range of the meaning of these terms. If one asks an average Muslim what he or she understands by Islam or the Islamic tradition, he or she is likely to refer to one or more of the following sources: the Qur'an (the Book of Revelations), the Sunnah (the practice of the Prophet Muhammad), Hadith (the sayings ascribed to the Prophet Muhammad), Fiqh (Jurisprudence), Madahib (Schools of Law), and the Shari'ah (the code of laws that regulates all aspects of Muslim life). If all of the above-mentioned sources of Islam formed a coherent, homogeneous body of knowledge, perhaps one could include all of them in the term Islam. But this is very far from being the case. Not only are there numerous problems of internal inconsistency within the area of Hadith and Sunnah and the Schools of Law, for example, but also it does not seem possible, in my opinion, to resolve the conflicts among the different "sources" of Islam.

The Islamic tradition, like the other major religious traditions of the world, comes from multiple sources. The most important among these sources are The Qur'an; Sunnah and Hadith; Ijma'; and Qiyas or Ijtihad. Given below are points of significance pertaining to each of these sources.

(1) The Qur'an: Muslims believe the Qur'an to be God's unadulterated Word transmitted through the agency of Angel Gabriel to the Prophet Muhammad, a Meccan Arab born in A.D. 570. The Qur'an consists of a series of revelations that the Prophet Muhammad received over a period of about 23 years. He conveyed these revelations without error or change to the first body of Muslims. The revelations were recorded during the lifetime of Muhammad, who recited the Qur'an in its entirety before his death. The Qur'an consists of a single, standardized text in Arabic, which, unlike some other sacred books, does not have multiple versions, though it has been translated into numerous languages. For Muslims the Qur'an is *the primary source* of normative Islam. The belief that there is no human element involved in the process of the transmission of revelation from God to humankind is what gives to the Qur'an its absolute authority.

(2) Sunnah and Hadith: Next to the Qur'an, the most important sources of the Islamic tradition are Sunnah or the practice of the Prophet Muhammad, and Hadith or the sayings attributed to the Prophet Muhammad. Since Islam, the youngest of the world's major religions, is fully historical, there is a good deal of information and documentation available with regards to the actions of the Prophet Muhammad. However, the area of Hadith, unlike that of Sunnah, is fraught with controversy. This has something to do with the fluid and changing nature of oral tradition itself, but there are also other reasons why many scholars of Islam have tended to express caution, if not skepticism, regarding the issue of the authenticity of individual ahadith (plural of hadith), or of Hadith literature as a whole.

The Arabian Peninsula, in which Islam arose, had been the home of nomadic tribes which had little experience of governance until they were unified into a Muslim ummah (community) by the new religion and its Prophet and left the shores of their homeland to encounter other cultures. The early Muslims had remarkable success in their outward march both eastward and westward and began the establishment of an empire stretching from Spain to India within the course of a century. However, in their encounter with other cultures that were very different from their own, they had to deal with a host of problems for which they had no ready-made solutions. It was natural for them to look for guidance in what they knew best—the Qur'an, and the example of the

Prophet Muhammad. Eagerness to use the Prophet's wisdom in resolving current issues led to a frantic search for ahadith. Soon there were millions of ahadith in circulation. This caused grave concern to the Muslim scholars of that time, some of whom set out to develop a system for the scientific study of the voluminous body of materials that comprises Hadith literature. Realizing that the vast majority of ahadith were not the words of the Prophet Muhammad, they established stringent rules for evaluating the authenticity of a hadith and the degree of reliability that could be attached to it.

Muhammad ibn Isma'il al Bukhari (A.D. 810–870) and Muslim bin al-Hajjaj (A.D. 817 or 821–875) were the compilers of the two most influential Hadith collections in Sunni Islam, which is followed by the majority of Muslims in the world. Although their work was thorough and painstaking, the area of Hadith literature remains problematic largely because the average Muslim lacks scientific knowledge of this discipline, which evolved to eliminate spurious or inauthentic ahadith.

With regards to the Hadith literature, a distinction needs to be made between those ahadith that are in conformity with the Qur'an and those that are not. Obviously the former must be accepted as "authentic" and the latter as "spurious." Those tenets of the Shari'ah that are based on the former confirm or reinforce Qur'anic teaching and, therefore, are binding on Muslims, but if there is anything in the Shari'ah that is based upon a hadith that can be shown to be contradictory to the Qur'an, then it is obviously not binding on Muslims. The situation regarding those areas of human life that are not directly covered by the Qur'an but are alluded to by the Hadith literature is more complicated. Not only must the relevant ahadith be tested for authenticity (in terms of the reliability of transmission) according to the technical criteria established by scholars with expertise in this area, but also the context and content of the ahadith must be scrutinized in order to determine whether the ahadith in question are merely descriptive or also normative. Muhammad Iqbal, modern Islam's most outstanding thinker, distinguishing between those ahadith that are of a purely legal character and those that are non-legal, observes:

> With regards to the former, there arises a very important question as to how far they embody the pre-Islamic usages of Arabia which were

in some cases left intact, and in others modified by the Prophet. It is difficult to make this discovery, for our early writers do not always refer to pre-Islamic usages. Nor is it possible to discover that the usages, left intact by express or tacit approval of the Prophet, were intended to be universal in their application. Shah Wali Ullah has a very illuminating discussion on the point. I reproduce here the substance of his view. The prophetic method of teaching, according to Shah Wali Ullah, is that, generally speaking, the law revealed by a prophet takes a special note of the habits, ways and peculiarities of the people to whom he is specifically sent. The prophet who aims at all-embracing principles, however, can neither reveal different principles for different peoples nor leave them to work out their own rules of conduct. His method is to train one particular people, and to use them as a nucleus for the building up of a universal Shari'at (Shari'ah). In doing so he accentuates the principles underlying the social life of all mankind, and applies them to concrete cases in the light of the specific habits of the people immediately before him. The Shari'at (Shari'ah) values (Ahkam) resulting from this application (e.g., rules relating to penalties for crimes) are in a sense specific to that people; and since their observance is not an end in itself they cannot be strictly enforced in the case of future generations. It was perhaps in view of this that Abu Hanifa, who had a keen insight into the universal character of Islam, made practically no use of these traditions. The fact that he introduced the principle of "Istihsan," i.e. juristic preference, which necessitates a careful study of actual conditions in legal thinking, throws further light on the motives which determined his attitude towards this source of Muslim law.[1]

In the absence of a Qur'anic dictum on a particular issue, the degree of authority or applicability that a hadith ought to have would depend, then, on a number of factors with most of which the average Muslim is totally unfamiliar.

Complex as the area of Hadith is, it has been pointed out by noted Islamicists, both Muslim and non-Muslim, that Hadith is very important as a source of law, and even of doctrine, in Islam. It has been the lens through which the Qur'an has been seen since the early centuries of Islam. Also, the significance of its emotive aspect is hard to overstate, as anything associated with Prophet Muhammad evokes a high degree of veneration among Muslims.

(3) Ijma' denotes consensus of the community and is regarded as being "perhaps the most important legal notion in Islam" by Muhammad Iqbal, who observes:

It is strange that this important notion, while invoking great academic discussion in early Islam, remained practically a mere idea, and rarely assumed the form of a permanent institution in any Muslim country. Possibly its transformation into a permanent legislative institution was contrary to the political interests of the kind of absolute monarchy that grew up in Islam immediately after the fourth Caliph. . . . It is, however, extremely satisfactory to note that the pressure of new world forces and the political experience of European nations are impressing on the mind of modern Islam the value and possibilities of the idea of Ijma'. The growth of republican spirit, and the gradual formation of legislative assemblies in Muslim lands constitutes a great step in advance. The transfer of the power of Ijtihad from individual representatives of schools to a Muslim legislative assembly which, in view of the growth of opposing sects, is the only possible form Ijma' can take in modern times, will secure contributions to legal discussions from laymen who happen to possess a keen insight into affairs. In this way alone we can stir into activity the dormant spirit of life in our legal system, and give it an evolutionary outlook.[2]

Traditional Islam has taken the position that the Ijma' of the first three centuries of Islam is "protected from error" and thus binding on all future generations and that in view of its infallibility and authority there is no need for any Ijma' in the present or the future. Some modern thinkers have challenged this position pointing out that "protection from error" is not to be understood in an absolute sense and does not amount to infallibility for all times as only Allah is infallible in an absolute sense; therefore, though the Ijma' of a particular period or place may be regarded as authoritative for that period or place it does not bind all Muslims of all times and places. In this context, Iqbal discriminates between a decision relating to a question of fact and the one relating to a question of law. In the former case, as for instance, when the question arose whether the two small Suras known as "Muavazatain" formed part of the Qur'an or not, and the Companions unanimously decided that they did, we are bound by their decision, obviously because the Companions alone were in a position to know the fact. In the latter case the question is one of interpretation only, and I venture to think, on the authority of Karkhi, that later generations are not bound by the decision of the Companions. Says Karkhi: The Sunnah of the Companions is binding in matters which cannot be cleared up by Qiyas, but it is not so in matters which can be established by Qiyas.[3]

To sum up this point, Ijma' that derives its sanction from a number of Qur'anic texts (e.g., Surah 2: Al-Baqarah: 43; Surah 3: Al-'Imran: 102; Surah 4: An-Nisa': 115) is an invaluable instrument of law-making by means of which Islam can become dynamic but it has been used—unfortunately—to keep Islam static through the insistence of the traditionalists who say that only the Ijma' of a particular time or group of people is to be considered a source of the Shari'ah. This attitude is not defensible either from the perspective of Qur'anic teaching, which condemns blind imitation of "tradition," or on grounds of human reason.

(4) Qiyas or analogical deduction is a form of Ijtihad that literally means "to exert." Describing Ijtihad as "the principle of movement in Islam," Iqbal says:

In the terminology of Islamic law, Ijtihad means to exert with a view to form an independent judgment on a legal question. The idea . . . has its origin in a well-known verse of the Qur'an; "And to those who exert We show Our path!" We find it more definitely adumbrated in a tradition of the Holy Prophet. When Ma'ad was appointed ruler of Yemen, the Prophet is reported to have asked him how he would decide matters coming up before him. "I will judge matters according to the Book of God," said Ma'ad. "But if the Book of God contains nothing to guide you?" "Then I will act on the precedents of the Prophet of God." "But if the precedents fail?" "Then I will exert to form my own judgment." The student of the history of Islam, however, is well aware that with the political expansion of Islam systematic legal thought became an absolute necessity, and our early doctors of law, both of Arabian and non-Arabian descent, worked ceaselessly until all the accumulated wealth of legal thought found a final expression in our recognized schools of Law. These schools of law recognize three degrees of Ijtihad: (1) complete authority in legislation which is practically confined to the founders of schools, (2) relative authority which is to be exercised within the limits of a particular school, and (3) special authority which relates to the determining of the law applicable to a particular case left undetermined by the founders. . . . The theoretical possibility of (the first) degree of Ijtihad is admitted by the Sunnis, but in practice it has always been denied ever since the establishment of the schools, inasmuch as the idea of complete Ijtihad is hedged around by conditions which are well-nigh impossible of realization in a single individual. Such an attitude seems exceedingly strange in a system of law based mainly on the groundwork provided by the Qur'an which embodies an essentially dynamic outlook on life.[4]

It is not surprising that the most profound of modern Muslim thinkers such as Syed Ahmad Khan and Iqbal stressed the tremendous importance of reopening the gates of Ijtihad at the same time as they advocated a return to the simplicity and universality of the Qur'an. Iqbal represents what I believe is the true spirit of Islam when he makes these observations concerning the exercise of Ijtihad:

I know the Ulama of Islam claim finality for the popular schools of Muslim Law, though they never found it possible to deny the theoretical possibility of a complete Ijtihad. . . . For fear of . . . disintegration, the conservative thinkers of Islam focused all their efforts on the one point of preserving a uniform social life for the people by a jealous exclusion of all innovations in the law of Shari'at (Shari'ah) as expounded by the early doctors of Islam. Their leading idea was social order, and there is no doubt that they were partly right, because organization does to a certain extent counteract the forces of decay. But they did not see, and our modern Ulama do not see, that the ultimate fate of a people does not depend so much on organization as on the worth and power of individual men. In an over-organized society the individual is altogether crushed out of existence. . . . The closing of the door of Ijtihad is pure fiction suggested partly by the crystalliza-tion of legal thought in Islam, and partly by that intellectual laziness which, especially in a period of spiritual decay, turns great thinkers into idols. If some of the later doctors have upheld this fiction, mod-ern Islam is not bound by this voluntary surrender of intellectual in-dependence . . . since things have changed and the world of Islam is today confronted and affected by new forces set free by the extraordi-nary development of human thought in all its directions, I see no rea-son why this attitude (of the Ulama) should be maintained any longer. Did the founders of our schools ever claim finality for their reasonings and interpretations? Never. The claim of the present gener-ation of Muslim liberals to re-interpret the foundational legal princi-ples, in the light of their own experience and altered conditions of modern life is, in my opinion, perfectly justified. The teaching of the Qur'an that life is a process of progressive creation necessitates that each generation, guided but unhampered by the work of its predeces-sors, should be permitted to solve its own problems.[5]

Having clarified what is meant by the sources of Islam, it needs to be underscored that despite Muslim claims that Islam has given women more rights than any other tradition, the Islamic tradition has, by and large, re-mained rigidly patriarchal. Muslim women, like women in other patriar-chal cultures, have seldom been able to acquire scholarship, particularly in the realm of religious thought. This means that the sources of Islam have been interpreted almost exclusively by Muslim men, who have arrogated to themselves the task of defining the ontological, theological, sociologi-cal, and eschatological status of Muslim women. It is hardly surprising that until now the majority of Muslim women who have been kept for cen-turies in physical, mental, and emotional bondage, have accepted this situ-ation passively. Here it needs to be mentioned that although the rate of literacy is low in many Muslim countries, the rate of literacy of Muslim women, especially those who live in rural areas where most of the popula-tion lives, is among the lowest in the world.

Between 1974 and 1984, I studied the Qur'anic passages relating to women and reinterpreted them from a non-patriarchal perspective. I was also observing during my frequent visits to Pakistan and my travels in other Muslim countries that alarming developments were taking place under the cover of so-called Islamization. A simple definition of Islamization is that it is the promulgation by the governments of some Muslim countries of laws that are designed to make them more Muslim. If one examines the contents of these laws, one finds that their primary focus is women. In order to understand the motivation underlying the Islamization process, it is useful to bear in mind that of all the challenges confronting the contemporary Muslim world, the greatest appears to be that of modernity. Unable to come to grips with modernity as a whole, many contemporary Muslim societies make a sharp distinction between two aspects of it. The first—generally referred to as modernization and largely approved of—is identified with science, technology, and a better standard of living. The second—generally referred to as Westernization and largely disapproved of—is identified with emblems of mass Western culture such as promiscuity, the breakup of family and community, latch-key kids, and drug and alcohol abuse. Many Muslims see emancipated women not as symbols of modernization but as symbols of Westernization, which is linked not only with the colonization of Muslim people by Western powers in the not-too-distant past but also with the continuing onslaught by Westerners and Westernized Muslims on "the integrity of the Islamic way of life."

Many traditional societies—including the Muslim—divide the world into private space (that is, the home, which is the domain of women) and public space (that is, the rest of the world, which is the domain of men). Muslims, in general, tend to believe that it is best to keep men and women segregated, in their separate, designated spaces, because the intrusion of women into men's space is seen as leading to the disruption, if not the destruction, of the fundamental order of things. If some exigency makes it necessary for women to enter into men's space, they must make themselves "faceless," or, at least, as inconspicuous as possible. This is achieved through veiling, which is thus an extension of the idea of the segregation of the sexes.

Women-related issues pertaining to various aspects of personal as well as social life lie at the heart of much of the ferment or unrest that characterizes the Muslim world. Many of the issues are not new, but the manner in which they are being debated today is. Much of this on-going debate has been generated by the enactment of manifestly anti-women laws in Muslim countries such as Pakistan, where General Muhammad Zia-ul-Haq promulgated the Hudood Ordinance (1979), the Law of Evidence (1984), and the Qisas and Diyat Ordinance (1990), which discriminate against women in a blatant manner. These laws, which pertained to women's testimony in cases of their own rape or in financial and other matters and to blood money for women's murder, aimed at reducing the value and status of women systematically, virtually mathematically, to less than those of men. The emergence of women's protest groups in Pakistan was very largely a response to the realization that forces of religious conservatism (aided by the power of the military government) were determined to cut the status of women down to half or less of men, and that this attitude stemmed from a deep-rooted desire to keep women in their place, which is understood as being secondary, subordinate, and inferior to that of men.

In 1983–84, I spent two years in Pakistan. It was the time when Islamization was at its peak and there was a deluge not only of anti-women legislation but also of anti-women literature. Reflecting upon what I was witnessing, I asked myself how it was possible for laws that were archaic and unjust to be implemented in a society that professed a passionate commitment to modernity. The answer came to me with stunning clarity. Pakistani society (or any other Muslim society for that matter) could enact or accept laws that specified that women were less than men in fundamental ways because Muslims, in general, consider it a self-evident truth that women are not equal to men.

Because at that time I was the only Muslim woman in Pakistan who was attempting to interpret the Qur'an systematically from a nonpatriarchal perspective, I was approached numerous times by women leaders (including the members of the Pakistan Commission on the Status of Women, before whom I gave testimony in May 1984) to state what my findings were and if they could be used to improve the situation of women in Pakistani society. I was urged by those spirited women, who were mobilizing and leading women's protests in the streets, to help them refute the arguments that were being used to make them less than fully human on a case-by-case or point-by-point basis. However, I knew through my long and continuing struggle with the forces of Muslim traditionalism (which were now being gravely threatened by what was described as "the onslaught of Westernization under the guise of modernization") that the arguments being broadcast to keep women in their place were only the front line of attack. Behind and below these arguments were others, and no sooner would one line of attack be eliminated than another one would be set up in its place. What had to be done, first and foremost, in my opinion, was to examine the theological ground in which all the anti-women arguments were rooted to see if, indeed, a case could be made for asserting that from the point of view of normative Islam, men and women were *essentially* equal, despite biological and other differences.

As a result of my study and deliberation, I came to perceive that not only in the Islamic, but also in the Jewish and Christian, traditions, there are three theological assumptions on which the superstructure of men's alleged superiority to women has been erected. These three assumptions are (1) that God's primary creation is man, not woman, because woman is believed to have been created from man's rib, hence is derivative and secondary ontologically; (2) that woman, not man, was the primary agent of what is customarily described as the "Fall," or man's expulsion from the Garden of Eden, hence all "daughters of Eve" are to be regarded with hatred, suspicion, and contempt; and (3) that woman was created not only *from* man but also *for* man, which makes her existence merely instrumental and not of fundamental importance.

It is not possible, within the scope of this essay, to deal exhaustively with any of the above-mentioned questions. However, in the following brief discussion of each question, an attempt is made to highlight the way in which sources of normative Islam have been interpreted to show that women are inferior to men. Of these three questions, the first is the most fundamental.

This is so because if man and woman have been created equal by God, who is the ultimate arbiter of value, they cannot become unequal *essentially* at a subsequent time. On the other hand, if man and woman have been created unequal by God, then they cannot become equal *essentially* at a subsequent time.

Muslims generally believe, as seriously as many Jews or Christians, that Adam was God's primary creation and that Eve was made from Adam's rib. Although this myth is obviously rooted in the Yahwists' account of creation in Genesis 2:18–24, it has no basis whatever in the Qur'an, which in the context of human creation speaks always in completely egalitarian terms. In none of the thirty or so passages that describe the creation of humanity (designated by generic terms such as an-nas, al-insan, and bashar) by God in a variety of ways is there any statement that could be interpreted as asserting or suggesting that man was created prior to woman or that woman was created from man. The Qur'an notwithstanding, Muslims believe that Hawwa' (the Hebrew/Arabic counterpart of Eve), who incidentally is never mentioned in the Qur'an, was created from the "crooked" rib of Adam. Adam, by the way, is not an Arabic term but a Hebrew one, meaning "of the soil" (from adamah, the soil). The Hebrew term Adam functions generally as a collective noun referring to the human species rather than to a male human being. In the Qur'an also, the term Adam refers, in twenty-one out of twenty-five instances, to humanity. Here it is of interest to note that though the term Adam mostly does not refer to a particular human being, it does refer to human beings in a particular way. As pointed out by Muhammad Iqbal:

Indeed, in the verses which deal with the origin of man as a living being, the Qur'an uses the words Bashar or Insan, not Adam, which it reserves for man in his capacity of God's viceregent on earth. The purpose of the Qur'an is further secured by the omission of proper names mentioned in the Biblical narration—Adam and Eve. The term Adam is retained and used more as a concept than as a name of a concrete human individual. The word is not without authority in the Qur'an itself.[6]

If the Qur'an makes no distinction between the creation of man and woman—as it clearly does not—why do Muslims believe that Hawwa' was created from the rib of Adam? Although the Genesis 2 account of woman's creation is accepted by virtually all Muslims, it is difficult to believe that it entered the Islamic tradition directly, for very few Muslims ever read the Bible. It is much more likely that it became a part of Muslim heritage through its assimilation in the Hadith literature. That the Genesis 2 idea of woman being created from Adam's rib did, in fact, become incorporated in the Hadith literature is evident from a number of ahadith. Of these, six are particularly important since they appear to have had a formative impact on how Muslims have perceived women's being and sexuality as differentiated from men's. The matn (content) of these six ahadith—three from Sahih Al-Bukhari and three from Sahih Muslim is given below:

- Treat women nicely, for a woman is created from a rib, and the most curved portion of the rib is its upper portion, so if you would try to straighten it, it will break, but if you leave it as it is, it will remain crooked. So treat women nicely.[7]
- The woman is like a rib, if you try to straighten her, she will break. So if you want to get benefit from her, do so while she still has some crookedness.[8]
- Whoever believes in Allah and the Last Day should not hurt (trouble) his neighbor. And I advise you to take care of the women, for they are created from a rib and the most crooked part of the rib is its upper part; if you try to straighten it, it will break, and if you leave it, it will remain crooked, so I urge you to take care of woman.[9]
- Woman is like a rib. When you attempt to straighten it, you would break it. And if you leave her alone you would benefit by her, and crookedness will remain in her.[10]
- Woman has been created from a rib and will in no way be straightened for you; so benefit by her while crookedness remains in her. And if you attempt to straighten her, you will break her, and breaking her is divorcing her.[11]
- He who believes in Allah and the Hereafter, if he witnesses any matter he should talk in good terms about it or keep quiet. Act kindly towards women, for woman is created from a rib, and the most crooked part of the rib is its top. If you attempt to straighten it, you will break it, and if you leave it, the crookedness will remain there so act kindly towards women.[12]

I have examined these ahadith elsewhere and have shown them to be flawed with regard to their formal (isnad) as well as their material (matn) aspects. The theology of woman implicit in these ahadith is based upon generalizations about her ontology, biology, and psychology contrary to the letter and spirit of the Qur'an. These ahadith ought, therefore, to have been rejected—because Muslim scholars agree on the principle that any hadith that is inconsistent with the Qur'an cannot be accepted. However, despite the fact that the ahadith in question contradict the teachings of the Qur'an, they have continued to be an important part of the ongoing Islamic tradition. Undoubtedly one of the major reasons for this is that these ahadith come from the two most highly venerated Hadith collections by Muhammad ibn Isma'il al Bukhari and Muslim bin al-Hajjaj. These two collections, known collectively as Sahihan (from sahih, meaning authentic), "form an almost unassailable authority, subject indeed to criticism in details, yet deriving an indestructible influence from the 'ijma' or general consent of the community in custom and belief, which it is their function to authenticate."[13] While inclusion in the Sahihan gives the ahadith in question much weight, their continuing popularity also tells us that they articulate something deeply embedded in Muslim culture—namely the belief that women are derivative creatures who can never be considered equal to men.

Many Muslims, like many Jews and Christians, would say that woman was responsible for the "Fall" of man or his expulsion from paradise, although nothing in the Qur'anic descriptions of the so-called Fall episode would warrant such an answer. Here it may be noted that—whereas in Genesis 3:6, the dialogue preceding the eating of the forbidden fruit by the human pair in the Garden of Eden is between the serpent and Eve (though Adam's presence is also indicated, as contended by feminist theologians) and this has provided the basis for the popular casting of Eve into the role of tempter, deceiver, and seducer of Adam—in the Qur'an, the Shaitan (Satan) has no exclusive dialogue with Adam's zauj (mate). In two of the three passages that refer to this episode, Surah 2: Al-Baqarah: 35–39 and Surah 7: Al-A'raf: 19–25, the Shaitan is stated to have led both Adam and zauj astray though in the former (verse 36), no actual conversation is reported. In the remaining passage, namely, Surah 20: Ta-Ha: 115–24, it is Adam who is charged with forgetting his covenant with God (verse 115), who is tempted by the Shaitan (verse 120), and who disobeys God and allows himself to be seduced (verse 121). If, however, one looks at all three passages as well as the way in which the term Adam functions generally in the Qur'an, it becomes clear that the Qur'an regards the act of disobedience by the human pair in al-jannah (the Garden) as a collective rather than an individual act for which exclusive, or even primary, responsibility is not assigned to either man or woman. Even in the last passage in which Adam appears to be held responsible for forgetting the covenant and for allowing himself to be beguiled by the Shaitan, the act of disobedience, that is, the eating from the "Tree," is committed jointly by Adam and zauj and not by Adam alone or in the first place.

That said, it is extremely important to stress that the Qur'an provides no basis whatever for asserting, suggesting, or implying that Hawwa', having been tempted and deceived by the Shaitan, in turn tempted and deceived Adam and led to his expulsion from al-jannah. This fact notwithstanding, many Muslim commentators have ascribed the primary responsibility for man's Fall to woman. There is hardly any doubt that Muslim women have been as victimized as Jewish and Christian women by the way in which the Jewish, Christian, and Islamic traditions have generally interpreted the Fall episode. However, it needs to be pointed out that the Qur'anic account of the episode differs significantly from the Biblical account and that the Fall does not mean in the Islamic tradition what it means in the Jewish, and particularly in the Christian, tradition.

To begin with, whereas in Genesis 3 no explanation is given as to why the serpent tempts either Eve alone or both Adam and Eve, in the Qur'an the reason why the Shaitan sets out to beguile the human pair in al-jannah is stated clearly in a number of passages. The refusal of the Shaitan to obey God's command to bow in submission to Adam follows from his belief that, being a creature of fire, he is elementally superior to Adam, who is a creature of clay. When condemned for his arrogance by God and ordered to depart in a state of abject disgrace, the Shaitan throws a challenge to the Almighty: he will prove to God that Adam and Adam's progeny are unworthy of the honor and favor bestowed on them by God, being, in general, ungrateful, weak, and easily lured away from the straight path by worldly temptations. Not attempting to hide his intentions to "come upon" human beings from all sides, the Shaitan asks for—and is granted—a reprieve until the Day of the Appointed Time. Not only is the reprieve granted but God also tells the Shaitan to use all his wiles and forces to assault human beings and see if they would follow him. A cosmic drama now begins, involving the eternal opposition between the principles of right and wrong or good and evil, which is lived out because human beings, exercising their moral autonomy, must now choose between the straight path and the crooked path.

In terms of the Qur'anic narrative, what happens to the human pair in al-jannah is a sequel to the interchange between God and Shaitan. In the sequel we learn that Adam and zauj have been commanded not to go near the Tree lest they become zalimin (transgressors). Seduced by the Shaitan, they disobey God. However, in Surah 7: Al-A'raf: 23, they acknowledge before God that they have done zulm (transgression) to themselves and earnestly seek God's forgiveness and mercy. They are told by God to go forth or descend from al-jannah, but in addressing them the Qur'an uses the dual form of address (referring exclusively to Adam and zauj) only once (in Surah 18: Ta-Ha: 123); for the rest, the plural form is used, which necessarily refers to more than two persons and is generally understood as referring to humanity as a whole.

In the framework of Qur'anic theology, the order to go forth from al-jannah given to Adam or the children of Adam cannot be considered a punishment because Adam was always meant to be God's viceregent on earth, as stated clearly in Surah 2: Al-Baqarah: 30. The earth is not a place of banishment but is declared by the Qur'an to be humanity's dwelling place and a source of profit to it. The al-jannah mentioned in the Fall story is not—as pointed out by Muhammad Iqbal—"the super-sensual paradise from which man is supposed to have fallen on this earth."[14]

There is, strictly speaking, no Fall in the Qur'an. What the Qur'anic narration focuses upon is the moral choice that humanity is required to make when confronted by the alternatives presented to them by God and the Shaitan. This becomes clear if one reflects on the text of Surah 2: Al-Baqarah: 35 and Surah 7: Al-A'raf: 19: "You [dual] go not near this Tree, lest you [dual] become of the 'zalimin'." In other words, the human pair is being told that if they go near the Tree, then they will be counted among those who perpetrate zulm. Commenting on the root ZLM, Toshihiko Izutsu says:

The primary meaning of ZLM is, in my opinion and of many of the authoritative lexicologists, that of "putting in a wrong place." In the moral sphere it seems to mean primarily "to act in such a way as to transgress the proper limit and encroach upon the right of some other person." Briefly and generally speaking *zulm* is to do injustice in the sense of going beyond one's bounds and doing what one has no right to.[15]

By transgressing the limits set by God, the human pair become guilty of zulm toward themselves. This zulm consists in their taking on the responsibility for choosing between good and evil. Here it is important to note that

> ... the Qur'anic legend of the Fall has nothing to do with the first appearance of man on this planet. Its purpose is rather to indicate man's rise from a primitive state of instinctive appetite to the conscious possession of a free self, capable of doubt and disobedience. The Fall does not mean any depravity, it is man's transition from simple consciousness to the first flash of self-consciousness, a kind of waking from the dream of nature with a throb of personal casuality in one's own being. Nor does the Qur'an regard the earth as a torture hall where an elementally wicked humanity is imprisoned for an original act of sin. Man's first act of disobedience was also his first act of free choice; and that is why, according to the Qur'anic narration, Adam's first transgression was forgiven. . . . A being whose movements are wholly determined like a machine cannot produce goodness. Freedom is thus a condition of goodness. But to permit the emergence of a finite ego who has the power to choose after considering the relative values of several courses of action open to him, is really to take a great risk: for the freedom to choose good involves also the freedom to choose what is the opposite of good. That God has taken this risk shows his immense faith in man, it is now for man to justify this faith.[16]

Because there is no Fall in the Qur'an, there is no original sin. Human beings are not born sinful into this world, hence do not need to be redeemed or saved. This is generally accepted in the Islamic tradition. However, the association of the Fall with sexuality, which has played such a massive role in perpetuating the myth of feminine evil in the Judaeo-Christian tradition, also exists in the minds of many Muslims and causes untold damage to Muslim women.

The Qur'an, which does not discriminate against women in the context of the Fall episode, does not support the view—held by many Muslims, Christians, and Jews—that woman was created not only from man but also for man. That God's creation as a whole is "for just ends" (Surah 15: Al-Hijr: 85) and not "for idle sport" (Surah 21: Al-Anbiya': 16) is one of the major themes of the Qur'an. Humanity, fashioned "in the best of moulds" (Surah 95: At-Tin: 4) has been created in order to serve God (Surah 51: Adh-Dhariyat: 56). God cannot be separated from service to humankind, or—in Islamic terms—believers in God must honor both Haquq Allah (rights of God) and Haquq al-'ibad (rights of creatures). Fulfillment of one's duties to God and humankind constitutes the essence of righteousness. That men and women are equally called upon by God to be righteous is stated unambiguously in a number of Qur'anic passages, such as the following:

> Believers, men
> And women, are guardians
> of one another: they impose
> What is just, and forbid
> What is evil: they observe
> Regular prayers, practice
> Charity, and obey
> God and his Apostle.
> Upon them will God pour
> His mercy: for God
> Is exalted in power and wise,
> God has promised to believers,
> Men and women, gardens
> Where rivers flow,
> To dwell therein,
> And beautiful mansions
> In gardens of everlasting bliss.
> But the greatest joy
> Is the good pleasure of God:
> That is the highest bliss.

The Qur'an makes clear that not only do men and women stand absolutely equal in the sight of God but also that they are protectors of each other. In other words, the Qur'an does not create a hierarchy in which men are placed above women, nor does it pit men against women in an adversary relationship. They are created as equal creatures of a universal, just, and merciful God whose pleasure it is that they live together in harmony and in righteousness.

Underlying the rejection in Muslim societies of the idea of man-woman equality is the deeply rooted belief that women who are inferior in creation (having been made from a crooked rib) and in righteousness (having helped the Shaitan in defeating God's plan for Adam) have been created mainly to be of use to men, who are superior to them.

The alleged superiority of men to women that permeates the Islamic (as well as the Jewish and Christian) tradition is grounded not only in Hadith literature but also in popular interpretations of some Qur'anic passages. Two Qur'anic passages—Surah 4: An-Nisa':34 and Surah 2: Al-Baqarah: 288—in particular, are generally cited to support the contention that men have "a degree of advantage" over women. Of these, the first reads as follows in A. A. Maududi's translation of the Arabic text:

Men are the managers of the affairs of women because Allah has made the one superior to the other and because men spend their wealth on women. Virtuous women are, thereof, obedient: they guard their rights carefully in their absence under the care and watch of Allah. As for those women whose defiance you have cause to fear, admonish them and keep them apart from your beds and beat them. Then, if they submit to you, do not look for excuses to punish them: note it well that there is Allah above you, Who is Supreme and Great.

It is difficult to overstate the impact of the general Muslim understanding of Surah 4: An-nisa': 34, which is embodied in Maududi's translation. As soon as the issue of women's equality with men is raised, the immediate response by traditionalists is, "But don't you know that God says in the Qur'an that men are 'qawwamun' in relation to women and have the right to rule over them and even to beat them?" In fact, the mere statement "ar-rijal-o qawwamun-a 'ala'an-nisa' " (men are qawwamun in relation to women) signifies the end of any attempt to discuss the issue of woman's equality with man in the Islamic ummah.

It is assumed by almost all who read Surah 4, verse 34, that it is addressed to husbands. The first point to be noted is that it is addressed to ar-rijal (men) and an-nisa' (women). In other words, it is addressed to all men and women of the Islamic community. Further, in relation to all the actions that are required to be taken, the plural and not the dual form (used when reference is made only to two persons) is found. Such usage makes clear that the orders contained in this verse were not addressed to a husband or wife but to the Islamic ummah in general.

The key word in the first sentence of this verse is qawwamun. This word has been translated variously as protectors and maintainers (of women), in charge (of women), having pre-eminence (above women), and sovereigns or masters (over women). Linguistically, the word qawwamun means breadwinners or those who provide a means of support or livelihood. A point of logic that must be made here is that the first sentence is not a descriptive one stating that all men as a matter of fact are providing for women, since obviously there are at least some men who do not provide for women. What the sentence is stating, rather, is that men ought to have the capability to provide (since "ought" implies "can"). In other words, this statement, which almost all Muslim societies have taken to be an actual description of all men, is in fact a normative statement pertaining to the Islamic concept of division of labor in an ideal family or community structure. The fact that men are qawwamun does not mean that women cannot or should not provide for themselves, but simply that in view of the heavy burden that most women shoulder in child bearing and rearing, they should not have the additional obligation of providing the means of living at the same time.

Continuing with the analysis of the passage, we come next to the idea that God has given the one more strength than the other. Most translations make it appear that the one who has more strength, excellence, or superiority is the man. However, the Qur'anic expression does not accord superiority to men. The expression literally means "some in relation to some," so that the statement could mean either some men are superior to some others (men and/or women). The interpretation that seems to me to be the most appropriate contextually is that some men are more blessed with the means to be better providers that are other men.

The next part of the passage begins with a "therefore," which indicates that this part is conditional upon the first: in other words, if men fulfill their assigned function of being providers, women must fulfill their corresponding duties. Most translations describe this duty in terms of the wife being "obedient" to the husband. The word salihat', which is translated as "righteously obedient," is related to the word salahiat (capability or potentiality). A women's special capability is to bear children, and she carries and protects the fetus (which is hidden from the eye) in her womb until it can be safely delivered.

What is outlined in the first part of this passage is a functional division of labor necessary for maintaining balance in any society. Men, who do not have to fulfill the responsibility of childbearing, are assigned the functions of being breadwinners. Women are exempted from the responsibility of being breadwinners in order that they may fulfill their function as child bearers. The two functions are separate but complementary and neither is higher or lower than the other.

The three injunctions in the second part of the verse were given to the Islamic ummah in order to meet a rather extraordinary possibility: a mass rebellion on the part of women against their role as child bearers—a function assigned to them by God. If all or most of the women in a Muslim society refused to bear children without just cause as a sign of organized defiance or revolt, this would mean the end of organized ummah. This situation must, therefore, be dealt with decisively. The first step to be taken is to find out the reasons for this act of defiance and to offer counseling. If this step is unsuccessful, the second step to be taken is isolation of the rebellious women from others. (It is to be noted here that the prescription is to leave the women in solitary confinement. By translating this line, "Keep them apart from your beds," Maududi is suggesting, if not stating, that the judging party is the husband and not the Islamic community—an assumption not warranted by the text.) If the second step is also not successful, then the step of confining women for a longer period of time may be taken by the Islamic community or its representatives. Here, it is important to point out that the Arabic word daraba, which is generally translated as "beating," has numerous meanings. When used in a legal context as it is here, it means "holding in confinement," according to the authoritative lexicon Taj al-'Arus. (In Surah 4: An-Nisa': 15, unchaste women are also prescribed the punishment of being confined to their homes.)

Although, through the centuries, Muslims have interpreted Surah 4: An-Nisa': 34 as giving men unequivocal mastery over women, a linguistically and philosophically/theologically accurate interpretation of this passage would lead to radically different conclusions. In simple words, this passage is saying that since only women can bear children (which is not to say that all women should bear children or that women's sole function is to bear children)—a function whose importance in the survival of any community cannot be questioned—they should not have the additional obligation of being breadwinners while they perform this function. Thus, during the period of a woman's childbearing, the function of breadwinning must be performed by men (not just husbands) in the Muslim ummah. Reflection on this Qur'anic passage shows that the division of functions mandated here is designed to ensure justice in the community as a whole. There are millions of women all over the world who are designated inaccurately as "single" parents (when, in fact, they are "double" parents) who bear and raise children singlehandedly, generally without much support from the community. This surely does not constitute a just situation. If children are the wealth and future of the ummah, the importance of protecting the function of childbearing and child raising becomes self-evident. Statistics from all over the world show that women and children left without the care and custodianship of men suffer from economic, social, psychological, and other ills. What Surah An-Nisa': 34 is ensuring is that this does not happen. It enjoins men in general to assume responsibility for women in general when they are performing the vitally important function of childbearing (other passages in the Qur'an extend this also to child rearing). Thus the intent of this passage, which has traditionally been used to subordinate women to men, is in fact to guarantee women the material (as well as moral) security needed by them during the period of pregnancy when breadwinning can become difficult or even impossible for them.

The second passage which mentions the so-called degree of advantage that men have over women is Surah 2: Al-Baqarah: 228, which reads:

> Divorced women
> Shall wait
> For a three-month period.
> Nor is it lawful for them

To hide what God
Hath created in their wombs,
If they have faith
In God and the last Day.
And their husbands
Have the better right
To take them back
In that period, if
They wish for reconciliation.
And women shall have rights
Similar to the rights
Against them, according
To what is equitable
But men have a degree
(of advantage) over them,
And God is Exalted in Power and Wise.

The advantage that men have over women in this context is that women must observe a three-month period called 'iddat before remarriage, but men are exempted from this requirement. The main reason why women are subjected to this restriction is because at the time of divorce a woman may be pregnant, and this fact may not become known for some time. As men cannot become pregnant, they are allowed to remarry without the waiting period.

In my judgment, the Qur'anic passages—in particular the two discussed above—on which the edifice of male superiority over women largely rests have been misread or misinterpreted, intentionally or unintentionally, by most Muslim societies and men. There is no question that if the Qur'an is read without patriarchal bias, it is extremely protective of the rights of women, especially within the home. There are more laws in the Qur'an about safeguarding the rights of all members of a family than on any other subject. The Qur'an recognized the weak and vulnerable situation of women at the time of the birth of Islam and aimed to uplift them in every way. This concern for women's empowerment was also central to the life and work of the Prophet Muhammad.

The revolution brought about by Islam in the nomadic society of Arabia, in which female children were often buried alive and in which women could be sold or inherited, is illustrated very well by the outstanding women who have inspired Muslim women through the centuries—such as Khadija and 'A'isha, the wives of the Prophet Muhammad, Fatima, his beloved daughter, and Rabi'a, the Sufi par excellence of the eighth century.

Khadija, known in the Muslim tradition as Tahira (the Pure) and Kubra (the Great), was the first and most important wife of Muhammad, who remained monogamous during her lifetime. When Muhammad entered Khadija's life as a young man, she was an older widow who owned property and engaged in trade. She employed Muhammad to take her merchandise to Syria and was so impressed by how well he executed his commission and by his personality that she offered him marriage. Muhammad accepted. Khadija supported him in every way and stood by him through the most difficult times of his life. She was the first person to accept the authenticity of his prophetic mission, and the Prophet Muhammad continued till the end of his life to remember her with the deepest love, respect, and gratitude.

'A'isha, beloved wife of the Prophet Muhammad, is very important in Muslim history not only because she became the Prophet's favorite wife after the death of Khadija but also because she is one of the major transmitters of the ahadith ascribed to him. According to a well-known saying, the Prophet said, "Learn half of the Deen (Principles of Faith) from me and the other half from 'A'isha." A multi-faceted, dynamic woman, 'A'isha is also to be remembered for her strong feminist consciousness, which is reflected in a number of her sayings.

Fatima, the youngest and only surviving child of the Prophet Muhammad and Khadija, is known in the Muslim tradition as Zahra (the Radiant One) and is greatly revered. She continued the bloodline of her father through her marriage to his cousin 'Ali, who is regarded as the first Imam of Shi'ite Muslims, who, after the Sunnis, are the most important sect in Islam. Fatima is the center of piety for many Muslims, who see her as a model to be emulated by all devout women.

Rabi'a's figure is shrouded in legends, including stories of miracles brought about by her intense devotion to God. But sketchy as the historical details of her life are, they point to an extraordinary personality. Probably a fourth (rabi'a) daughter, she was born into extreme poverty. Orphaned at a young age, she was sold into slavery for a paltry sum. She served her master by the day but fasted much and spent most of the night in praying to God. Becoming aware of her profound piety, her master released her from bondage.

Among the devotees of Rabi'a, who lived a celibate, highly austere life, were spiritual and temporal leaders of her time. But though many sought her prayers or guidance, she solicited no help from anyone, including God. Her prayers, including the following, reflect her all-consuming passion for God, which makes even Heaven and Hell irrelevant: "O my Lord, if I worship Thee from fear of Hell, burn me in Hell, and if I worship Thee from hope of Paradise, exclude me thence, but if I worship Thee for Thine own sake then withhold not from me Thine Eternal Beauty."

Rabi'a, the most outstanding Sufi saint in an age of saints, whose name has become a symbol for women who attain the highest spiritual station in any age, has been a source of inspiration to many mystics, including her biographer Farid-ud-din 'Attar who, in his famous poem "The Conference of the Birds," pays her the high compliment of being the Crown of Men (Taj ar-Rijal).

As I look back on my life's journey, I can identify some figures who have been a source of inspiration to me. Among them, perhaps none ranks higher than the poet-philosopher Iqbal, from whom I learned what I consider to be the core of the message of the Qur'an. The outstanding women of early Islam are also very important to me, as are the two real-life women who have had the greatest impact on me—my mother and my daughter. As I think about the debt I owe to those who have helped to shape my mind and soul and the course of my life, I remember my duty to present and future Muslim girls and women and renew my commitment to do what I can to help them achieve self-actualization. I have come a long way since my journey as a feminist theologian began in Stillwater in 1974. My Odyssean venture to make sense of my own life as a Muslim woman through my study of the sources of my religious tradition, history, and culture has taken me from one end of the world to the other. It was been a hard but rewarding quest, which goes on as the struggle to create a world free of injustice and inequity continues.

8

Goddess Spirituality and Wicca

By Wendy Griffin

MY FIRST ENCOUNTER with Goddess Spirituality was in the late 1980s, when a large red-headed student in my Women and Power class stood up and announced she was a feminist Witch and Dianic priestess, and invited the entire class to a ritual celebrating the spring equinox. Being somewhat leery, but definitely curious, I asked a colleague to go with me. We ended up studying and doing research with my student's coven for over a year.

I had read about witchcraft as an occult practice years before, but what I had read was unrelated to either spirituality or feminism. The experience with the coven was different. These women were clearly feminists and believed that, just as the personal was political, so was the spiritual. Women's sexuality and gender politics were central to their analysis. They saw themselves as liberating women's souls and helping to heal women and the planet from the wounds of patriarchy.

There was no sudden conversion on my part, no Road to Damascus experience, just a slow recognition that I was familiar and comfortable with some of the ideas the Witches were sharing with us. It took some time for me to realize the spiritual nature of their practice. I was not a spiritual seeker; I had been an atheist since my early teens. But I had been raised by a spiritual mother who never called what she did "religion." At her summer camp for girls in northern Wisconsin, we would have Sunday twilight meditations by the lake, silent torch-lit processions of women through silver birch groves, and pageants of re-created myths around the campfire. I grew up surrounded by strong, competent, beautiful, empowered women who were at peace with their environment. Encountering Goddess Spirituality was like coming home.[1]

Today I practice my spirituality within a Dianic coven and, at the same time, I celebrate the Wheel of the Year with my life-partner, who, until he met me, was a "solitary" Witch. Although he believes Deity exists, for me the Goddess is a human construct, a metaphor that represents the Web of Life that connects us all. One of the major tenets of Goddess Spirituality is that one does not need to believe in the Goddess to experience Her. I do not believe, but I *have* experienced Her.

THE ROOTS

For a young religion, the history of Goddess Spirituality is fairly complex. In part, this is because the practice today is made up of various distinct strands that might even be considered a family of religions. To explore all of these and do them justice would take a book unto itself.[2] I have chosen to focus on a very few threads that have made the most significant contributions to Goddess Spirituality as we begin the new millennium. The major element that these strands have in common is an honoring of a female representation of Divinity, a Goddess who is simultaneously both one and many[3] and who is immanent in Nature. There is no one name for these spiritual practitioners of this Goddess or even one everyone agrees upon for the practice. Some call themselves pagans,[4] some Wiccans, Witches, or Gaians, and some have no word at all for themselves. Sometimes the strands are called Women's Spirituality, Feminist Spirituality, Paganism, or Witchcraft. All four of these labels attempt to address specific communities within Goddess Spirituality and none are without problems. The majority of religions today are profoundly gendered, some enforcing traditional gender roles, others transforming gender identity. Profoundly spiritual women, many of whom are feminists, have addressed these issues of gender within the context of their own traditional religions that do not revere female divinity. Thus to call Goddess Spirituality *Women's* Spirituality may say very little indeed. And although women do outnumber men, there are men who call upon the Goddess and attend rituals in her name.

The label of Feminist Spirituality is every bit as misleading. Although there are strong elements of feminism in the practice and writings, there are women who believe in the Goddess and are not feminists. They are uninterested in identifying as such, especially younger practitioners. This is even more prominent among the male practitioners, as might be expected. Feminism has influenced some of the strands much more significantly in the United States than in other countries, and even there some who reap the benefits of feminism believe there is no longer a need for it.

For the moment, Goddess Spirituality will have to suffice when speaking of the larger tapestry of the Goddess traditions in the West. The tapestry is of a religion, a varied collection of beliefs, a family of spiritualities, a spiritual journey, and a social movement. In order to see this, we need to examine the individual strands and ideas that go into the weaving.[5] I begin with Witchcraft, for though it is not the whole of the practice, it is a major part and gives shape and color to the greater whole.

THE CRAFT OF THE WISE

The milieu that gave birth to much of contemporary Witchcraft and paganism can be traced back to the late sixteenth century in Scotland and the founding of Freemasonry.[6] Like the medieval craft guilds, Freemasonry had a mythical history and a body of secret knowledge that was taught to initiates. What distinguished it was that it admitted members who were not working in a specific trade, its historical claims were greater, and it was more concerned with the ethical and moral considerations behind Masonic tradition than the trade itself. As Freemasonry spread to England and beyond, it became known as "the Craft" and began to incorporate degrees of initiation. The initiations themselves grew more ritualistic, the five-pointed star called a pentagram was adopted as a major symbol and the four cardinal points of the compass were given esoteric significance and employed in ritual. The eighteenth century saw tremendous growth in

Freemasonry, not only in numbers, but in elaborate rituals and rich symbolic lore as well.

The nineteenth century presented intellectuals with a choice between an orthodox Christianity and the new science, where humans were suddenly but a small part of a vast, mechanized universe. The occult offered a middle path that promised to combine scientific experimentation with the romantic appeal of "ancient wisdom."[7] The British revival of ritual magic began with the founding of the Societas Rosicruciana in Anglia to study the occult sciences. Members of this English Rosicrucian Society were of a specific elite: Christian men who had achieved the highest grade in Freemasonry. The Society for Psychical Research was founded shortly after the Rosicrucian Society, drawing its own elite, including Prime Minister William Gladstone and the poet Alfred Lord Tennyson. On its heels came the Theosophical Society, its offspring the Hermetic Society, and then the Hermetic Order of the Golden Dawn.

The Golden Dawn claimed to trace its knowledge back to ancient philosophers and mysteries. It trained initiates in what were believed to be mystical and magical systems, blending together elements from Freemasonry, Christianity, the cabbala, Tantra, Egyptian mythology, Greco-Egyptian texts, and ceremonial magic. Members learned ritual magic that promised to give them control of or alignment with elemental powers that could be used for practical purposes and specific goals. This was not a religious society but a magical one, where deities were neither worshipped nor invoked to intercede in human affairs, but used to represent certain desirable qualities and empower the practitioner.[8] Envisioned as universal, the presiding female deity wore only the lunar horns of Isis. Though not the only goddess identified with this figure, Isis was extremely important, as Egypt was believed by many to have been the home of magic. The major male god was Pan, favorite of the nineteenth-century poets who saw him as the gentle yet powerful and protective god of the sylvan countryside.

Pan's chosen status can be attributed to several things. In 1862, a retired French historian and anti-Catholic named Jules Michelet published *La Sorcière*. This book claimed that witchcraft was what had survived from an ancient pagan religion, brutally oppressed and driven underground by the Church. Witches, who had once been great healers, held religious sabbaths and worshipped Pan, the god of fertility, whom the Church had confused with Satan. Although never accepted by scholars, the book became a popular best seller and has never been out of print. Pan, frolicking in the woods, was a god of Nature, wild, rebellious, and joyful. His appeal to English romantics at a time when England was undergoing rapid industrialization and urbanization was strong. Within a fairly short time, Pan became the Horned God that some strands of Goddess Spirituality still honor today.

At the turn of the twentieth century, millions of British men and hundreds of women had been initiated and were working in secretive groups that handed down knowledge and practices called the Craft, secrets that were believed to go back to the beginning of recorded history.[9] Then another small book appeared that was to be one of the most important texts of contemporary paganism. *Aradia: Gospel of the Witches* was a collection of stories, spells, and invocations purportedly used by Italian Witches, practitioners of the Old Religion, "the faith of millions in the past."[10] Charles Leland, an American journalist, reportedly received the handwritten manuscript from a young woman named Maddelena, who served as his informant and then disappeared from his life after handing over the Gospel. The book explains how the Goddess Diana was first "before all creation; in her were all things; out of herself, the first darkness, she divided herself; into darkness and light she was divided. Lucifer, her brother and son, herself and her other half, was the light."[11] From this union was born a daughter, Aradia, whom Diana sent to teach humanity Witchcraft and destroy oppression. Leland refers to Aradia as the Messiah, often confused with and reflecting her divine mother. That it was a female sent to teach Witchcraft was understandable, he wrote, "For every woman is at heart a witch."[12]

The idea that Witches were secret practitioners of an ancient religion that passed down esoteric knowledge to initiates was a natural fit. Even the newly formed British Folk Lore Society proclaimed its truth, and when respected Egyptologist Margaret Murray deviated from her established field of scholarship and presented her new work on Witchcraft at the Society's meetings, it was easily accepted. Published in 1921, Murray's *The Witch Cult in Western Europe* argued that witchcraft was a widespread pagan fertility cult that worshipped a horned god of nature. Covens made up of 13 Witches met regularly and held sabbats, religious holidays on the old quarter days that began the Celtic agricultural seasons. Twelve years later, the book appeared in the popular press, slightly reworked to be openly celebratory and painting the Old Religion as a profoundly life-affirming one. Murray attempted to show that the Horned God of the Greenwood was the oldest of all male deities and could be traced across Europe and the Near East, all the way back to the Stone Age. Pan was simply one aspect of this God; perhaps a more significant one was the horned Gallic deity Cernunnos or Herne. The budding goat horns of Pan were also the spreading antlers of the sacred stag.

Shortly after the popular version of *The Witch Cult* was published, a retired civil servant by the name of Gerald Gardner returned to England after spending many years in Ceylon, North Borneo, and Malaya. Fascinated by folklore and the supernatural, he had written several monographs while there, including one on the use of a Malay ceremonial knife. He settled down on the outskirts of the New Forest in southern England, where according to his later writings, he met a woman by the name of Old Dorothy and was initiated into her coven of witches. In 1949, he published *High Magic's Aid,* a novel that represented some of the coven's beliefs and practices. The picture was remarkably similar to Murray's, including a primary male divinity. However, in Gardner's novel, a priestess was necessary to work with the priest in order to invoke deity.

Significantly, the year before in 1948, the acclaimed English poet Robert Graves had published *The White Goddess.* Presenting his work not as fictive narrative but as an authentic work of history, Graves linked the changing aspects of the moon to a universal Goddess, envisioning her as Maiden, Mother, and Crone. He argued that she was the earliest European deity, and, using what he called the historical grammar of poetic myth, he attempted to reveal the secrets held for thousands of years by Her initiates. The Triple Goddess was real, he insisted, and when enough people believed in Her again, Her reign would begin in earnest.

Shortly after the British laws against witchcraft were repealed in 1951, Gardner began to give press interviews, and in 1954 he published *Witchcraft Today,* which was presented as a factual account of English Witchcraft. The religion he described was a nature-based one in which Goddess and God were both venerated. Practitioners were organized into covens led by a High Priestess with the help of her High Priest. The Goddess was invoked into the High Priestess through a ritual act called Drawing Down the Moon. The belief in the necessity of male/female polarity (the opposition and balance of the masculine and feminine) was reflected in training, initiation, and the practice of ritual magic. Major religious festivals consisted of eight sabbats held on the four days that marked the beginning of the agricultural seasons and the four solar festivals celebrating the solstices and equinoxes. Witches worked with energy within sacred circles that had quarters cast in the four directions, each of which had esoteric meanings and was linked to one of the four elements. They practiced techniques conducive to trance and ecstasy, used ritual tools, and maintained a cult of secrecy, notes of which were kept in a Book of Shadows. Gardner called this religion Wicca.[13]

Doreen Valiente, who was initiated as a Witch in 1953, became Gardner's High Priestess. She noticed that some passages in the rituals handed to him by the New Forest Witches were suspiciously similar to those of other occult groups, in particular to those of England's leading ritual magician Aleister Crowley. Crowley, former member of the Golden Dawn and the Ordo Templi Orientis, argued that magic was related to physics, not religion. It was "the art or science of causing change in conformity with will."[14] Magic occurred through putting oneself in harmony with an interconnected universe. When challenged by Valiente, Gardner responded that the Witches' ceremonies had been incomplete and he was obliged to "flesh them out" with writings and practices of others in order to make them viable. Valiente, a writer of lyrical beauty, removed portions she felt inappropriate or objectionable and helped to write some of the ritual invocations that are still used today. Due to internal disagreements, she and a group of supporters eventually left Gardner to form their own coven.

Although Gardner's story of the New Forest coven was accepted by practitioners initially, it was vulnerable to challenge.[15] Drawing on the work of those before him, and adding considerable new information and insight, British historian Ronald Hutton's research reveals that Gardner was very involved in other occult groups before Witchcraft, including Crowley's Ordo Templi Orientis, where he was a member of the highest level and apparently had Crowley's approval to attempt to revive it shortly before the publication of *High Magic's Aid* in 1949. Gardner also sat on the governing councils of both the Ancient Druid Order and the Folk Lore Society.[16]

It should be no great surprise then to discover that Gardner's Wicca included elements from other magical traditions. Like Freemasonry, there

were degrees of initiation, knowledge, and skills in "the Craft" marked by
Wiccan ceremonies, a belief that all these were handed down from ancient
times, an occult significance given to the four directions, and the use of
the pentagram as a major symbol. Like the Golden Dawn, Wicca involved
women on an equal basis, performed magic for practical ends, celebrated
seasonal rites, and drew divinity from or into human beings. Similar relationships were assigned among the four elements and the four directions,
and the working tools for ritual magic were essentially the same, with the
ceremonial knife (called an "athame" by Gardner) given special importance. From Crowley came the blessing called the "five fold kiss," the celebration of the human body, and the Wiccan code of ethics, or Rede.[17] A
major Wiccan invocation is clearly adapted from Leland's *Aradia* and the
image of the Horned God included Murray's Cernunnos.

Wicca was a new counter-cultural religion under the label of the Old
Religion,[18] one that sacralized Nature and the human body, understood
Divinity to be immanent rather than solely transcendent, and saw human
sexuality as a way of celebrating the Divine. Hutton believes this religion
was probably the result of a particular combination of major cultural
trends that had developed in society since 1800, trends that are still in
force today.

> In religious terms, it might be said that he [Gardner] was contacted
> by a divine force which had been manifesting with increasing
> strength during the previous two hundred years, and that it worked
> through him to remarkable effect. A secular way of saying the same
> thing, more commonly found among historians, is that cultural forces
> which had been developing for a couple of centuries combined in
> his emotions and ideas to reproduce a powerful, and extreme, re-
> sponse to the needs which they represented.[19]

By the early 1960s in England, networks of covens began to spread,
and different styles or traditions of Witchcraft were emerging. Individuals
appeared who claimed to have inherited their religion or to have been initiated into a tradition unrelated to Wicca. In some cases, people left Gardnerian covens, as they came to be called, and began their own versions of
the Craft; among the most noted was Alexandrian Witchcraft, named after
Alex Sanders. These innovations and newly appeared traditions were not

greeted enthusiastically by Gardnerians, who believed their practice was an ancient one, handed down through centuries of persecution. And by Gardner's death in 1964, the Wiccan community was torn with low-level conflict, a phenomenon sometimes referred to as Witch Wars.

In 1970 the Pagan Front was formed in England to promote unity within Witchcraft and to promote the Old Religion itself within the wider society. Supported by leaders of three different traditions, it held its first national meeting in London in 1971. The inaugural speech was given by Doreen Valiente. For a time the organization published a newsletter called *The Wiccan* and served as a contact service for people in search of a coven or training in the Craft. In 1981, the Pagan Front became the Pagan Federation with regional councils and, eventually, an elected governing committee. Leonora James, a Cambridge-trained philosopher, brought intellectual rigor as the new editor of *The Wiccan,* and forged links between the organization and academic scholars. James suggested that magical techniques were a way of focusing the conscious mind, enabling it to connect with the unconscious mind. This is what would allow practitioners to transform themselves and the world around them. The move away from a strictly fertility cult of Gardner grew even stronger when Vivianne Crowley, a Jungian psychologist trained in both Gardnerian and Alexandrian traditions, became the first secretary of the Pagan Federation in the late 1980s. Between the two women, Wicca gained an intellectual respectability it had not possessed before.

Vivianne Crowley's contributions are important in the development of Wicca as a mature religion. Her nine books explore both the practice and meaning of Wicca and of contemporary paganism. They have been translated into German and Dutch, and will soon appear in French, Norwegian, and Bulgarian. The growth of Wicca in Europe can be seen in the annual Pan-European Wiccan Convention, an organization she began in 1990 that holds a conference in a different country of northwest Europe every year. She and her husband Chris Crowley set up and led the Wicca Study group, providing classes and workshops in England, Germany, and Norway for almost a decade. In addition to her teaching and writing, Crowley has been very active in interfaith dialogue. Building on the work of Janet and Stewart Farrar, she teaches that healing is an important part of Wiccan practice and belief and that training leads to personal wholeness.[20] There is a deeply felt need for Wicca, she says.

It is to counteract imbalance—between women and men, between men and their inner feminine, between humankind and the world we inhabit—that the archetype of the Goddess has arisen in the world today. Long-buried in the human psyche, the Goddess has awoken and in dreams, visions, art and literature pursues us. Some ignore her call, but many answer and through religion, magic, art, music, poetry, craft and vision they come to Her. The Goddess lives and all who desire may serve at Her altar.[21]

Druids and other pagans joined the Pagan Federation, and membership grew from a few hundred to thousands. As publicity increased and grew more favorable in the 1990s, pagan chaplains were recognized by hospital and prison services, and at least one served in a British university. The first academic conference on paganism in contemporary Britain was held at the University of Newcastle in 1994, and academic scholars began doing research and publishing in the field.

Scholars suggest that all religions mythologize their own origins, and Witches in Britain now typically speak of the Old Religion as a metaphor rather than a reality. Although there is a growing tendency to refer to themselves as pagans instead of Witches, the revelations concerning the origins of Wicca have not disillusioned practitioners. Frederic Lamond, initiated by Gardner in 1957, insisted that it wasn't Gardner's magnetic personality that attracted followers, as he lacked the charisma of great religious leaders. Nor was it the power in what Gardner said or wrote, according to Lamond, but a

power reaching out from the experience of the rituals and magical workings themselves, and from the deities to whom they were dedicated, especially the goddess.[22]

As for being disillusioned, Lamond summed it up in 1997 when he asked,

Does it matter whether a religious or magical tradition is three or three thousand years old if it works in helping us discover the divine spark within ourselves and cast effective spells?[23]

WITCHCRAFT IN AMERICA

Gardnerian Witchcraft was brought to the United States in 1962 by Raymond and Rosemary Buckland. Although there is some disagreement among Witches if this was the first tradition in America, it is the first for which there is undisputed evidence. The first Gardnerian coven was founded in 1964, and the following year, the Church of Wicca was establish in Missouri, receiving tax-exempt status in 1972. This status is significant as it entails certain privileges and benefits that are protected by the courts' interpretations of the states' and federal constitutions. A recognized nonprofit religious organization has the right to ordain clergy to legally "marry and bury" and have representatives in hospitals, prisons, and the military when requested. In addition, there are significant postage and tax benefits, which, depending on state and county laws as well as federal, may provide some exemptions on things like real estate or social security paid on ministerial salaries. Perhaps more importantly, the religious nonprofit tax-exempt status signifies that the state recognizes the religion as a legitimate one, deserving of protection and privilege. When the State of Georgia granted tax-exempt status to the Ravenwood Church of the Old Religion in 1982, there was an immediate challenge to the decision. Its status was upheld by the Georgia Supreme Court. It was a battle that was fought more than once,[24] sometimes in a colorful fashion not untypical of Witches, as in 1970 when Italian Witch Leo Martello and the American Civil Liberties Union took the New York City Parks Department to court for a permit to hold a Witch-In. Over one thousand people showed up to celebrate the victory and take part.

One year after the Bucklands arrived in America, Betty Friedan published *The Feminine Mystique*. Although it took a few years for feminism and Witchcraft to meet, when they did there was an immediate attraction on the part of those feminists who were beginning to question male authority in general, and male spiritual authority in particular. However, for many years the attraction was not mutual.

The feminist spin to Witchcraft first became visible on Halloween, 1968. A group of black-clad women calling themselves WITCH disrupted and, in a dramatic fashion, hexed a New York brokerage firm, the Chase Manhattan Bank, and the Morgan Guaranty Trust. Within weeks covens had sprung up in Boston, Chicago, San Francisco, Washington, DC, North Carolina, Oregon, and Texas. In Chicago, WITCH hexed the Transit Authority for raising fares. In Washington DC, the United Fruit Company was hexed for "slave-labor practices abroad and sex discrimination in hiring at home."[25] These covens were locally based, and, though they all used the acronym WITCH, in one place it meant Women's International Terrorist Conspiracy from Hell, in another Women Infuriated at Taking Care of Hoodlums, Women Inspired to Commit Herstory, and so on. Calling themselves the striking arm of the Women's Liberation Movement, the covens were mainly concerned with doing feminist guerrilla theater. Although they called themselves "witches" and their groups "covens," they were not Wiccan and were not held together by a religious or spiritual belief system, but by the same radical feminism that was resulting in other actions across the country. They took the name WITCH from I Samuel 15:23, which says, "For rebellion is as the sin of witchcraft." As women rebelling against patriarchy, the symbol of the witch was a particularly powerful one for them. They frequently passed out cards to women which read in part, "You are a witch by saying aloud, 'I am a witch,' three times and thinking about that. You are a witch by being female, untamed, angry, joyous, and immortal."[26]

The witch that these women claimed as their symbol was hardly Glenda the Good from the Land of Oz.[27] The witch was the rebellious woman, empowered with secret knowledge. The witch was also a symbol of women's victimization and later resiliency when faced with the evils of institutionalized male dominance. The manifesto of WITCH accepted uncritically the writing of Matilda Joselyn Gage, first-wave feminist and political activist who, almost one hundred years earlier, had claimed that nine million women were put to death for the crime of Witchcraft. Familiar with Michelet's *La Sorcière,* Gage had come to the conclusion that Witches were pagan priestesses of an ancient religion, specialized in healing, and persecuted by the Church in order to stamp out female independence.[28] WITCH, despite its brief life span, linked irrevocably the second wave of American feminism and the symbol of the witch.

The religion of Witchcraft spread in America. New covens were formed by people who had been initiated and trained in Wicca. Others were spontaneously created, using rituals and magical techniques created from a combination of research and inspiration. Within traditions, coven members added their own elements, while some began new traditions altogether, and some simply practiced on their own, gathering information from books that were starting to appear on the market. Beginning in the early 1970s, different groups organized pagan conferences and festivals. Featured speakers shared stories and songs, and large rituals generated a tremendous cross-fertilization of ideas and practices. Among the first such events were Gnostican and national Witchmeets sponsored by Llewellyn Publications. Simply having an "in-house" publisher who was himself Wiccan helped to spread the word about the new Old Religion. According to Chas Clifton, former editor at Llewellyn,

> . . . Llewellyn as a publishing house has done a lot to define American paganism for good or ill. Their conscious philosophy is to publish lots of entry-level books . . . in a "shotgun" approach to see what catches on—and also to dominate bookshelf space in stores.[29]

It was a successful approach for both Witchcraft and Llewellyn, which grew from a small publisher of astrology books in 1901 to a mid-size publisher employing over 100 people and publishing more than 500 authors, specializing in the promotion of books on various Craft traditions.

One charismatic woman who created a new tradition was Zsuzsanna Budapest. A Hungarian immigrant who had lived in Chicago and studied with the improvisational theater group Second City, Budapest and her husband and sons moved to New York in order for her to attend the American Academy of Dramatic Arts. In an interview I did with her in 1991, she told me she heard about WITCH and tried, but was unable, to locate them. In 1970, Budapest went to southern California on a three-week vacation. She never returned.

On the Winter Solstice of 1971, a year after she arrived in California, Budapest and six other women created the Susan B. Anthony Coven Number 1, a group of separatist feminist Witches. According to former member Barbara Chesser, the group was originally a writing and study group. Although Budapest says that her mother was a Witch who taught her many of the practices back in Hungary, Chesser claims that she herself discovered many of them through research for her Ph.D. in anthropology, and it was she who brought them to the coven. Budapest began to develop the role of the autonomous High Priestess, one without a High

Priest, and the group of women began to experiment with religious ritual, combining European and British folk customs with creative improvisation. Then the women decided to go public.

> I said we should gather and celebrate ourselves. Well, that was a novel idea, celebrating ourselves along with the seasons, celebrate ourselves with the Goddess, celebrate ourselves *as* the Goddess. All of this was brand new. They [women not in the coven] didn't relate to the concept of the Goddess. . . . I snuck it by them because we gave the best of parties and they came and what happened to them was very good. They got filled up and went home and they told everybody that the Witches give the best of parties. They didn't realize those were rituals for the Goddess, and then eventually I told them what was going on. . . . It took many years of just passing it as a party for the season instead of saying this is a ritual for the Goddess.[30]

Budapest claims there were some gatherings where more than 700 women attended,

> dancing on the mountaintop, jumping over fire with their clothes off, I mean those were good times. Huge big full moon in our faces. That was ecstasy to be had![31]

This new Wiccan tradition saw the Triple Goddess as an autonomous deity. It did not celebrate a divine male principle; practitioners were also spiritual separatists. Men were not allowed. In creating this kind of space where women felt safe to experiment and to simply be women without the social constraints imposed upon them in mixed groups, the religion reflected the many women's consciousness-raising groups that were gaining in popularity. As such, it caught on among women looking for spiritual experience, and more covens formed. Budapest simply called it Wicca until the mid-70s,[32] after which time it became known as Dianic Witchcraft, probably after the Goddess of the witches in Leland's *Aradia*.[33] The fact that the Goddess Diana avoided contact with men made the name especially appropriate. Clearly, the practice was based upon or at the very least profoundly influenced by Gardnerian Wicca.[34] From the beginning, the Dianic Craft incorporated distinctive Gardnerian elements such as the five-fold kiss used in blessing, the set of ritual tools that included the use and name of the athame, the language and manner of casting the circle, the association of the elements with the four directions, the eight sabbats, and the concept of the Triple Goddess, which Gardner borrowed from Robert Graves.

Budapest opened an occult supply store and began to give classes and lectures. More and more women came to the rituals she and her group organized. Her rituals were broken up twice and participants arrested for trespassing, as the mountaintops they danced on in ecstasy didn't belong to them. Budapest, however, declared that the real reason they were arrested was because the police couldn't believe that hundreds of women could get together and have a wonderful time without a single man among them.[35] Then, in 1975, Budapest was arrested for doing a tarot reading. It made her and Dianic Witchcraft famous.

To the mainstream feminist movement, Goddess feminists had been seen as anti-political and the still nascent Goddess Movement a drain on time and energy that should be better invested in working for women's liberation. Feminist Witches were worse than an embarrassment, they were dangerous because they made the women's movement look too weird and too lesbian. What Budapest referred to as "womyn's religion"[36] got no positive mention in the women's press until Budapest herself was thrown into jail. A small article in *Ms.* made her seem to be a feminist hero. She was a martyr, a victim of and a threat to patriarchal oppression, a real Witch. Although she lost the case, which was based on a law against fortune telling, she considered it a "badge of honor" to be arrested for "prophesying the future, for being a prophet."[37] The California Supreme Court later struck down the law under which she was convicted.

The Feminist Book of Lights and Shadows, written and published by a "hard-working collective of wimmin" in 1979, is dedicated to "Diana, Virgin Huntress of the Night" and to Masika Szilagyi, Budapest's mother, who is credited with being Budapest's inspiration for teaching the Craft to "wimmin." Republished in 1980 as Volume One of Budapest's *Holy Book of Women's Mysteries,* it contains the manifesto of the Susan B. Anthony Coven #1. It affirms a belief in an ancient peaceful era when the earth was seen as Mother and women were Her priestesses. It explains that "aggressive males" exiled from matriarchies were responsible for the invention of rape and the subjugation of women, that a political revolution was impossible without a spiritual one, and that feminist Witches were part of a necessary change in universal consciousness. Members of the coven committed themselves to joy, self-love, life-affirmation, to teaching other women the techniques of magic and Witchcraft, and to the Goddess of Ten Thousand Names.[38]

Budapest's group was unapologetically religious and claimed there was a body of knowledge called magic that could be learned. This made its manifesto significantly different from that of WITCH, demonstrating the "progression from radical feminism to feminist religion."[39]

Budapest has always been highly skilled at blending together myth and history into moving narrative. Whether she was taught Witchcraft by her mother and is a "hereditary" Witch, created a new tradition with a group of feminist women in concert with the times, or was inspired by the Divine, she is acknowledged today as the Mother of the Dianic Craft. When she moved to northern California in 1980, she left behind a new High Priestess,[40] Ruth Rhiannon Barrett, who went on to form Circle of Aradia (CoA). CoA is a large religious congregational community, not a coven. As a registered nonprofit religious organization, it is run by a board of directors, just as is required of any legally recognized church or temple in the United States. Besides offering large public Goddess rituals to the women's community, it provides classes on a variety of topics, largely on the basic techniques of Witchcraft, but also on things like Goddess herstory, tool making, and drumming. Literally thousands of women have taken classes in the Dianic Craft in the twenty-two years CoA has been in existence.

Another significant source for Dianic teaching is the Reformed Congregation of the Goddess-International (RCG) incorporated in Wisconsin in 1984. RCG publishes a widely read quarterly newspaper, sponsors two conferences and national gatherings a year, and provides a six-year training curriculum called Cella. This is an organized program of supervised self-directed spiritual development activities for women, with specific paths or areas of specialization. Training is currently going on in the states of California, Indiana, Minnesota, New York, Washington, Wisconsin, Texas, and Washington, DC. Regardless of where the training takes place, all students are required to participate in an internship in the Mother House in Wisconsin. Women do not have to be Dianics to participate, though most are, but only Dianics may become priestesses of the Congregation.

Although not initially limited by sexual orientation, over time the Dianic tradition became more a practice for lesbian Witches. In part, this depended on the personalities involved in individual covens. The nature of women's covens is such that very intimate emotional relationships are forged there, and people are usually attracted to a particular coven because they have a friend who is a member and feel they have something in common with the group. At the very least, it is a place where women hope to feel safe, though this may not always prove to be true. In addition, this was during the 70s and early 80s, when a great deal of sexual experimentation was going on in America. Although in some groups tensions did not exist between lesbian and heterosexual women, in others lesbians refused to even participate in rituals with heterosexual women. Of course, these same tensions could also be seen in the political women's movement at the time. By the 90s, these conflicts had typically ceased to exist, and sexual orientation was no longer an issue for Dianics in most American groups. Although the groups remain firmly closed to men, the number of heterosexual women increased significantly, and now the Dianic Craft is no longer predominately lesbian.

Other Witches were initially dismissive of Dianic Witches, declaring them far "too Dianic," meaning too political, too feminist, and too lesbian.[41] For some time there was considerable tension, as the majority of Witchcraft traditions emphasized a belief in the necessity of male/female polarity in order to work magic. These groups did not consider the Dianic practice legitimate. In addition, Wiccans still argued that their religion was an ancient one, brought back by Gardner after centuries of Christian oppression. It wasn't until recently that the origins of the Craft were researched or understood. In light of the earlier understandings, the Dianic Craft was not only seen as an upstart, but as a warped caricature of their Craft. Covenant of the Goddess (COG), which formed in California as an umbrella organization in 1975 to gain legal recognition for Witchcraft as a religion, accepted Dianic covens in the early 80s, and this conflict was fairly well resolved in the United States by the late 80s. COG represented Witches from any tradition and created a formal but flexible national network.

Circle Sanctuary, founded in 1974 and granted religious tax-exempt status in 1980, was another significant network, one that accepted a large variety of Goddess traditions. Circle published a newsletter, which has since turned into a quarterly magazine, and holds regular training, rituals, and one of America's oldest pagan summer festivals on its 200-acre nature preserve in the wilds of Wisconsin.

At first, most women came to feminist Witchcraft and Goddess Consciousness through feminism. Starhawk, author of *The Spiral Dance* (1979), came to feminism and Witchcraft at about the same time. Through her writing and her position as first national president of COG, Starhawk effectively became the bridge between the various traditions within Witchcraft.[42] She had some training in Faery Witchcraft, commonly believed to be an American tradition, and elements of this combined with her personal experiences in her widely read first book. In 1980, she teamed with another member of a coven she belonged to in order to teach a class in magic based on *The Spiral Dance*. The class was so popular that more members of her original coven joined in the teaching, and students who had graduated from the classes began forming their own covens. Some of the teachers joined with some of the students to publish a small newsletter and organize public rituals in San Francisco. By the end of 1980, this group had formed the Reclaiming Collective.

From the very beginning, Reclaiming was unusual in that it worked through consensus.[43] There was neither High Priestess nor High Priest. All of the Collective's activities, from designing classes to organizing participation in public political protests, were done in this manner. Many people today assume that Starhawk is the group's leader, but although she has always been the primary thealogian and is the most famous of the Reclaiming Collective, the group has no leader, and she herself has always acknowledged that much of her own thinking grows out of the community and is informed by others.[44]

Like the Dianic Craft, the Reclaiming Collective linked together the spiritual and the political, but this was done in a very direct way that involved a public display of magical protest and action. Many of the members of the Collective and people who attended the public sabbats participated in anti-nuclear civil disobedience in such places as the Lawrence Livermore Lab, Diablo Canyon, and the Vandenburg Air Force Base. Their political commitment was based firmly on their religious beliefs, and some of the activist Witches, including Starhawk, were arrested for acting on these beliefs

Another element that Reclaiming had in common with the Dianic Craft was its innovative form of ritual magic. Unlike Wiccans who traced their lineage back to Gardner, Witches trained in the Reclaiming Tradition did not believe that sexual polarity was always necessary, and they prided themselves on incorporating spontaneity into their practice. Macha NightMare writes,

> When I first began learning Craft, the most powerful lesson I learned from my early working was that if I listened with my heart, if I experienced in my bones and blood, if I could recognize the divine in my own image in a mirror and in the feel of Sun on my skin, wind in my hair, then I could tap into that inner women's wisdom which was innate. I learned that my sacred ritual acts—however they might be performed, whatever words, gestures, tools, symbols were used—are those of a priestess of the Goddess if I will them to be. I feel this when the hair on my arms stands up, my scalp tingles, and I feel rushes of energy up and down my spine. In the face of such experience, I *know* that I am tapping into a rich, vibrant source that reaches deep into the center of the earth, far out into the celestial, and to the core of my soul.[45]

The Reclaiming classes were so popular that in 1985, the Collective offered a summer "intensive," a week of concentrated classes held within sacred space. The success of these was such that the Collective began to rent space in rural areas, and soon the intensives came to be known as Witchcamps. Over time, the teachers were invited to other states and countries, including Florida, Missouri, Michigan, Pennsylvania, Texas, Vermont, West Virginia, Canada, England, Germany, and Norway. The people trained in those camps in turn trained others in their own communities, and the teachings spread. One result of this was that Starhawk and the Reclaiming Collective contributed greatly to making American Witches in general more feminist and more political than British Witches.[46]

In the meantime, Starhawk was finishing work on a Master's degree in clinical psychology and feminist therapy. Her thesis was published in 1982 as *Dreaming the Dark: Magic, Sex and Politics.* Her 1987 book *Truth or Dare: Encounters with Power, Authority and Mystery* explored some of the Collective's magical techniques and provided tools for others to engage in direct magical activism. Although neither book was as popular as *Spiral Dance,* they provided a deepening understanding of Goddess Spirituality to readers. In fact, Starhawk was the first to write a comprehensive theology of Witchcraft and to articulate its ethos. There is more than just a touch of irony in the fact that the two leading, and certainly the two most lyrical, theologians of this religion introduced to the modern world by a man are women, Starhawk and Vivianne Crowley.[47]

Today, Witchcraft is a fully developed nature-based mystery religion. Sabbats, held eight times a year, serve to link the individual and the group to each other and to Nature, and offer participants a regular opportunity to reflect on their own personal growth and goals. Focus on the lunar cycle reinforces the dynamic human cycle of birth, life, death, and rebirth, whether the last is seen as reincarnation or the natural recombining of DNA. The reenactment of reconstructed myths provides meaning and allows Witches to link the divine within them to the divine around them in the natural world and denies the separation between the sacred and the secular. Their celebration of the human body and sexuality provides truth messages about immanence and integration, challenging notions about mind/body dualism, and their spiritual practice makes permeable the boundary between religion and magic.

THE GODDESS IN AMERICA

The Reclaiming and Dianic traditions have blurred the divisions between Witchcraft and the less structured, looser spiritual weave of other Goddess celebrants. With the Dianic training and focus upon an autonomous female deity and Reclaiming's public rituals and Witchcamps, some of which are women-only, many women who don't identify as Witches have learned to incorporate magical techniques and Craft beliefs into their spiritual practice. But the original framing lay elsewhere.

In 1971, in the same year that Budapest's coven announced its presence, feminist theologian Mary Daly was invited to be the first woman ever to preach at a Sunday service at Harvard's Memorial Church. Daly had already gained some academic fame and notoriety from her feminist

critiques of patriarchal religion, but those earlier critiques had been a call
for reform. By 1971, Daly had moved from her reformist position and
turned her Harvard sermon into a "Call for an Exodus" from patriarchal
religion.

> We can give physical expression to our exodus community, to the
> fact that we must go away . . . We cannot really belong to institu-
> tional religion as it exists. It isn't good enough to be token preachers.
> It isn't good enough to have our energies drained and co-opted.
> Singing sexist hymns, praying to a male god breaks our spirit, makes
> us less than human.[48]

Her sermon concluded when she left the pulpit and literally, and symbolically, walked out of the church. According to Daly, hundreds of people
got up and followed her out the door.[49] Later that year, she wrote, "The
women's movement will present a growing threat to patriarchal religion
less by attacking it than simply leaving it behind."[50]

By 1973, she began to use female imagery in articulating the Divine
and urged women to create religious rituals for themselves, for each to
feel her own way in her spiritual journey. In the same year, Barbara
Ehrenreich and Deirdre English condemned the Catholic and Protestant
Churches for the persecution of witches, writing that the essential character of the historical witch-hunts was "that of a ruling class campaign of
terror directed against the female peasant population." They were somewhat more circumspect in their estimate of people put to death for the
crime of witchcraft than other writers, saying only that there were "thousands upon thousands of executions."[51] Their major argument was that the
"crimes" for which these women were really convicted were those that
dealt with female sexuality and the unauthorized practice of medicine or
midwifery. By 1978, Daly had incorporated this concept into her work,
along with Gage's figure of nine million witches and Graves's vision of the
Triple Goddess, and these concepts became commonly accepted parts of
American Goddess lore.

WomanSpirit magazine began to publish in 1974 as a quarterly created
by Ruth and Jean Mountaingrove in Oregon. They were aided by a
changing collective of women in various states. *WomanSpirit* had a significant impact during its ten years of publication. The magazine provided a

forum for women to explore their spirituality through poetry, art, articles about personal experiences, descriptions of rituals, and discussions among women. As the writing collective was geographically diverse, the articles reflected what was happening around the country. The editors wrote,

> We feel we are in a time of ferment. Something is happening with women's spirituality. We don't know what it is, but it's happening to us and it's happening to other people. *WomanSpirit* is trying to help facilitate this ferment.[52]

An event even more significant than the publication of *WomanSpirit* also occurred in 1974. Marija Gimbutas published *Gods and Goddesses of Old Europe,* reprinted eight years later as *The Goddesses and Gods of Old Europe.* In it, the archeologist argued for the existence of a prehistoric, peaceful, agrarian culture that was matrifocal and worshipped "a Goddess incarnating the creative principle as Source and Giver of All."[53] This idea was not totally new; it was first suggested in 1849 by German scholar Eduard Gerhard, but not widely accepted until 1901, when Sir Arthur Evans decided that prehistoric Crete had worshipped a single female deity who was both Virgin and Mother with a divine child. Within a few years, other scholars announced similar findings in Europe, and Sir James Frazer, author of the *Golden Bough,* extended the idea to Western Asia, adding the image of a male son as consort who dies and returns like the grain. By the first decade of the twentieth century, textbooks argued that the worship of Olympian deities had been preceded by universal worship of a Great Mother Goddess, an idea that gave substance to Robert Graves's work that would follow.[54]

Gimbutas's contribution was to posit that this Goddess civilization was invaded over a period of two thousand years by horse-back riding, patriarchal warriors from a proto-Indo-European culture. During this time, goddesses, "or more accurately the Goddess Creatrix in Her many aspects, were largely replaced" by the male-dominated pantheon of the Indo-Europeans.[55] In her later work, Gimbutas attempted to decipher a language in the symbol system used in the art of what she called Old Europe.[56] Although her work, especially her later work, has been severely attacked on several fronts,[57] her books, the ideas, and the stunning photographs they contained were devoured by women looking for symbols to express their own spiritual experiences. The myth of the "Golden Age of Matriarchy" was and continues to be embraced by some practitioners of Goddess Spirituality, who draw their inspiration from what they believe is long-denied human history. Others stress that, in spite of her somewhat problematic methodology and some of her conclusions, Gimbutas's contribution cannot be overestimated.[58] Believing that male dominance and warfare have always existed leaves little hope for change. Through her use of archeo-mythology, Gimbutas helped to develop a new paradigm that allows people to envision a peaceful, egalitarian future based on spiritual values that resonate with contemporary human concerns as we enter the twenty-first century.

Merlin Stone's *When God Was a Woman* (1978) gave the nascent Goddess movement an even greater sense of historical legitimacy. Unlike Gimbutas, she focused primarily on the Near and Middle East, with particular attention to the Bronze Age, but she too found evidence of widespread veneration of female deities. In addition, she wrote about women as priestesses and prophets, as performers of sacred sexual rites in the temple, as keepers of sacred snakes, and as Goddess worshippers as late as 600 B.C.E. The book is her explanation for the "suppression of women's rites." She explored myth and religious dogma to argue that historical events and political attitudes led to the development of the story of the expulsion from Paradise, the blaming of the Fall on Eve, and the resulting devaluation of women. Although she specifically said in the introduction that the book was not intended as a historical text, it was taken as one by her many readers.

The first conference that envisioned Deity as female took place in Boston in 1976. It began with a ritual in an old church led by a group of Witches, who cast a circle and invoked the Goddess.[59] The next goddess conference occurred in 1978 at the University of California in Santa Cruz. Five hundred people attended "The Great Goddess Reemerging Conference" and heard scholar Carol Christ explain "Why Women Need the Goddess." Religious symbols that are almost exclusively male keep women in a state of psychological and physical dependence on male authority and create the impression that female religious power is illegitimate, Christ argued. But simply rejecting the objectionable symbols on a conscious level doesn't work because they continue to work at a deeper level unless they are replaced with new symbols that have meaning. She urged women to "develop a theory of symbol and thealogy congruent with their experience at the same time that they 'remember and invent' new symbol systems."[60] The symbol of the Goddess was offered as one that would legitimize and celebrate female power, female will, female bodies, and the bonds among women. There was no need to believe in the Golden Age of Matriarchies of the past or to try and imagine what might have been; women began to weave together dreams of what might be.[61]

Women rewrote the ancient myths, consciously transforming them to reflect the values in which they believed. In some cases, these reconstructed myths were presented as reflecting earlier stories, before invaders came and brought with them their patriarchal pantheon of divinities. Myth is sacred narrative, providing truth messages about the nature of reality and humanity's position within it. Traditional Greek mythology described Pandora as Zeus's punishment to men, a girl whose insatiable curiosity was the cause of all of humanity's ills. Spretnak (1978) presented Pandora as the Earth Goddess bringing humanity an abundance of gifts in Her great jar. In another reconstructed myth, Persephone wasn't captured and carried off by Hades but descended into the underworld of her own will to do her own work of receiving and renewing the dead. Plaskow (1979) envisioned a conversation between Eve and Lilith, Adam's first wife in Hebraic tradition. The first two women in the world shared secrets, formed bonds, and established sisterhood. Stone (1979) collected stories of goddesses from around the world, providing multicultural models for women. Novelist Marion Zimmer Bradley (1982) rewrote the Arthurian legend from the perspective of a priestess, a new mythic interpretation that presented the story as the clash between Goddess and Christian cultures in ancient Britain.

Language was refashioned as well. Naomi Goldenberg (1979) coined the term *thealogy* to refer originally to feminist Witchcraft, but it quickly was broadened in scope to cover all of Goddess Spirituality. Building on amateur historian Robert Briffault's speculations in 1927, she asserted that the word "virgin" meant a female who was independent, regardless of whether or not she was sexually active. Women who had never heard of Briffault confidently adopted the usage of the term.

The first anthologies appeared that brought together scholars, thealogians, poets, political activists, novelists, visual artists, and practicing Witches. *Womanspirit Rising* (Christ and Plaskow 1979) and then *The Poli-*

tics of Women's Spirituality (Spretnak 1982) presented the diversity of women's insights about and encounters with Goddess Spirituality. It addressed the accusation from some feminists that Goddess Spirituality was an apolitical "cop-out" by arguing not only that patriarchal spirituality is unhealthy for the female psyche but that spirituality is an intrinsic dimension of the human experience. If the personal were political, how then could spirituality be any less so?

While it might appear as though all these publications from the late 1970s and early 1980s drew from the work of Gimbutas, that analysis would be simplistic. The reality of the "time of ferment" noted in *Woman Spirit* was that there were artists working independently with Goddess imagery, academics challenging the gendered nature of mainstream religion and religious iconography, and women giving workshops on myth, magic, and menstruation. The bubbling up of these ideas across the country was a cauldron from which came an explosion of creativity. Many of these books were beautifully written and easily read, which added to their growing popularity. Source and reference books such as Barbara Walker's (1983) *Woman's Encyclopedia of Myths and Secrets,* promised to reveal hidden history and provide women with new symbols and language to give voice to their spiritual journeys. Riane Eilser's (1988) *The Chalice and the Blade* provided an egalitarian vision of the past that was a pledge to the future. Although the information offered to women in these texts and others like them was vulnerable to scholarly challenge, it was nevertheless inspiring. There were striking photographs and illustrations in books and the new Goddess magazines, performance art, installations in small galleries, a "reclaiming" of Middle Eastern dance forms, and music everywhere. As women explored the "Goddess Within," they were exploring the artist within as well. In workshops for example, women not only learned the stories of Isis, but they made sistrums to play when they invoked her in the rituals they were beginning to create. Rituals that were "frequently islands of beauty and magic in a sea of ordinary time" acknowledged significant events in women's lives, such as a first menstrual period, a birth, a divorce.[62] Women's groups often celebrated the Sabbats as well; Spring Equinox became the reunion of mother and daughter through the myth of Persephone; Samheim (the Celtic Halloween) was the time of the Crone. The Goddess was their energy and their Muse.

Workshop leaders came from various sources; Witches, thealogians, authors, and artists gave presentations on what they knew best. Others came from the Unitarian Universalist Church. *Cakes for the Queen of Heaven* was a program developed by Shirley Ranck in 1986 as one of several actions taken by the Church to implement the "Resolution on Women and Religion" adopted by its General Assembly. This ten-week course was intended to help women explore female religious history and its meaning for their lives. Packaged and sold nationally as a set, the workshop and slides were made available to facilitators around the country, both in and outside of the Church. A multicultural program called "Rise Up and Call Her Name" was added a few years later and included other religions and Goddesses from non-Western cultures in response to the accusation that Goddess Spirituality was a whites-only movement.

THE GODDESS IN BRITAIN

The same ferment was occurring simultaneously in England. A handful of women who were members of the London Women's Liberation Movement got together in 1975 and formed the Matriarchy Study Group (MSG) with the intention of questioning the assumption that God had always been perceived as male. These mostly young, college-educated, working-class women[63] set out to look for historical evidence of matriarchal social organization in a scholarly manner. The members each took a different area of twentieth-century writings to study and report on to the collective. They were influenced by American feminists who began to publish in this field. Stone's *When God was a Woman*, for example, had appeared in Britain in 1975 as *The Paradise Paper*. The Matriarchy Study Group decided to publish its own research in the spring of 1977. *Goddess Shrew*, the first publication, was done in journal format and included articles that ranged from birth control practices in ancient Egypt to myths of virgin births from a variety of religious traditions. Its major emphasis, however, was on the argument that approximately 5,000 years earlier, there had been a "Patriarchal Takeover" that lasted roughly 2,000 years, which resulted in the suppression of a widespread, woman-based culture, along with its attending religious imagery, myths, and leadership roles for women. Because so much evidence had been lost, the journal informed its readers that it would ". . . look to poetry and myth, to trees and stones, to the form of the landscape . . . and dedicate our inspiration to the Muse."[64]

Goddess Shrew was given a small mention in a national newspaper and suddenly letters poured in from all over England asking for copies, as well as letters from clergymen, some supporting it and more denouncing it and demanding that its publication be stopped. The resulting publicity helped sell more than 5,000 copies of that first issue. The collective continued to publish, and similar groups began to form elsewhere. Although all of these started as study groups with a political base and not as spiritual groups, some began to do religious rituals. Tensions between individual personalities arose, exacerbating the growing divergence between those who wished to do what they saw as scholarly work and those who wanted spiritual practice. The original Matriarchy Study Group, after intensive work for five years, reached burnout and disbanded. With its demise, the Matriarchy Reclaim and Research Network (MRRN) was formed in 1981 to serve as an umbrella for a variety of groups, including those that practiced magic, those that wanted to do spiritual ritual, and those that preferred to study. It began publishing a newsletter on the eight Wiccan festivals, an unbroken record of publication that continues today. But people began to lose interest in the study groups and wanted direct experience of the female Divine rather than the intellectual study of prehistory.

The idea of a separatist women's culture began to attract some attention from another source in England about the same time. Monica Sjoo, a Swedish-born artist living in England, focused on a monotheistic Goddess by fusing the images of the Neolithic Great Goddess with the mother goddesses of the early Bronze Age, resulting in the publication in 1981, with Barbara Mor, of a lengthy book on *the* "Mother Goddess." The book influenced many women both in Britain and beyond, and firmly established the idea that the Goddess was not something completely external to the self, but something within as well. They wrote, "For a woman to be able to recognize and love the Goddess she must be able to love herself and the Goddess in other women. . . . Feminism means the rebirth of the Goddess within us."[65]

Visits by American members of Reclaiming encouraged the British women, who no longer felt they were an isolated group struggling to provide evidence for the existence of the Goddess. Inspired by the visitors'

stories and Starhawk's writings of Goddess rituals among American
Witches of both sexes, many of the women wanted to "make bonds" with
Wiccans. However, the strong British Wiccan resistance to feminism and
the question of single-sex rituals prevented that. Nevertheless, Jean Freer,
an American Dianic, gave a talk at a women's Goddess celebration and invited people to join a Dianic grove,[66] and many did. They held rituals and
offered classes for women who were interested in learning more about
ancient goddesses and techniques of magic. In this manner, the radicalized
tradition of Dianic Wicca came to England. Unlike the American Dianic
Craft, it was never particularly well accepted. Not only did traditional
Wicca have an established presence, but the British separatist Goddess
Movement was growing.

    In September of 1981, the same year that the MRRN was formed,
women began camping outside the U.S. Air Force base at Greenham
Commons, protesting the deployment of ground-launched cruise missiles.
Determined to make visible the threat of nuclear war, the women established a peace camp where supporters could join, on a temporary basis,
those who had given up their comfortable lives to camp out, year round,
in the rain and snow, enduring the taunts of soldiers and the ridicule of
the press. At times thousands of women would show up to encircle the
base and stand witness at its nine gates. They hung pictures of their mothers and children on the fence, wove a huge yarn web around the 20-mile
perimeter to emphasize that everything is connected in a fragile web of
life, and held mirrors up to the fence to reflect the "death-dealing energy
back on itself."[67] Once in 1983, a group of 44 women even infiltrated the
base itself and danced on top of a missile silo in the cold dawn. In sum,
they performed acts of magic, sometimes drawing directly upon the works
of Budapest and Starhawk. The Goddess was with them at Greenham
Commons. Although the overt action and intent involved a political
struggle at Greenham, a feminist Goddess Spirituality evolved there that
grew to overlap the antiwar activity.[68] Much of this was due to the presence of women from the MRRN, who participated in the consciousness-
raising groups at Greenham. Kathy Jones, who went on to be a key figure
in the Glastonbury Goddess community, reports that several members of
her women's group were at Greenham as well, and she credits that experience as one of the most important elements that began to bring the
knowledge of the Goddess "back" into people's awareness. Greenham was

unique for many reasons, not the least of which was that it was one of the few places initially where groups of black and white women joined together in Goddess Spirituality.

In the mid-1980s, Shan Jayran appeared on the British scene. Trained as a Dianic Witch, having traveled and lived and worked in a variety of communities, including a separatist lesbian one, she claimed a colorful past and brought an eclectic perspective to British Goddess Spirituality. Founding the House of the Goddess (HOG), she provided training and rituals in her London home. In 1987, House of the Goddess held a Halloween event in Battersea Town Hall that was the largest gathering of Goddess celebrants modern Britain had ever seen. Almost 1,400 people attended from a variety of different Goddess traditions. This event set the stage for the large public Goddess events organized by others that were to follow.

In 1983, after her participation at Greenham, Kathy Jones was inspired to create a play to honor the women and publicize what was happening there. She drew upon the myth of the rape of Persephone, seeing Pluto as the military/industrial complex that is "raping Nature and her daughters, stealing her bounty, putting nothing back, then seducing us all with material goods, so that we come to love him for the things he gives us."[69] This was the first of many put on by Ariadne Productions in Glastonbury, believed to be the site of the ancient island of Avalon. Jones calls these "sacred dramas," organized by the community for the community much like passion plays. They are a deliberate reworking of ancient myths within a magical ritual setting whose ". . . purpose is to inscribe a mythic framework for an equal partnership between women and men, where all human beings are empowered to be truly themselves. Our plays, performances and videos give direct expression to long hidden aspects of the divine feminine—Goddess, and to the divine masculine—God, as images, archetypes, muse and transforming divinities."[70] When I interviewed her in 1997, Jones said proudly, "We are making magic!"

In addition to sacred drama, Glastonbury is the home of the Isle of Avalon Foundation, a charitable organization founded by Jones to serve the eclectic Goddess community that looks to the town as a source of information, education, and spiritual experience. The Foundation, dedicated to helping people find their individual spiritual paths, offers evening talks, classes, and weekend workshops on a variety of spiritual and New Age topics. Glastonbury is the site of the first Christian shrine in England, and has a romantic history that weaves together tales of pagan deities, Christians visionaries, and the magic of King Arthur's Court. Its reputation as a place of spiritual pilgrimage was revived with the publication of Marion Bradley's *The Mists of Avalon,* the popularity of which ensured that many who might not otherwise be exposed to the reconstructed history would learn of the struggle between ancient Goddess Spirituality and patriarchal Christianity. Jones told me in 1997 that this book is one of the "huge" reasons thousands of women come to Glastonbury every year looking for the Goddess and hoping to experience her there. And Goddess imagery is everywhere, from sacred drama to the surrounding landscape to tourist souvenirs. The Glastonbury Goddess community is also rather unusual in that it has a solid core of men who are supportive and actively involved. An annual Goddess Conference, organized by Jones and Tina Redpath, is open to both women and men, and draws people from all over Britain, as well as from America, Australia, and the European continent.

These international conferences and events have recently been joined by international "Goddess tours," group pilgrimages to ancient temples, wells, and ruins. Whether or not priestesses ever led egalitarian communities in the worship of a Great Goddess in the "Golden Age," contemporary priestesses in various nations are leading a growing community in celebrating Her in Her many manifestations today. According to Asphodel Long, of the original MSG, "the movement is immature, brash and sometimes silly. But it has immense power and veracity, and to my way of knowing should be recognized as an authentic voice of deity."[71]

THE GODDESS OF TEN THOUSAND NAMES

Before discussing the challenges for Goddess Spirituality, it is important to mention an organization that has growing implications for the wider Goddess milieu. In Ireland on the spring equinox in 1976, Lawrence Durdin-Robertson, his wife Pamela, and his sister Olivia Robertson founded the Fellowship of Isis (FOI). Cousins of the poet Robert Graves, the trio drew more from the heritage of Freemasonry and the nineteenth-century Romantics than from either Witchcraft or the feminist Goddess research occurring on both sides of the Atlantic. Isis was the Goddess of Ten Thousand Names, and as such, she was to represent all goddesses, and though the gods are also venerated, the Fellowship was founded to give a common framework for all those who honored the Goddess. The Robertsons believed strongly that a Goddess Movement was necessary to counter the influence of male-dominated religion. But, Olivia stresses, "the Goddess is not fighting patriarchy, She is re-introducing matriarchy. This is a loving way."[72]

It was an unlikely group, one that claimed descent from Scota, legendary Queen of the Scots. Lawrence was a former Anglican Vicar, his wife, Pamela, a mystic who insisted on the equality of all beings. Olivia had written seven novels and studied in London to be a medium and healer. In 1963, they had turned the family castle in Clonegal, Ireland, into the Clonegal Centre for Meditation and Study.

The Fellowship of Isis was unique in that, from its inception, it was envisioned as a forum where Witches, Druids, Hindus, and Shintoists could be joined by Christians and Jews in celebrating the "reemergence" of the religion of the Goddess. Like other strands within Goddess Spirituality, FOI insisted that the abandonment of the Goddess was responsible for much of the horror of the modern world. But there were no vows, no commitments to secrecy, and members were free to maintain other religious allegiances. Membership was open to anyone who agreed with the four basic principles. The first was the belief that the religion of the Goddess had been neglected for too long and was needed to ameliorate conditions in today's world. The second consisted of a statement that FOI would have no ecclesiastical hierarchy. Although this is often easier to proclaim than practice, this principle served to emphasize the validity of the experiential aspects of spirituality. A sincere believer was the authority of her or his own religious practice. The titles that emerged in the organization over time were designed to go with increased responsibilities and FOI does not consider this to be ranking, though clearly some prestige and power have accrued to the titles. The third principle addressed the forum's multi-faith nature. It was a reminder that FOI was not attempting to start a new religion, simply recognizing that the Goddess was already emerging and, indeed, in some places had never been forgotten. The last, and not the least important point of agreement, announced that joy and pleasure were gifts from the Goddess and should be celebrated as part of

Her worship. There was no room for asceticism and no sacrifices, whether real or symbolic.[73]

The Fellowship became international almost immediately, spreading from Ireland to Britain and the United States. A small notice printed in *Gnostica* magazine in the United States one year after FOI's founding drew the first American members and within a very short time groups had formed in Washington, DC, Chicago, and San Francisco. Although solitary practitioners have always been welcomed members, FOI began to create community through its Iseums, local groups that offer spiritual rituals, such as initiation and other celebratory rites. Considered to be "hearths" of the Goddess, each Iseum is dedicated to the Goddess or Goddess and God of the founder's choice, and, as such, is believed to be shaped by the characteristics of the presiding deity. For example, one Iseum in the southwestern United States that is dedicated to Diana the Huntress is a sanctuary for desert wildlife and focuses on attunement with the Earth and all her creatures. Another in Victoria, Australia, is dedicated to the Egyptian Goddess Hathor and emphasizes healing. Iseums may teach initiate level classes and, if the head is ordained within the Fellowship, may also offer training for the priesthood. Each priestess or priest is free to serve the Goddess in any way the individual sees fit and is authorized to perform ceremonies "received" by Olivia in meditation and published for the community. Iseums are currently located in Australia, British Columbia, Ireland, Nigeria, South Africa, United States, and Yugoslavia. The membership of FOI is spread across 95 countries, with Nigeria claiming the most members.

Typically, the training for priesthood is offered through a Lyceum, or school, all of which are chartered through the College of Isis at Clonegal Castle in Ireland. However, like the Iseums, they are shaped by the attributes of the deity to whom they are dedicated. Until very recently, Lyceums demonstrated considerable variation in practice and focus, depending on the belief system of the individual who conducted the training. In 1999, there was an attempt to standardize the curriculum to some extent and now all Lyceums are required to provide courses centered around the FOI liturgy. Like Freemasonry, training is marked by 32 structured degrees or levels, with an added 33 that marks a "spontaneous mystical awakening."

In 2000, Olivia, in her eighties and the only survivor of the three original founders, announced she would share the responsibility and authority in FOI with an authoritative archpriesthood, made up of 32 individuals on four different continents. It is planned that when an existing member of the archpriesthood retires, a replacement will be chosen by the consensus of the remaining ones. The organization's literature still insists that this is not a hierarchy, but a division of responsibility. How this will function in reality remains to be seen.

FOI is growing in popularity in the United States, especially among women in the loosely structured Goddess Movement. The Church of Isis, associated with FOI, is registered federally as a nonprofit religious organization, giving it a legal recognition few other groups in Goddess Spirituality have achieved. Anyone who is initiated into the priesthood through the Church may obtain legal ministerial credentials and the benefits that may accrue from setting up an affiliated Iseum. One of the strengths of FOI is the mutable nature of its Iseums. All too often, however, that also means there is little accountability or few standards for training. Just as there seems to be a general move away from using the word "Witch" and toward the word "Priestess" or "Priest," there appears to be a move away from the more rigorous and time-consuming training demanded by Witchcraft and toward whatever might be required by individual Iseums. This is particularly true of women practicing Goddess Spirituality in groups where there is no "legitimate" clergy.

The inclusiveness of the organization continues to be a significant attraction. It functions just as the founders intended, allowing those who honor the Goddess to come together in a way that many other groups do not. It was this spirit of inclusion that allowed the Fellowship to be one of the organizers of the Parliament of World Religions in Chicago in 1993, along with COG, Circle Sanctuary, the pagan EarthSpirit community, and other, more traditional, religious groups.

"There is no 'party line' of Goddess worship; rather, each person's process of perceiving and living Her truth is a movement in the larger dance. . . ."[74] Though Charlene Spretnak was referring specifically to what was then called women's spirituality with those words, it certainly holds true for Witches as well. The religion is based on what one does rather than on what one believes.[75] Several years ago when a colleague and I examined how doing research in this field had affected us, I wrote that I did not believe in a divinity but I had experienced Her.[76] By that I meant that I had known those moments of magic when I sensed the Mystery and felt connected to a Greater Whole. For some the Goddess is simply an intellectual concept or an archetype. Patricia Monaghan, poet and author of numerous Goddess books, reminds us that there are also "those for whom She is an emotional construct, a way of understanding the varying voices of the emerging self."[77]

For some She is more concrete, and belief in Her comes with certain responsibilities. "Serving the life force means working to preserve the diversity of natural life, to prevent the poisoning of the environment and the destruction of the species," writes Starhawk.[78] This is especially appropriate for a pagan deity immanent in Nature, one who teaches believers "to consider themselves and their place in the web of things, to honor the richness and enhance the diversity of life."[79] Kathy Jones told me that "the Goddess is returning inextricably into people's consciousness all over the planet. It isn't always overt, it can be in an ecological awareness."[80] Certainly in terms of the environment, Goddess celebrants seem to be working for Her and becoming more political.

For still others, the Goddess is an Entity, one who may or may not have a male consort, one who is immanent and who may also be transcendent in an interconnected universe. In spite of a tendency on the part of a small minority to pray to or worship Her, She is not usually understood in terms of an external deity who intervenes. Starhawk tells us that the Goddess doesn't rule the world, She *is* the world.[81] Hutton points out that Witchcraft attempts to draw out and enhance divinity within each of us. He does not suggest that the Goddess and God are imaginary, though he says they may indeed be

passionate projections of the human heart and mind. . . . It may equally well be true, however, that human belief has actually given them life, or else that they have always existed and have been perceived anew because people now have need of them.[82]

But if an entity, Starhawk argues the Goddess is also "constantly changing form and changing face. Her images do not define or pin down a set of attributes; they spark inspiration, creation, fertility of mind and spirit."[83]

Budapest envisions the Goddess as "all that is female in the Universe . . . the Universe herself is the Goddess. It's almost like being a cell on your own body. . . . We are part of Her, there is no separation of the two. . . . It's an energy, it's a force, instead of a force, let me call Her a flow. The flow is with us."[84] This "flow" can also be understood as Mary Daly does, when she writes that the word "Goddess" is a verb, a "Metaphor for Ultimate/Intimate Reality, the constant Unfolding Verb of Verbs in which all be-ing participates, Metaphor of Metabeing."[85] If we can comprehend how light can be simultaneously both a particle and a wave, then we can understand that the Goddess is the flowing of energy that links all things, that flows through all things, and so is all things. She is the singer and the song, the dancer and the dance, the weaver and the web She weaves.

A dear friend of mine, a Dianic Witch, recently lost her 89-year-old father to cancer. His death was long and hard in coming. She sat next to his bed as he drifted in and out of a morphine-induced state. In order to strengthen herself and, possibly, help his passing, she occasionally read passages out loud from *The Pagan Book of Living and Dying*.[86] Her father had been a nominal Christian all his life and simply assumed that his daughter was as well. He never learned otherwise, as he was too far into his "crossing" to maintain lucidity. However, at one point, inspired by something she read or perhaps a morphine dream, he suddenly spoke up clearly and forcefully.

"We all drink of the same milk," he said. It was one of the last things he ever said.

PROBLEMS AND CHALLENGES

A major strength of an experiential religion that has no agreed-upon authoritative text may also be a major problem, especially when there is no centralized form of governance. When "each [celebrant] is the priestess of her own religion,"[87] no one can gainsay another's truth. This flexibility may be conducive to a lack of accountability and responsibility. While

some people argue for karmic judgment, others want more immediate solutions to situations in which an individual violates the trust of others or
is simply unstable in ways that bring conflict or unethical standards to the
community.[88] There are a few forums for dealing with these problems—
for example, COG has had a standing ethics committee and recently
tightened both the membership and the grievance processes to deal with
potential problems, and Olivia Robertson has the authority to expel
someone from the Fellowship. However, actions such as these are extremely rare. Nevertheless, tensions do arise within covens and Goddess
groups. In the case of the former, the High Priestess has the final word on
resolution and there is no appeal. In the latter case, it depends on how the
group is organized, but the outcome is often painful. Thus, there continue
to be occasional Witch Wars, and the more intimate the group involved,
the more wrenching the result may be.

Other challenges have to do with the gender roles in spiritual practice. Goddess Spirituality "encourages a psychological range and flexibility
which few other modern philosophies or techniques of self-development
can provide for their female adherents."[89] Although this is true for
women, and although there is tremendous emphasis on healing and
wholeness for everyone, the role available for men does not seem to allow
them to reflect on or grow into the wholeness of their lives. At the very
least it is considerably more limiting than the image of the Triple Goddess
is for women. For example, I once participated in a ritual where a young
horned Cernunnos symbolically battled an older one, who was defeated
and driven way vanquished. Privileging male youth and virility as the primary aspects of male divinity leaves many if not the majority of men out.
There has been an attempt to incorporate the image of masculine nurtu-
rance into the godhead, most notably in the mythic image of the Green
Man, the God of Vegetation believed to be represented in Medieval foli-
ate heads. But both the Horned God and the Green Man are used as entities, identities whole unto themselves, rather than part of the natural cycle
of men's lives.

At a conference on the Ambivalent Goddess, held at King Alfred's
College in Winchester, England, in 1997, I heard Shan Jayran explore a vision of pagan masculinity that might address my concerns. Although she
did not speak to the limited potential for men, she saw the God as War-

rior, Protector, and Sacred Fool, the latter in the Shakespearean sense in which the Fool is the wisest man in the King's court. I have not seen this creative approach elsewhere, nor have I seen discussion on this issue. The kind of Triple God envisioned by Jayran, whether it is this particular one or not, would allow room for the growth and change that real men go through, and allow them to experience and identify with the Divine throughout their lives.

A different issue is that among some women's Goddess groups, there is no role for men at all. This may be much less acceptable to younger women today than it was in the 1970s and 80s. Recently, a group of young women who were going through Cella priestess training left, arguing that "feminism is passé." They abandoned the separatist vision of the Dianics, not Goddess Spirituality. Although I strongly disagree with their understanding of feminism, I often encounter this reaction among my beginning students in women's studies. It takes them some time to see that being pro-woman does not mean being anti-male. However, perhaps some rethinking is called for. Women-only groups and rituals can be very empowering, inspirational, and, yes, magical, as I have written in the past.[90] I, for one, would certainly not want to see them disappear. But privileging lesbian women by allowing them to share their spirituality with their loved ones and forbidding heterosexual women from doing the same thing is problematic in the very least.[91] There may indeed be a need for space and time for single-sex groups in order to explore the Mysteries. But if women and men are to live together in whatever way we do on this fragile planet, surely there is a need for us to come together as well. A thealogy that totally excludes one sex is likely to be damaging to both, as we have clearly seen.

There is a genuine danger in reifying gender roles, as is done too often in Goddess Spirituality. Wholeness implies developing our full potential, not just the socially constructed part that was assigned to us based on biological sex. In a similar manner, linking women's spirituality and creativity primarily to the act of birthing and making it the major sacrament as frequently occurs is quite limiting.[92] Rather than empowering women with a new vision of the sources of women's power, this uses what is really rather conservative iconography. In its emphasis on fertility, it affirms women's traditional roles and ignores powerful aspects of the Divine long associated with goddesses: the gift of rhythm (Inanna), the science of agriculture (Isis), spinning and weaving (Nephtys), education and knowledge (Nidaba), war (Parbutta), justice (Xenia), and courage (Alencica), to name just a few.

Finally, an increasing fragmentation within Goddess Spirituality may be interpreted in different ways. Are people turning away from the Goddess or is the tapestry still being woven? The phenomenon may suggest a spiritual community still struggling to find meaning or perhaps searching for a matrix through which to explore and contain their spiritual experiences. According to religious scholar Wade Clark Roof, this splintering of religious understandings reflects what is going on in other communities of faith. He has concluded that we live in a culture of spiritual quest where religious identities are malleable and multifaceted.[93]

Starhawk, however, believes that the considerable crossover among members, where a Witch in one tradition may become an unaffiliated Goddess celebrant and then a priestess in FOI, is a stitching of small networks that joins circles to other circles and strengthens the whole.[94] Sociologist Michael York refers to this as SPINS,[95] a network structure that helps to maintain continuing functional viability. He argues that it rests on interpersonal ties among like-minded people, ties among leaders who may change circles, activities of spokespeople, large gatherings, and a sharing of beliefs through books, magazines, workshops, and the like,[96] all of which are present in the Goddess community.

In the fifteen years since I was first introduced to Goddess Spirituality, I have seen people who have dropped out of groups. A very small number disappear. More of them have joined or even begun new groups, some seem to "take a sabbatical," and a considerable number have found different ways of exploring their spirituality, through things like graduate degrees in religious studies or psychology. I suspect the spiritual impact of this last group will be significant in ways we have yet to imagine.

I was recently a guest at a dedication of five young women who had been studying in a local lyceum for two years. The dedicants told me they were Witches and had been working together as a coven for some time. Their sponsor was a FOI priestess who had been involved with the occult since the 60s and who, for many years, had been a Dianic Witch. Each of the young women dedicated herself that day to a different goddess, none of them, incidentally, to Isis. The youngest, a married Latina Witch who had just turned 20, dedicated herself to the Aztec Goddess of her fore-mothers. Such is the eclectic and protean nature of this living spirituality. And so the weaving continues.

Notes

INTRODUCTION

1. Diana L. Eck, *A New Religious America: How a "Christian Country" Has Become the World's Most Religiously Diverse Nation* (San Francisco: Harper San Francisco, 1994).

2. Bruce G. Trigger, *Early Civilizations: Ancient Egypt in Context* (Cairo: American University in Cairo Press, 1993) 53.

3. Trigger 55–60; Eli Sagan, *At the Dawn of Tyranny: The Origins of Individualism, Political Oppression and the State* (New York: Vintage, 1985) 277ff; Robert Bellah, "Religious Evolution" in Roland Robertson, ed. *Sociology of Religion* (Baltimore: Penguin, 1969) 262–92.

4. Bellah 267ff.

5. Katherine K. Young, "Introduction" in Arvind Sharma ed. *Religion and Women* (Albany: State University of New York Press, 1994) 14–23.

6. Paul Nathanson and Katherine K. Young, *Transcending Misandry* (Montreal: McGill-Queen's University Press, forthcoming).

7. H. Patrick Glenn, *Legal Traditions of the World: Sustainable Diversity in Law* (Oxford: Oxford University Press, 2000) 12–14.

8. Katherine K. Young, "Introduction" in Arvind Sharma ed. *Today's Woman in World Religion* (Albany: State University of New York Press, 1994).

9. Arvind Sharma, *To the Things Themselves: Essays on the Discourse and Practice of the Phenomenology of Religion* (New York: Walter de Gruyter, 2001) 113–19; 169–71; 250–61; Katherine K. Young, "Introduction" in Arvind Sharma and Katherine K. Young, eds. *Feminism and World Religions* (Albany: State University of New York Press, 1999) 18–22.

10. Paul Nathanson and Katherine K. Young, *Spreading Misandry: The Teaching of Contempt for Men in Popular Culture* (Montreal: McGill-Queen's University Press, 2001).

CHAPTER TWO

1. For a fuller description of the Indian Buddhist nuns and an analysis of why the order eventually died out, see Nancy Auer Falk, "The Case of the Vanishing Nuns: the Fruits of Ambivalence in Ancient Indian Buddhism," *Unspoken Worlds: Women's Religious Lives*, ed. by Nancy Auer Falk and Rita M. Gross (Belmont, CA: Wadsworth, 2001), pp. 196–206.

2. Mount Koya was also closed to women until relatively recently.

3. Soto is one of the main Zen lineages in Japan; the other is the Rinzai lineage, usually said to have been founded by Eisei. The major difference between the two is their methods of practicing meditation. Soto stresses quiet mindful sitting, whereas Rinzai is famous for koans, riddles, or puzzles upon which students meditate. Both stress equally the importance of meditation practice and awakening to one's own Buddhahood.

4. Diana Y. Paul, *Women in Buddhism: Images of the Feminine in Mahayana Tradition* (Berkeley: Asian Humanities Press, 1979), p. 308.

5. Quoted by Janice Dean Willis in "Nuns and Benefactresses: The Role of Women in the Development of Buddhism," *Women, Religion, and Social Change.* ed. by Yvonne Hadad and Elison Banks Findley (Albany: State University of New York Press, 1985), p. 75.

6. Chatsumarn Kabilsingh, *Thai Women in Buddhism* (Berkeley: Parallax Press, 1991), p. 26.

7. Luis O. Gomez, tr. *The Land of Bliss: The Paradise of the Buddha of Measureless Light* (Honolulu: University of Hawaii Press, 1996), p. 74 (Vow # 35).

8. Anguttaranikaya v,6,5. Quoted by Cornelia Dimmitt Church, "Temptress, Housewife, Nun: Women's Role in Early Buddhism," *Anima: An Experiential Journal* I:2 (Spring 1975), p. 55.

9. Liz Wilson, *Charming Cadavers: Horrific Figurations of the Feminine in Indian Buddhist Hagiographic Literature* (Chicago: University of Chicago Press, 1996), p. 94.

10. Ibid., p. 23.

11. Andrew Schilling and Anne Waldman, tr. *Songs of the Sons and Daughters of the Buddha* (Boston: Shambhala, 1996), pp. 50–51.

12. Though this motif is widespread, one of the best known and influential episodes is found in the Lotus Sutra. The eight-year-old Naga princess, who is already enlightened, changes her physical form into that of a male when a skeptical elder declares that such an accomplishment would be impossible. For an introduction to and translation of the texts, see Paul, pp. 185–90. For a feminist discussion of the text, see Gross, pp. 67–71.

13. Quoted in Paul, p. 230.

CHAPTER THREE

1. "Pai" has been translated as "worship," which has a stronger sense of ancestors than "gods," and is therefore not entirely correct. I have chosen to use "venerate" because it has a stronger sense of "respect" with a correspondingly weaker sense of divinity in the persons or objects being "venerated." It is true that pai is used with spirits or shen, as in pai shen, the worshipping of spirits; but pai is also often used with fang as in pai-fang, to visit. Both the nuances of "venerate" and "worship" are therefore contained in pai tsu-hsien. I appeal here to the Confucian philosopher Hsün-tzu's idea of the different levels of understanding.

2. T'uan means united, together, collective; nien is year, annual; fan can be used as rice, meal; so that "annual family dinner" would be a reasonable translation.

3. When a woman marries, she marries out of her family (chia-ch'u); whereas when a man marries, he takes a wife into his family (ch'ü).

4. For a more detailed exposition on this, see the section on Buddhism in Tak-ling Terry Woo, "Religious Ideals, Beliefs, and Practices in the Lives of Women During the Reign of T'ang Ming Huang," Ph.D. Diss., University of Toronto, 2000.

5. I am not suggesting that all Chinese believe in this explanation of the ritual. Hsün-tzu's assessment of the different levels of understanding is again helpful here. One might expect a sage (sheng-jen) and an exemplary person (chün-tzu) to understand this ritual quite differently than the average person.

6. Ritual or ritual enactment (li) is one of the central tenets of Confucianism.

7. Taylor writes that self-cultivation has always been a part of Confucianism. In the classical tradition it was with an eye to becoming an exemplary or virtuous person, chün-tzu; in Neo-Confucianism it was to become a sage. (1986:22) The concepts of self-cultivation and investigation of things both come from The Great Learning (Ta Hsüeh).

8. I am using Roger Ames's translation here. Legge translated chün-tzu as "gentleman," which is not quite right because the Chinese is ungendered. An alternative translation is "virtuous person," but this is not entirely satisfactory either because it is too general and confluent to power and virtue (te), and benevolence or compassion (jen), which is suggestive of all social values. (Dawson, xxi)

9. In academic terms, I might say that my exercise here is at once "confessional and subjective" by taking a personal interest in the future of Confucianism; and "objective and scholarly" in describing the traditional beliefs and practices for women in Confucianism.

10. Taylor 1990, 130–131.

11. Ibid., 127. Taylor quotes Tu Wei-ming: "Self-realization entails the task of bearing witness to the dimension of humanity which is communal and, in the ultimate sense, transcendent."

12. Confucius (551–479 B.C.E.) is not recorded as having spoken a great deal about filial piety in The Analects (Lün Yu). When he did, he was often speaking with Tseng Tzu. For this reason, Tseng Tzu is believed by some to have recorded The Classic on Filial Piety, on which The Classic on Filial Piety for Women is based. The origin of The Classic on Filial Piety, like the woman's classic, is unclear. Another tradition has it that it was written by Confucius; another that it was bequeathed by the seventy disciples; and yet another that it was apocryphal from the Han—this last scenario is unlikely to be true since there is reference to it in The Spring and Autumn Annals of Mr. Lu (Lü-shih Ch'ün-ch'iu). (Wang 1–2) It is, nevertheless, accepted that this classic comes from the Confucian school. There are records to show that two versions of the same text, the Old and New Texts (named after their scripts), existed during the Han dynasty. (Wang 3) An early mention of filial piety is made in The Records of Rituals (Li Chi), also known as The Book of Rituals, compiled around 206 B.C.E to 8 C.E. In the section "The Essence of Sacrifice" (Chi T'ung), it is stated: Therefore, a filial son should serve his parents in three ways: to feed them when they are alive, to mourn them when they die and to offer sacrifices to them when mourning is over. . . . Sacrifice is meant to be the perpetuation of feeding one's parents and the continuation of filial piety. (Huang 28–29) The place of a woman in this is as a wife and daughter-in-law. Almost a millennium after The Book of Rituals, the Neo-Confucian Ch'eng I (1033–1108) writes that during his day, people "are careful in choosing sons-in-law but careless in selecting daughters-in-law. . . . The choice of a daughter-in-law is very important. Why should it be neglected?" (Chu and Lu, 173) Then some six hundred years after Ch'eng I, Chang Po-hsing (1651–1725) explains Ch'eng I's comments in this

way:[Women] confine themselves to their own private quarters. It is difficult to know their character. Furthermore, taking a daughter-in-law in marriage is to continue the family line. Some ancient people predicted whether a family would prosper or decline on the basis of the virtuous or vicious character of the daughter-in-law. The matter is of utmost importance. (Ibid., 173–174) Put simply, if a daughter-in-law who actually manages the family is not filial and obedient (hsiao-shun), then her children, grandchildren, and great grandchildren will un- likely be filial either because the root example they are modeling themselves on is deficient.

13. This is at the end of Section 1 in the Nü Hsiao Ching. (Woo 192)

14. On answering a question about why "the learning of the great man consists in loving the people,"Wang in part says this:"Therefore, only when I love my father, the father of others, and the fathers of all men can my humanity really form one body with my father, the fathers of others, and the fathers of all men. When it truly forms one body with them then the clear character of filial piety will be manifested" (Chan 273).

15. I am dating this to 1911, when China became a Republic.

16. I am simply describing the mechanic of ritual in dynastic China; I am neither endors- ing nor rejecting the traditional ideas about women.

17. For example, Confucianism has become irrelevant in Joseph Levenson's estimation. He argues in his essay on the Well-field that with Communism, the disruption of Confucianism is complete; he writes that ". . . Marx is the Classic, not the Rituals of Chou or Chou-li . . . And where Marx and Mao judge no Shao is judging yet, no Mencius and no Confucius" (Levenson 287).

18. These include Liu Hsiang's Biographies of Women (Lieh Nü Chuan), Pan Chao's Ad- monitions to Women (Nü Chieh), Lady Cheng's The Classic on Filial Piety for Women (Nü Hsiao Ching), and Sung Jo-hsin's The Analects for Women (Nü Lun Yu).

19. Nivison quotes Julia Ching's translation of Kant on Chinese philosophy:"Their teacher Confucius teaches in his writings nothing outside a moral doctrine designed for the princes . . . [concluding that] a concept of virtue and morality never entered the heads of the Chi- nese." (65) And Fingarette, who finally arrives at a very different assessment of Confucius, be- gins his Preface with this:"When I began to read Confucius, I found him to be a prosaic and parochial moralizer; his collected sayings, the *Analects,* seemed to me an archaic irrelevance." (vii) These are just two examples of one particular strain of Western opinions of Confucianism.

20. This refers to the period before the Han dynasty in the third century B.C.E.

21. Mou 27.

22. I am not suggesting that China never experienced religious strife; and I certainly do not want to give the impression that Confucians have never mounted campaigns against their reli- gious rivals who were most often the Buddhists and Taoists. However, the degree and fre- quency of violence associated with religious conflict have been smaller and less frequent when compared with the Western religions.

23. I have avoided ethnic and national identity here. Many, other than "Han" Chinese, have been Confucian. The label "Han" is in itself problematic since it encompasses historically "mixed" groups from what are now the northern, southern, western, and eastern parts of China.

24. I refer here to the notion that one can only be a Jew, Christian, or Muslim at one time; that one cannot simultaneously be a Christian Jew, or a Muslim Christian, or a Jewish Muslim.

25. This is a rather complicated issue. Suffice it to note here that the performance of ritual based on social hierarchy is at the heart of Confucianism and that this doctrinal focus on hier- archy contrasts greatly with the Western focus on equality before God.

26. I am encouraged by recent publications from Susan Mann, *Precious Records: Women in China's Long Eighteenth Century,* 1997; Lisa Raphals, *Sharing the Light: Representations of Women and Virtue in Early China,* 1998; Robert Cutter and William Cromwell, *Empresses and Consorts,* 1999; Sherry J. Mou (ed.), *Presence and Presentation: Women in the Chinese Literati Tradition,* 1999; and Dorothy Ko, *Every Step a Lotus: Shoes for Bound Feet,* 2001.

27. T'ang has "man" here; I have changed it to the gender-neutral "human being."

28. I am referring to Classical Confucianism here. Neo-Confucianism shifted the concept of the Ultimate to Principle or li. As noted earlier, Confucianism has no revealed scriptures, though it does have a strong tradition of the "sacred" and the "divine." See footnote 14.

29. Lau 194. I am dealing with the ideal here and not the practice. Many have treated the words of Confucius, for example, as God-given truth so that they might as well have been revealed truth.

30. Rituals for filial piety (hsiao) and more specifically ancestor veneration are a primary part of these sacrificial rites.

31. I have changed Watson's translation of chün-tzu from gentleman to exemplary person.

32. Watson 89.

33. Ibid. 36.

34. Ibid.

35. I have change Watson's "his" to "her."

36. Watson 82.

37. Watson uses "the heavens." To be consistent with my other references I have capitalized Heaven and made it singular. (82)

38. The small person or hsiao-jen is one who is selfish, profit-minded, seeking the best for herself, and resorts to any means to amass what she wants. Hsün Tzu quotes an old text that says "Order is born from the chün-tzu, disorder from the hsiao-jen." (Watson 36)

39. Tu 127.

40. Woo 193.

41. Ibid. 199.

42. This is Chen Yu-shih's insight from an unpublished paper delivered at a conference on Women and Confucianism held at the University of Hawaii in 1993. I thank Professor Tu Wei-ming for permission to use this material.

43. I am of course grossly oversimplifying here. He may be independently wealthy, and he may also be very well trained in a particular skill, thereby making it easy for him to return to the workforce and earn a good living.

44. See Ames and Rosemont; they propose a new translation of jen as "authoritative conduct."

45. Woo 196.

46. Ibid. 195.

47. Again, I am grossly oversimplifying here. Both spouses may be working; and they may share their chores; however, a Confucian will likely suggest that the two can never be entirely "equal." Here lies the crux of the matter: the senior member is obliged to look after the junior one; and the junior one is obliged to be loyal to the senior one. One weakness in the Confucian system, as Lee Rainey, Professor of Chinese Religions at the Memorial University in Newfoundland, suggested in a private conversation on 19 June 2000, is in the lack of sanctions against the senior member. In other words, if the husband does not perform his duties within the traditional relationship, the wife has little recourse.

48. Tradition has it that the Nü Hsiao Ching was written by a Lady Ch'eng, the wife of a certain Chen Miao, who was a minor official during Brilliant Emperor or T'ang Ming Huang's reign. She presents this to Hsüan-tsung on the occasion of her niece's marriage to his son Yung Wang. It is not clear if this is a true source of the treatise. The Classic is not mentioned in the official histories nor T'ang literature; and there is no record of a Yung Wang. The earliest date ascribed to the Classic is an illustration by Yen Li-pen who died in 673, before Hsüan-tsung was born. Some have argued that it was probably written close to or during the Sung dynasty.

49. In traditional Chinese culture, not only in Confucian beliefs, a person was thought to have two souls: the heavenly soul (yang; hun), which becomes the spirit, and the earthly soul (yin; kuei), which becomes the ghost.

50. Woo 152.

51. Ames and Rosemont 49.

52. Woo 193–94 and Lün Yu.

53. Chan, 180.

54. Lün Yu 1:2 in Ames and Rosemont 71.

55. On following the Way, Mencius said: "Those who are obedient to Heaven are preserved; those who go against Heaven are annihilated." (4:A:7 in Lau 120)

56. Ibid. 30.

57. Ibid. 195.

58. The women of the imperial household are associated with "Kuan-sui," the title of the first ode in the Shih Ching, which is symbolic of a happy marriage, and a unicorn's hoof or lin-chih, which is suggestive of having many sons. (Woo 192) Ch'eng Hao uses this same ode to explain that a happy marriage and progeny are necessary before "the laws and systems of the [Offices of the Chou] Chou kuan can be put into practice."

59. Lün Yu 12:19.

60. Woo 193.

61. Ibid. 194.

62. Lün Yu 1:12 in Ames and Rosemont 30.

63. Ibid. 93.

64. Lün Yu in Fingarette 79.

65. Chan Wing-tsit translated this as "son" (181); I have neutralized it to "child."

CHAPTER FIVE

1. Mary Daly, *Beyond God the Father* (Boston: Beacon Press, 1973).

2. S. Ackerman, *Under Every Green Tree: Popular Religion in Sixth-Century Judah*, Harvard Semitic Monographs 46 (Atlanta: Scholars Press, 1992); idem., "Isaiah," *The Women's Bible Commentary*, ed. C. A. Newsom and S. H. Ringe (London: SPCK; Louisville: Westminster/John Knox, 1992), pp. 161–68; idem., "The Queen Mother and the Cult in Ancient Israel," *Journal of Biblical Literature* 112 (1993): 385–401.

3. Rachel Adler, "I've Had Nothing Yet, So I Can't Take More," *Moment* 8 (September 1983): 22–26.

4. Robert Seltzer, *Jewish People, Jewish Thought* (New York: Macmillan, 1980).

5. See the study by Saul M. Olyan, *Asherah and the Cult of Yahweh in Israel* (Atlanta: Scholars Press, 1988).

6. David Noel Freedman, "Yahweh of Samaria and His Asherah," *Biblical Archeologist* (December 1987): 241–50.

7. Tikvah Frymer-Kensky, *In the Wake of the Goddesses: Women, Culture, and the Biblical Transformation of Pagan Myth* (New York: Free Press, 1992).

8. See footnote 1.

9. Phyllis Trible, *God and the Rhetoric of Sexuality* (Philadelphia: Fortress Press, 1978).

10. Anthony Saldarini, "Babatha's Story," *Biblical Archeological Review* 24, no. 2 (March/April 1998): 28–33, 36–37, 72–74.

11. Ross S. Kraemer, *Her Share of the Blessings: Women's Religion among Pagans, Jews and Christians in the Greco-Roman World* (New York: Oxford University Press, 1992); idem., *Maenads, Martyrs, Matrons, Monastics: A Sourcebook on Women's Religions in the Greco-Roman World* (Philadelphia: Fortress Press, 1988). See also Barbara Nathanson, "Toward a Multicultural Ecumenical History of Women in the First Century/ies C.E.," in *Searching the Scriptures: A Feminist Introduction*, ed. Elisabeth Schüssler Fiorenza (New York: Crossroad, 1993).

12. See Charlotte Elisheva Fonrobert, *Menstrual Purity: Rabbinic and Christian Reconstruction of Biblical Gender* (Stanford: Stanford University Press, 2000).

13. Judith Hauptman, *Re-reading the Rabbis: A Woman's Voice* (Boulder, CO: Westview Press, 1998). For a far more critical perspective, see Rachel Biale, *Women and Jewish Law: An Exploration of Women's Issues in Halakhic Sources* (New York: Schocken Books, 1984).

14. Judith Wegner, *Chattel or Person? The Status of Women in the Mishnah* (New York: Oxford University Press, 1988). See also Tal Ilan, *Jewish Women in Greco-Roman Palestine: An Inquiry into Image and Status* (Tübingen: J. C. B. Mohr [Paul Siebeck], 1995).

15. David M. Feldman, *Birth Control in Jewish Law: Marital Relations, Contraception, and Abortion as Set Forth in the Classic Texts of Jewish Law* (New York: New York University Press, 1968).

16. Howard Eilberg-Schwartz, *The Savage in Judaism: An Anthropology of Israeli Religion and Ancient Judaism* (Bloomington: Indiana University Press, 1990); Daniel Boyarin, *Carnal Israel: Reading Sex in Talmudic Culture* (Berkeley: University of California Press, 1993); Miriam Peskowitz, *Spinning Fantasies: Rabbis, Gender, and History* (Berkeley: University of California, 1997).

17. Bernadette Brooten, *Women Leaders in the Ancient Synagogue: Inscriptional Evidence and Background Issues* (Scholars Press, 1982).

18. Talmud Bavli Megillah 23a.

19. Mordechai Friedman, "Marriage as an Institution: Jewry under Islam," in *The Jewish Family: Metaphor and Memory*, ed. David Kraemer (New York: Oxford University Press, 1989); Avraham Grossman, "Medieval Rabbinic Views on Wife-Beating, 800–1300," *Jewish History* 5 (1991): 53–62.

20. S. D. Goitein, *A Mediterranean Society: The Jewish Communities of the Arab World as Portrayed in the Documents of the Cairo Geniza*, 5 vols. (Berkeley: University of California Press, 1967–1988).

21. Shaye Cohen, "Purity and Piety: The Separation of Menstruants from the Sancta," in *Daughters of the King: Women and the Synagogue*, ed. Susan Grossman and Rivka Haut (Philadelphia: Jewish Publication Society, 1992).

22. Susan E. Shapiro, "A Matter of Discipline: Reading for Gender in Jewish Philosophy," in *Judaism Since Gender*, ed. Miriam Peskowitz and Laura Levitt (New York: Routledge, 1997).

23. Elliot R. Wolfson, *Circle in the Square: Studies in the Use of Gender in Kabbalistic Symbolism* (1995). See also Judith R. Baskin, "From Separation to Displacement: Perceptions of Women in Sefer Hasidim," *Association for Jewish Studies Review* 19, no. 1 (1994): 1–10.

24. Chava Weissler, *Voices of the Matriarchs: Listening to the Prayers of Early Modern Jewish Women* (Boston: Beacon Press, 1998).

25. Renee Levine Melammed, "Sephardi Women in the Medieval and Early Modern Periods," in *Jewish Women in Historical Perspective*, ed. Judith R. Baskin (Detroit: Wayne State University Press, 1998*); Heretics or Daughters of Israel? The Crypto-Jewish Women of Castile* (New York: Oxford University Press, 1999).

26. For example, see Libby Garshowitz, "Gracia Mendes: Power, Influence, and Image," in *Power of the Weak: Studies on Medieval Women*, ed. Jennifer Carpenter and Sally-Beth MacLean (Urbana: University of Illinois Press, 1995); see also *The Memoirs of Gluckel of Hameln*, trans. Marvin Lowenthal (New York: Schocken Books, 1977).

27. Howard Adelman, "Wife-Beating Among Early Modern Italian Jews, 1400–1700," *Proceedings of the Eleventh World Congress of Jewish Studies*, vol. 1 (. Jerusalem: The World Union of Jewish Studies, 1994), 135–142.

28. Ada Rapoport-Alpert, "On Women and Hasidism: S. A. Horodecky and the Maid of Ludmir Tradition," in *Jewish History: Essays in Honor of Chimen Abramsky*, eds. A. Rapoport-Alpert and S. J. Zipperstein (London: P. Halban, 1988).

29. Charlotte Baum, Paula Hyman, and Sonya Michel, *The Jewish Woman in America* (New York: Dial Press, 1976); Susan Glenn, *Daughters of the Shtetl: Life and Labor in the Immigrant Generation* (Ithaca: Cornell University Press, 1991); Linda Kuzmack-Gordon, *Women's Cause: The Jewish Women's Movement in England and the United States, 1881–1933* (Columbus: Ohio State University Press, 1990).

30. Michael Berkowitz, *Zionist Culture and West European Jewry Before the First World War* (New York: Cambridge University Press, 1993).

31. Deborah Bernstein, *The Struggle for Equality: Urban Women Workers in Pre-State Israeli Society* (New York: Praeger, 1987).

32. Marion A. Kaplan, *The Jewish Feminist Movement in Germany: The Campaigns of the Jüdischer Frauenbund, 1904–1938* (Westport, CT: Greenwood Press, 1979); *The Making of the Jewish Middle Class: Women, Family, and Identity in Imperial Germany* (New York: Oxford University Press, 1991).

33. Paula Hyman, "Immigrant Women and Consumer Protest: The New York City Kosher Meat Boycott of 1902," *American Jewish History* 70 (September 1980), 91–105.

34. Esther Fuchs, *Israeli Mythogynies: Women in Contemporary Hebrew Fiction* (Albany: State University of New York Press, 1987).

35. Naomi Seidman, *A Marriage Made in Heaven? The Sexual Politics of Hebrew and Yiddish* (Berkeley: University of California Press, 1997).

36. For feminist criticisms of Levinas, see Simone de Beauvoir, *The Second Sex*, trans. H. M. Parshley (New York: Vintage Books, 1952), p. xix. See Tina Chanter, "Feminism and the Other," in *The Provocation of Levinas: Rethinking the Other*, eds. Robert Bernasconi and David Wood (London and New York: Routledge, 1988), 32–56; Luce Irigaray, "Questions to Emmanuel Levinas: On the Divinity of Love," trans. Margaret Whitford, Catherine Chalier, "Ethics and the Feminine," and Tina Chanter, "Antigone's Dilemma," in *Re-Reading Levinas*, eds. Robert Bernasconi and Simon Critchley (Bloomington: Indiana University Press, 1991), 109–46; Robert Manning, "Thinking the Other Without Violence? An Analysis of the Relations Between the Philosophy of Emmanuel Levinas and Feminism," *Journal of Speculative Philosophy* 5, no. 2 (1991): 132–43; Stella Sandford, "Writing as a Man: Levinas and the Phenomenology of Eros," *Radical Philosophy* 87 (1998): 6–17; Ze'ev Levi, "Woman and the

Feminine in the Philosophy of Levinas," in *The Other and Otherness: Problems in the Philosophy of Emmanuel Levinas* [Hebrew] (Jerusalem: Magnes Press, 1997), 204–19.

37. Marion A. Kaplan, *The Jewish Feminist Movement in Germany: The Campaigns of the Jüdischer Frauenbund, 1904–1938.*

38. Renate Bridenthal, Atina Grossmann, and Marion A. Kaplan, eds., *When Biology Became Destiny: Women in Weimar and Nazi Germany* (New York: Monthly Review Press, 1984).

39. David Biale, *Eros and the Jews: From Biblical Israel to Contemporary America* (New York: Basic Books, 1992), and Sander Gilman, *The Jew's Body* (New York: Routledge, 1991). See also Nancy A. Harrowitz, *Antisemitism, Misogyny, and the Logic of Cultural Difference: Cesare Lombroso and Matilde Serao* (Lincoln: University of Nebraska Press, 1994).

40. Studies of women's experiences during the Holocaust, as victims, perpetrators, and bystanders, have been collected in several anthologies, including Esther Katz and Joan Miriam Ringelheim, *Women Surviving the Holocaust: Proceedings of the Conference* (New York: Institute for Research in History, 1983); Carol Rittner and John K. Roth, eds., *Different Voices: Women and the Holocaust* (New York: Paragon House, 1993); and Dalia Ofer and Lenore J. Weitzman, eds., *Women in the Holocaust* (New Haven: Yale University Press, 1998).

41. Michael Berkowitz, "Transcending 'Tzimmes and Sweetness': Recovering the History of Zionist Women in Central and Western Europe, 1897–1933," in *Active Voices: Women in Jewish Culture*, ed. Maurie Sacks (Urbana: University of Illinois Press, 1995) and Myra Glazer, ed., *Burning Air and a Clear Mind: Contemporary Israeli Women Poets* (Athens: Ohio University Press, 1981).

42. Pamela Nadell, *Women Who Would Be Rabbis: A History of Women's Ordination, 1889–1995* (Boston: Beacon Press, 1998).

43. Tamar El-Or, *Educated and Ignorant: Ultraorthodox Jewish Women and Their World*, trans. Haim Watzman (Boulder, CO: Lynne Rienner Publishers, 1993).

44. Lynn Davidman, *Tradition in a Rootless World: Women Turn to Orthodox Judaism* (Berkeley: University of California Press, 1991; Debra R. Kaufman, *Rachel's Daughters: Newly Orthodox Jewish Women* (New Brunswick: Rutgers University Press, 1991).

45. Marcia Falk, *The Book of Blessings: New Jewish Prayers for Daily Life, the Sabbath, and the New Moon Festival* (San Francisco: Harper, 1996).

CHAPTER SIX

1. Saiving 1.

2. Most women have anecdotes to illustrate this experience. At a reception for five new faculty members, including myself, in 1972, someone began a conversation by asking me, "And what does your husband teach?"

3. The ignoring of Stanton's book is an example of how women's scholarship was excluded from serious consideration until the 1960s. Stanton's discovery of the different treatment of the two sexes in the Bible was contemporaneous with Hermann Gunkel's discovery of different styles of writing to identify northern and southern tribes in the Pentateuch. His discovery revolutionized the study of the Bible; Stanton's is not treated as revolutionary in histories of Biblical scholarship.

4. Carr observes that "with some exceptions, the modern church completely resisted the full equality of women. . . . And yet, as [the encyclical] *Pacem in Terris* notes, the secular emancipation of women took place first and more rapidly in Christian societies. Why? Could it be

the message of the gospel, submerged in oppressive cultural forms, acted as a leaven in surprising ways?" (34)

5. In the Western church, Mary Magdalen is conflated with the prostitute who washes Jesus' feet with her tears of repentance. The Eastern church did not make this mistake and portrayed Mary Magdalen as a close friend of Jesus who understood him better than some other friends and who was a leader among the apostles, especially after the death of Jesus. See King.

6. Elizabeth Schüssler Fiorenza 298.

7. Ibid. 177–78.

8. Kadel 16, 20.

9. Dewey 23.

10. Ibid.

11. Chadwick 22–23.

12. Cloke 6–7.

13. Quoted in LaPorte 7–8.

14. Ibid. 29.

15. Cloke 2.

16. This "gap" between what one thinks and what one does amounts to what today we call ideology in the sense of those values, predispositions, and interests that are largely hidden to us and that prompt the particular direction we take in all of our unreflective action. More destructively the gap is the scotosis or blind spot that allows injustices and abuses of power to persist in society for centuries—long beyond what any reasonable people would imagine could be tolerated. Nevertheless, those who blame the past for the world's evils often forget that lapses from the original vision during their own era are attributable both to those who lack the vision as well as those who possess but betray it. The gap also reveals the insufficiency of either power or law alone to right wrongs.

17. Brock and Harvey 45.

18. Cloke.

19. Ibid. 17.

20. Ibid. 22.

21. Ambrose (X, 371).

22. Elm 194–96.

23. Ibid.

24. Ibid. 187.

25. Burrus 24.

26. Carolyn Walker Bynum 33.

27. Ibid. 42.

28. Morris 213. Even though he does not say so, it is reasonable to think that Morris's numbers designate only men's monasteries because a few pages later he uses exclusively male language to describe other religious orders: "In Cluniac and Benedictine houses, the best-trained monks were those who had entered as boys, had been fully instructed in the complications of chant and ceremonial, and had seen society only from the cloister. The Cistercians and Premonstratensians, by contrast, were recruited from among adults, men who had lived in society and rejected its values" (220). Morris's essay reveals the erasure by academicians of women's presence in religious traditions.

29. Thompson 55.

30. Ibid.

31. Abelard XV, 71.

32. Crawford 46.
33. Kavanaugh I:84.
34. Ibid. I:328.
35. Weber 35.
36. Greenblatt 25.
37. O'Brien 456.
38. Carr 21.
39. Cone 154.
40. Wetherilt 1.

CHAPTER SEVEN

1. Muhammad Iqbal, *The Reconstruction of Religious Thought in Islam* (Lahore: Shaikh Muhammad Ashraf, 1971), pp. 171–72.
2. Ibid., pp. 173–74.
3. Ibid., p. 175.
4. Ibid., pp. 148–49.
5. Ibid., pp. 151–78.
6. Ibid., p. 83.
7. M. M. Khan, translation of *Sahih Al-Bukhari* (Lahore: Kazi Publications, 1971), p. 346.
8. Ibid., p. 80.
9. Ibid., p. 81.
10. A. H. Siddiqui, translation of *Sahih Muslim* (Lahore: Shaikh Muhammad Ashraf, 1972), p. 752.
11. Ibid.
12. Ibid., pp. 752–53.
13. Alfred Guillaume, *The Traditions of Islam* (Khayats: Beirut, 1966), p. 97.
14. Muhammad Iqbal, *Reconstruction of Religious Thought in Islam*, p. 84.
15. Toshihiko Izutsu, *The Structure of the Ethical Terms in the Koran* (Tokyo: Keio Institute of Philosophical Studies, Mita, Siba, Minatoku, 1959), pp. 152–53.
16. Muhammad Iqbal, *Reconstruction of Religious Thought in Islam*, p. 85.

CHAPTER EIGHT

1. For a detailed description of this process, see Foltz and Griffin (1996).
2. Journalist and High Priestess Margot Adler (1986) has done the best job of this task thus far.
3. See Long (1997).
4. All Witches are pagans and honor the Goddess, but pagan is a larger category, and not all pagans are Witches.
5. Jorgenson and Russell (1999) see these as separate and distinct spiritualities. Others point to a blurring of boundaries of belief among them, the similarities in practice and the individuals who cross comfortably from one group's ritual to another (Griffin 1995; York 1995; Ellwood and McGraw 1999; Gottschal 2000).

6. Historian Ronald Hutton (1999) has done an impressively thorough job of exploring this history and is the source of much of the information presented here.

7. Ibid.

8. Hutton believes this distinction to be critical.

9. Ibid.

10. Leland (1990:109).

11. Ibid. 18.

12. Ibid. 114.

13. Originally spelled Wica, its etymology was believed to be related to the word *wisdom*. Today, it is commonly understood to refer to changing things by "shaping or bending" energy with the mind or human will.

14. Hutton (1999:174).

15. That was challenged by Janet and Stewart Farrar, in collaboration with Doreen Valiente in the early 1980s, Aiden Kelly (1991), and most recently, by Ronald Hutton (1999).

16. Hutton (1999).

17. This had been significantly modified, however. Crowley's Law of Thelema was, "Do what thou wilt shall be the whole of the Law. Love is the Law, Love under Will." The Wiccan Rede is, "An as it harm none, do what thou wilt."

18. There are also Witches who call themselves Traditional or Hereditary Witches who say their religion was passed down to them through their families. Hutton believes that these practices usually turn out to have derived from the same components from which Wicca developed.

19. Hutton (1999:239–240).

20. Crowley (2000).

21. Crowley (1990:64–65).

22. Hutton (1999:250).

23. Lamond (1997:18).

24. On October 30, 1985, Congress finally defeated an attempt to remove tax-exempt status from Wiccan churches. In 1999, a similar issue was brought up when Congressman Bob Barr discovered that there were Wiccan covens performing religious services on U.S. military bases. Unaware that the official U.S. Army Chaplain's Handbook had included a section on Wicca since 1978, Barr tried to force them off the bases and failed.

25. Morgan (1970:306f)

26. Ibid. (606).

27. As religious scholar Cynthia Eller (1993:55) points out, "By choosing this symbol, feminists were identifying themselves with everything that women were taught not to be: ugly, aggressive, independent and malicious."

28. Gage (1893).

29. Clifton (2000).

30. Budapest (1991).

31. Ibid.

32. According to Hutton (1999).

33. There was another tradition also called Dianic that had both women and men. However, Budapest's version of the Craft grew to the point where the other group became known as McFarland Dianics, after its founder, and many Witches today are unaware that male Dianics exist.

34. See Hutton (1999) for more details on this.

35. Budapest (1991).

36. Alternate spellings of the word "woman" were popular in the 70s and 80s and represented a separatist stance from men and the masculine.

37. Budapest (1991).

38. Although Budapest doesn't mention her, this was also one of the titles of the Egyptian Goddess Isis.

39. Eller (1993:57–58)

40. Like the Fellowship of Isis, a discussion of which will follow, many Dianics insist that the title High Priestess does not indicate a hierarchical status, but what a woman is called who has agreed to take on more responsibilities. Other Dianics feel uncomfortable with this title and insist that their covens be ruled by consensus. However, there one may find Elder Priestesses, a title which, they argue, simply means they have been around and involved for a long time.

41. Lozano and Foltz (1990).

42. Eller (1993).

43. Some other groups also use this procedure today.

44. NightMare (2000). See below for a description of the origin and evolution of the term *thealogy*—used now to refer to Goddess Spirituality.

45. NightMare (1998:16).

46. Canadian professor of the psychology of religion (University of Ottawa) Naomi Goldenberg (1979) was among the first to note that, although not all North American covens called themselves feminist, all of them supported feminist ideology to some degree.

47. Significantly, they both have advanced degrees in psychology, as does Selena Fox, founder of Circle Sanctuary.

48. In King (1993:163).

49. Daly (1992).

50. In Eller (1993:47)

51. Ehrenreich and English (1973:7).

52. Adler (1986:186).

53. Gimbutas (1974:9).

54. Hutton (1999).

55. Gimbutas (1974:9).

56. Gimbutas (1989).

57. These arguments continue today, even within Goddess Spirituality. For excellent examples of this, see *The Pomegranate: A New Journal of Neopagan Thought,* numbers 6, November 1998, and 7, February 1999.

58. It should be pointed out that Gimbutas was an acknowledged and respected expert on the prehistory of the Slavs, the Balts, and Eastern European Bronze Age cultures.

59. Adler (1986).

60. Christ (1982:77).

61. It needs to be stressed that the great majority of feminist researchers into ancient cultures never argued for a Golden Age of Matriarchy but posited for the existence of cultures that were matrifocal and/or matrilinear, fairly egalitarian, and in which Divinity was seen as female and sometimes male. For an early clarification of this, see Spretnak's Response, in her 1982 *Politics of Women's Spirituality.*

62. Eller (1993:92)

63. In personal correspondence to me, Long suggests that despite family background, college education in the United Kingdom effectively moves someone from working to middle class. However, and in spite of living what might be considered middle-class lives, the women themselves insisted that they were working class (Komatsu 1986).

64. Matriarchy Study Group (1977:4).

65. Sjoo and Mor (1981:5).

66. A grove is a group numbering over 13.

67. McAllister (1988:28).

68. See Long (1994) for a review of the research on the Greenham experience.

69. Jones (1996:13).

70. Ibid. (6).

71. Long (1997:28).

72. Robertson (1975:9).

73. Lawrence disliked the image of the "sacrificed, tortured and bleeding Christ." Olivia reports that one day, before founding the Fellowship, she discovered her brother unnailing Jesus from a crucifix in the family chapel. It was this act of "kindness" that told her she should work with him on reintroducing the religion of the Goddess (Robertson 1975:17).

74. Spretnak (1982:xvii).

75. This was first pointed out by Adler (1986).

76. Foltz and Griffin (1996).

77. Monaghan (1997:5).

78. Starhawk (1979:11).

79. Harvey (1996:169).

80. Jones (1997).

81. Starhawk (1979).

82. Hutton (1999:51).

83. Starhawk (1979:9).

84. Budapest (1991).

85. Daly (1987:76).

86. Starhawk, Macha NightMare, and the Reclaiming Collective (1997).

87. Goldenberg (1979:93).

88. I am not suggesting that there should be a body to whom clergy or leaders *should* be responsible, only pointing out that challenges exist when this is not the case.

89. Goldenberg (1979:99).

90. Griffin (1995, 2000).

91. Thanks to Patricia Monaghan, who shared this insight over dinner one night.

92. This has been a continuing argument of Asphodel Long's (see King 1993).

93. Roof (1999).

94. Starhawk (1987).

95. Segmented Polycentric Integrated Networks.

96. York (1995).

Bibliography

CHAPTER ONE

Andal. 1971. "Nacciyar Tirumoli." In ed. Annangaracariyar, P. B., *Nalayira tivviyap pirapantam*. Kanchi:V. N. Tevanatan.

Bhagavad Gita. See Miller.

Bhuttat, Alvar. 1971. "Irantam Tiruvantati." In ed. Annangaracariyar, P. B., *Nalayira tivviyap pirapantam*. Kanchi:V. N. Tevanatan.

Davidman, Lynn and Tenenbaum, Shelley. 1994. *Feminist Perspectives on Jewish Studies*. New Haven:Yale University Press.

Dehejia,Vidya. 1990. *Art of the Imperial Cholas*. New York: Columbia University Press.

Doniger,Wendy and Smith, Brian, trans. 1991. *The Laws of Manu*. London: Penguin Books.

Findly, Ellison Banks. 1985. "Gargi at the King's Court: Women and Philosophic Invention in Ancient India." In ed. Haddad,Y.Y. and Findly, E. B., *Women, Religion, and Social Change*. Albany: State University of New York Press, pp. 37–58.

Kane, Pandurang Vaman. 1953–1974. *History of Dharmasastra (Ancient and Mediaeval Religious and Civil Law)*, vols. I-V. Poona, India: Bhandarkar Oriental Research Institute.

Kishwar, Madhu. "From Manusmriti to Madhusmriti: Flagellating a Mythical Enemy." Internet article. http://www.infinityfoundation.com/ECITmythicalframeset.htm

Leslie, Julia. 1983. "Essence and Existence: Women and Religion in Ancient Indian Texts." In ed. Holden, Pat, *Women's Religious Experience*. London: Croom Helm.

Lorenzen, David. 1999. "Who Invented Hinduism?" *Comparative Studies in Society and History*, vol. 41, no. 4 (1999), pp. 630-659.

Manu Smirti. See Doniger,Wendy.

McGee, Mary. 1995. "Bahina Bai: The Ordinary Life of an Exceptional Woman, or, the Exceptional Life of an Ordinary Woman." *Journal of Vaisnava Studies*, vol. 3, no. 4, pp. 111-148.

Mehta, Vatsala. "The Hindu Widow with Special Reference to Gujarat." Master's Thesis, University of Bombay, 1956.

Miller, Barbara Stoler, trans. 1986. *The Bhagavad Gita: Krishna's Counsel in Time of War*. New York: Columbia University Press.

Narayanan, Vasudha. 1995. "Tiruvenkatam in the Fifteenth Century." *Journal of Vaisnava Studies*, vol. 3, no. 3, pp. 91-108.

_____. 1999. "Brimming with Bhakti, Embodiments of Shakti." In ed. Sharma, Arvind and Young, Katherine K., *Feminism in World Religions*. Albany: State University of New York Press.

_____. 2001. "Casting Light on the Sounds of the Tamil Veda: Tirukkoneri Dasyai's Garland of Words." In ed. Patton, Laurie L., *Jewels of Authority: Women and Text in the Hindu Tradition*. New York: Oxford University Press.

Natya Shastra. See Rangacharya.

O'Flaherty, Wendy Doniger. 1975. *Hindu Myths*. Hammondsworth: Penguin.

Orr, Leslie. 2000. *Donors, Devotees, and Daughters of God: Temple Women in Medieval Tamilnadu*. New York: Oxford University Press.

Patton, Laurie L. 2001. *Jewels of Authority: Women and Text in the Hindu Tradition*. New York: Oxford University Press.

Pearson, Anne. 1996. *Because It Gives Me Peace of Mind: Ritual Fasts in the Lives of Hindu Women*. Albany: State University of New York Press.

Pillai Lokacarya. 1966. *Srivacana Bhusanam*, sutra 29. In ed. Annangaracariyar, P. B., *Srimatvaravaramunintra krantamalai*. Kanchi: V. N. Tevanatan.

Pintchman, Tracy. 1998. "When Vows Fail to Deliver What They Promise: The Case of Rajavanti." Paper presented at the American Academy of Religion, Orlando, Florida.

Poykai, Alvar. 1971. *Mutal Tiruvantati*. In ed. Annangaracariyar, P. B., *Nalayira tivviyap pirapantam*. Kanchi: V. N. Tevanatan.

Ramanujan, A. K. 1967. *The Interior Landscape*. Bloomington: Indiana University Press.

_____. 1982. "The Lives of Female Saints." In ed. Hawley, John Stratton and Wulff, Donna, *The Divine Consort: Radha and the Goddesses of India*. Berkeley Religious Studies Series, vol. 3.

Rangacharya, Adya, ed. and trans. 1996. *The Natyasastra*. Delhi: Munshiram Manoharlal.

Rig Veda. Rig III.31.1. Oral tradition; usually identified by these numbers.

Tharu, Susie and Lalita. 1991. *Women Writing in India: 600 B.C. to the Present*. New York: Feminist Press.

Vishnu Purana. See H. H. Wilson.

Wilson, H. H., trans. 1840. *The Vishnu Purana: A System of Hindu Mythology and Tradition*. London: J. Murray.

Young, Katherine K. 2002. "Om, the Vedas, and the Status of Women with Special Reference to Srivaishavism." In ed. Patton, Laurie L., *Jewels of Authority: Women and Text in the Hindu Tradition*. New York: Oxford University Press, pp. 84–121.

CHAPTER TWO

Works Cited

Church, Cornelia Dimmitt. "Temptress, Housewife, Nun: Women's Role in Early Buddhism," *Anima: An Experiential Journal* I:2 (Spring 1975).

Falk, Nancy Auer. "The Case of the Vanishing Nuns: the Fruits of Ambivalence in Ancient Indian Buddhism," *Unspoken Worlds: Women's Religious Lives*, ed. by Nancy Auer Falk and Rita
M. Gross (Belmont, CA: Wadsworth, 2001), pp. 196–206.

Gomez, Luis O., tr. *The Land of Bliss: The Paradise of the Buddha of Measureless Light* (Honolulu:
University of Hawaii Press, 1996).

Gross, Rita M. *Buddhism after Patriarchy: A Feminist History, Analysis, and Reconstruction of Buddhism* (Albany: State University of New York Press, 1993).

_____, "Buddhism," *Women in Religion,* ed. by Jean Holm (London: Pinter Publishers, 1994),
pp. 1–29.

Kabilsingh, Chatsumarn. *Thai Women in Buddhism* (Berkeley, CA: Parallax Press, 1991).

Paul, Diana Y. *Women in Buddhism: Images of the Feminine in Mahayana Tradition* (Berkeley: Asian
Humanities Press, 1979).

Schelling, Andrew and Waldman, Anne, tr. *Songs of the Sons and Daughters of the Buddha*
(Boston: Shambhala, 1996).

Willis, Janice Dean. "Nuns and Benefactresses: The Role of Women in the Development of
Buddhism," in *Women, Religion, and Social Change*, ed. by Yvonne Hadad and Elison Banks
Findley (Albany: State University of New York Press, 1985), p. 75.

Wilson, Liz. *Charming Cadavers: Horrific Figurations of the Feminine in Indian Buddhist Hagiographic Literature* (Chicago: University of Chicago Press, 1996).

Recommended Readings

Dowman, Keith, tr. *Sky Dancer: The Secret Life and Songs of the Lady Yeshe Tsogyel* (London:
Routledge and Kegan Paul, 1984). This somewhat difficult book is an account of one of
the most important female Vajrayana Buddhists.

Gross, Rita M. *Buddhism After Patriarchy: A Feminist History, Analysis, and Reconstruction of Buddhism* (Albany: State University of New York Press, 1993). The most extensive discussion of
women and Buddhism.

Paul, Diana Y. *Women in Buddhism: Images of the Feminine in Mahayana Tradition* (Berkeley, CA:
Asian Humanities Press, 1979). Carefully introduced selections from important Mahayana
texts.

Robinson, Richard H. and Johnson, Willard L. *The Buddhist Religion: a Historical Introduction,*
4th edition (Belmont, CA: Wadsworth Publishing Company, 1997). The most complete
and useful textbook on the Buddhist history and doctrine.

Skilton, Andrew. *A Concise History of Buddhism* (Birmingham, England: Windhorse Publications, 1994). A shorter, more accessible history of Buddhism.

Snellgrove, David and Richardson, Hugh. *A Cultural History of Tibet* (Boulder: Prajna Press,
1980). An accurate and readable history of Tibet and Tibetan Buddhism.

Strong, John S. *The Experience of Buddhism: Sources and Interpretations* (Belmont, CA: Wadsworth
Publishing Co., 1995). An extensive and useful selection of Buddhist texts.

Swearer, Donald K. *The Buddhist World of Southeast Asia* (Albany: State University of New York
Press, 1995). A very useful account of contemporary Theravada Buddhism.

Tsomo, Karma Lekshe, ed. *Sakyadhita: Daughters of the Buddha* (Ithaca, NY: Snow Lion, 1988).
A very useful summary of the contemporary status of women, especially nuns, in the Buddhist world.

Williams, Paul, *Mahayana Buddhism: The Doctrinal Foundations* (London: Routledge, 1989). Complete and accessible survey of Mahayana Buddhist thought.

CHAPTER 3

Ames, Roger T. and Rosemont, Henry Jr. (trans.). 1998. *The Analects of Confucius: A Philosophical Translation.* New York: Ballantine Books.

Bodde, Derk. 1939. "Types of Chinese Categorical Thinking" in Charles Le Blanc and Dorothy Borei (eds.), *Essays on Chinese Civilization by Derk Bodde.* Pp. 141–160. Princeton: Princeton University Press.

Chai, Ch'u and Chai, Winberg. 1965. "*Hsiao Ching*" in Ch'u Chai and Winberg Chai, *The Sacred Books of Confucius and other Confucian Classics.* Pp. 323–334. New Hyde Park, NY: University Books.

Chan, Wing-tsit (trans.). 1963. *Instructions for Practical Living and Other Neo-Confucian Writings by Wang Yang-ming.* New York and London: Columbia University Press.

Chen, Ivan (trans.). 1920. *The Book of Filial Piety Including the Twenty Four Examples.* First edition published 1908. London: John Murray.

Ching, Julia. 1997. *Mysticism and Kingship in China: The Heart of Chinese Wisdom.* Cambridge: Cambridge University Press.

Chu Hsi and Lu Tsu-ch'ien (comps.). 1175. Wing-tsit Chan (trans.). 1967. *Reflections on Things at Hand.* New York and London: Columbia University Press.

Dawson, Raymond. 1993. *Confucius: The Analects.* Oxford, New York: Oxford University Press.

Dobson, W. A. C. H. (trans.). 1963. *Mencius.* Toronto: University of Toronto Press.

Fingarette, Herbert. 1972. *Confucius: the Secular as Sacred.* New York: Torchbooks.

Graham, Angus Charles. 1989. *Disputers of the Tao: Philosophical Argument in Ancient China.* La Salle, Ill.: Open Court.

Huang, Chichung (trans.). 1997. *The Analects of Confucius.* New York, Oxford: Oxford University Press.

Lau, D. C. (trans.) 1970. *Mencius.* Middlesex: Penguin Books.

Legge, James (trans.). 1971. *Confucius. Confucian Analects. The Great Learning and the Doctrine of the Mean.* First published in 1893 by Clarendon Press, Oxford. New York: Dover Publications.

Levenson, Joseph R. 1960. "Ill Wind in the Well-field: The Erosion of the Confucian Ground of Controversy" in Arthur F. Wright, *The Confucian Persuasion.* Pp. 268–287. Stanford: Stanford University Press.

Mou Tsung-san. 1981. "Confucianism as Religion" in Douglas Lancashire. *Chinese Essays on Religion and Faith.* Pp. 21–43. San Francisco: Chinese Materials Centre.

Murray, Julia. 1988. "The Ladies' Classic of Filial Piety and Sung Textual Illustration: Problems of Reconstruction and Artistic Context" in *Ars Orientalis.* 18:95–129. Ann Arbor: Dept. of History of Art, University of Michigan.

Nivison, David S. 1996. *The Ways of Confucianism.* Edited and with an introduction by Bryan W. Van Norden. Chicago and La Salle, Ill.: Open Court.

T'ang, Chun-i. 1981. "Spirit of Religion and Modern Man" in Douglas Lancashire. *Chinese Essays on Religion and Faith.* Pp. 44–52. San Francisco: Chinese Materials Centre.

Taylor, Rodney L. 1990. *The Religious Dimensions of Confucianism*. Albany: State University of New York Press.

———. 1986. *The Way of Heaven*. Leiden: E. J. Brill.

Traylor, Kenneth L. 1988. *Chinese Filial Piety*. Bloomington, Ind.: Eastern Press.

Tu Wei-ming. 1998. "Probing the 'Three Bonds' and 'Five Relationships' in Confucian Humanism" in Walter H. Slote and George A. DeVos (eds.). *Confucianism and the Family*. Albany: State University of New York Press.

Wang, Te-shih (ed.). 1972. *Hsiao Ching chin-chu chin-i*. (A Modern Annotated Interpretation of *The Classic on Filial Piety*)

Watson, Burton (trans.). 1963. *Hsün Tzu: Basic Writings*. New York: Columbia University Press.

Wilhelm, Richard (trans.). 1967. *The I Ching or Book of Changes*, rendered into English by Cary F. Baynes. Princeton: Princeton University Press.

Woo, Tak-ling T. 2000. *Religious Ideals, Beliefs and Practices in the Lives of Women During the Reign of T'ang Ming Huang*. Ph.D. Dissertation. University of Toronto.

CHAPTER 4

Research into the history of women in Taoism is based on the following Chinese sources:

Chinese Sources

TT: from The Taoist Canon (Cheng T'ung and Wan Li addendum)
TTCH: from Hsiao T'ien-shih's Tao-tsang ch'ing-hua (Essentials of the Taoist Canon)
NC: non-canonical texts
TT: Ch'ing-ching ching (Scripture of Cultivating Stillness)
TTCH: Ch'ing-ching yüan-chun k'un-yüan ching (The Celestial Ruler Sun Pu-erh's Scripture on Cultivating Stillness for Women)
TT: Han Wu-ti nei-chuan (The Inner Chronicles of Han Wu-ti)
TTCH: Hsi Wang-mu nü-hsiu cheng-t'u shih tse (Mother Empress of the West's Ten Precepts on the True Path of Women's Practices)
TTCH: Hsiu-chen p'ien-nan tsan-cheng (Answers to Questions Concerning Cultivation)
TTCH: Hung-shih hsien-fo ch'i-tsung (Hung's Chronicles of the Wondrous Lives of the Immortals and Boddhisattvas)
TTCH: K'un-ning miao-ching (Cultivating Stillness for Women)
TT: Lieh-hsien chuan (Biographies of the Immortals)
NC: Lieh-hsien ch'üan-chuan (Complete Biographies of the Immortals)
TT: Li-shih chen-hsien t'i-tao tung-chien (Comprehensive History of the True Immortals)
TTCH: Ling-yuan ta-tao ke (Song of the Luminous Origin of the Great Tao)
TT: Mu t'ien-tzu chuan (The Legends of King Mu)
TTCH: Ni-wan-li tsu-shih nü-tsung shuang-hsiu pao-fa (The Teacher Li Ni-wan's Precious Raft of Women's Paired Practice)
TTCH: Nü-kung Cheng-fa (Correct Methods for Women's Practice)
TTCH: Nü chin-tan fa-yao (Essentials of the Golden Elixir Method for Women)

TT: San-tung yü-shu (The Jade Writ of the Three Caverns)
TT: Shang-ch'ing huang-ting nei-ching yü ching (The Yellow Court Classic of Internal Images of the High Pure Realm)
TT: Shen-hsien chuan (Chronicles of the Immortals)
TTCH: Sun Pu-erh yüan-chun fa-yü (The Celestial Ruler Sun Pu-erh's Oral Teachings)
TT: Ta-tung chen-ching (The Sacred Scriptures of the Great Cavern
TT: Yüan-shih shang-chen chung-hsien chi (Records of the Most High Realized Beings of the Primal Beginning)
TT: Yün-chi ch'i-ch'ien (Seven Bamboo Satchels of the Cloud Scrolls)
TT: Yung-cheng chi-hsien chuan (The Record of the Assembly of Immortals of the Celestial City)

Recommended Readings

For the non-Chinese reader, the following is an introductory list of readings on the topic:

Cleary, Thomas. trans. and ed. 1989. *Immortal Sisters: Secrets of Taoist Women*. Boston: Shambhala. A collection of poems of female practitioners of internal alchemy, including the writings of Sun Pu-erh.

Kohn, Livia. trans. and ed. 1993. *The Taoist Experience*. Albany: State University of New York Press. A good collection of a wide range of subjects from the Taoist Canon, including biographies of the Mother Empress of the West and several female immortals.

Laughlin, Karen, and Eva Wong. 1999. "Feminism and/in Taoism," in *Feminism and World Religions*, Arvind Sharma and Katherine K. Young, eds. Albany: State University of New York Press. A view of Taoist philosophy and practice from the perspective of feminism.

Robinet, Isabelle. 1993. *Taoist Meditation*. Albany: State University of New York Press. Probably the best scholastic study of Shang-ch'ing Taoism.

Porter, Bill. 1993. *The Road to Heaven*. San Francisco: Mercury House. An interesting travelogue. Porter interviews female and male Taoist and Buddhist hermits in China.

Wile, Douglas, trans. and ed. 1992. *Art of the Bedchamber: The Chinese Sexual Yoga Classics Including Women's Solo Meditation Texts*. Albany: State University of New York Press. An excellent translation of texts on sexual alchemy and female internal alchemy.

Wong, Eva, trans. 1990. *Seven Taoist Masters*. Boston: Shambhala. The dramatized story of how Sun Pu-erh and her fellow students attained enlightenment and immortality.

_____. 1997. *The Shambhala Guide to Taoism*. Boston: Shambhala. An account of the history, systems, and practice of Taoism for the non-specialist and non-practitioner of the Taoist arts.

_____. 2002. *Tales of the Taoist Immortals*. Boston: Shambhala.

CHAPTER 6

Abelard. *Historium Calamitatum*. c. 1135.

Ambrose, "Concerning Virgins." In *Nicene and Post-Nicene Fathers, Second Series*. Vol. VI, ed. P. Schaff and H. Wace. London and Oxford: Charles Scribner's Sons, 1893.

Brock, Sebastian P. and Susan Ashbrook Harvey, intro. and trans., *Holy Women of the Syrian Orient*. Berkeley: University of California Press, 1987.

Burrus, Virginia. *The Making of a Heretic: Gender, Authority, and the Priscillianist Controversy.* Berkeley: University of California Press, 1995.

Carr, Anne. *Transforming Grace: Christian Tradition and Women's Experience.* San Francisco: Harper and Row, 1988.

Chadwick, Henry. "The Early Christian Community." In John McManners, pp. 21–69.

Clark, Elizabeth. *Women in the Early Church.* Wilmington: Michael Glazier, 1983.

Cloke, Gillian. "This Female Man of God": Women and Spiritual Power in the Patristic Age, AD 350–450. London: Routledge, 1995.

Cone, James H. *Martin and Malcolm and America.* Maryknoll: Orbis, 1992.

Crawford, Patricia. *Women and Religion in England 1500–1720.* London: Routledge, 1993.

Elm, Susanna. "*Virgins of God": The Making of Asceticism in Late Antiquity.* Oxford: Oxford University Press, 1994.

Dewey, Joanna. "From Oral Stories to Written Text." In *Women's Sacred Scriptures.* Kwok Pui-Lan and Elizabeth Schüsseler Fiorenza. *Continuum* 1998/3, 20–28.

Isasi-Diaz, Ada María and Yolanda Tarango. "Mujerista Theology." In Ruether and Keller.

Goldstein, Valerie Saiving. "The Human Situation: A Feminine View." *Journal of Religion* 40 (1960), 100–112.

Judge, E. A. "The Earliest Use of Monchos for "Monk" (P. Coll. Youtie 77) and the Origins of Monasticism." *Jahrbuch für Antike und Christentum* (1977), 72–89.

Kabel, Andrew. *Matrology: A Bibliography of Writings by Christian Women From the First to the Fifteenth Centuries.* New York: Continuum, 1995.

Kavanaugh, Kieran and Otilio Rodriguez. *The Collected Works of St. Teresa of Avila.* Vols. I and II. Washington: Institute of Carmelite Studies, 1976–1980.

King, Karen L. "Canonization and Marginalization: Mary of Magdala." In *Women's Sacred Scriptures, Concilium* 1998/3, 28–36.

LaPorte, Jean. *The Role of Women in Early Christianity.* Lewiston, NY: Edwin Mellen Press, 1982.

Laurence, Anne. "A Priesthood of She-Believers: Women and Congregations in Mid-seventeenth Century England." In Sheils and Wood.

Mayr-Harting, Henry. "The West: The Age of Conversion (700–1050)." In McManners.

McEnroy, Carmel E. *Guests in Their Own House: The Women of Vatican II.* New York: Crossroad, 1996.

McManners, John, ed. *The Oxford History of Christianity.* Oxford: Oxford University Press, 1990.

Morris, Colin. "Christian Civilization (1050–1400)." In McManners.

O'Brien, Susan. "Lay-Sisters and Good Mothers: Working-class Women in English Convents, 1840–1910." In Sheils and Wood.

Po-Chia Hsia, R., *The World of Catholic Renewal 1540–1770.* Cambridge: Cambridge University Press, 1998.

Sheils, W. J. and Diana Wood. *Women in the Church: Papers of the Ecclesiastical History Society.* London: Basil Blackwell, 1990.

Thompson, John Lee. *John Calvin and the Daughters of Sarah: Women in Regular and Exceptional Roles in the Exegesis of Calvin, His Predecessors, and His Contemporaries.* Geneva: Librairie Droz S.A.

Thompson, Sally. *Women Religious: The Founding of English Nunneries after the Norman Conquest.* Oxford: Clarendon, 1991.

Weber, Alison. *Teresa of Avila and the Rhetoric of Femininity.* Princeton: Princeton University Press, 1990.

Wetherilt, Ann Kirkus. *That They May be Many: Voices of Women, Echoes of God*. New York: Continuum, 1994.

Further Reading

Bynum, Carolyn Walker. *Holy Feast and Holy Fast: The Religious Significance of Food to Medieval Women*. Berkeley: University of California Press, 1987.

Carr, Anne E. *Transforming Grace: Christian Tradition and Women's Experience*. San Francisco: Harper and Row, 1988.

Cloke, Gillian. *"This Female Man of God": Women and Spiritual Power in the Patristic Age, AD 350–450*. London: Routledge, 1995.

Fitzgerald, Kyriaki Karidoyanes. *Women Deacons in the Orthodox Church*. Boston: Holy Cross, 1998.

Kadel, Andrew. *Matrology: A Bibliography of Writings by Christian Women from the First to the Fifteenth Centuries*. New York: Continuum, 1995.

Murphy, Cullen. *The Gospel According to Eve*. New York: Houghton Mifflin, 1998.

Ruether, Rosemary Radford and Rosemary Skinner Keller, eds. *In Our Own Voices: Four Centuries of American Women's Religious Writing*. San Francisco: HarperCollins, 1995.

Salisbury, Joyce E. *Church Fathers, Independent Virgins*. London: Verso, 1991.

Schüssler Fiorenza, Elizabeth. *In Memory of Her: A Feminist Theological Reconstruction of Christian Origins*. New York: Crossroad, 1983.

CHAPTER 8

Adler, Margot. 1986. *Drawing Down the Moon*. Revised and expanded edition. Boston: Beacon Press.

Bradley, Marion Zimmer. 1982. *The Mists of Avalon*. New York: Ballantine.

Budapest, Zsuzsanna. 1980. *The Holy Book of Women's Mysteries, Vol. 1*. Revised edition. Oakland, CA: Susan B. Anthony Coven No. 1.

———. 1991. Taped interview by author. June 17. Oakland, California.

Christ, Carol. 1982. "Why Women Need the Goddess: Phenomenological, Psychological, and Political Reflections," in *The Politics of Women's Spirituality*. Charlene Spretnak, ed. Garden City, NY: Anchor Press. Pp. 71–86.

——— and Judith Plaskow, eds. 1979. *Woman Spirit Rising*. San Francisco: Harper and Row.

Clifton, Chas. 2000. April 17. Personal E-mail communication. Used with permission.

Crowley, Vivianne. 1990. "Priestess and Witch," in *Voices of the Goddess*. Caitlin Matthews, ed. Wellingborough, Northamptonshire, England: Aquarian Press. Pp. 45–66.

———. 2000. "Healing in Wicca," in *Daughters of the Goddess: Studies of Healing, Identity and Empowerment*. Wendy Griffin, ed. Walnut Creek, CA: AltaMira Press. Pp. 151–165.

Daly, Mary. 1987. *Websters' First New Intergalactic Wickedary of the English Language*. Boston: Beacon Press.

———. 1992. *Outercourse*. San Francisco: HarperSanFrancisco.

Ehrenreich, Barbara and Diedre English. 1973. *Witches, Midwives, and Nurses: A History of Women Healers*. 2d edition. Old Westbury, NY: The Feminist Press.

Eller, Cynthia. 1993. *Living in the Lap of the Goddess: The Feminist Spirituality Movement in America*. New York: Crossroads Press.

Ellwood, Robert and Barbara McGraw. 1999. *Many Peoples, Many Faiths: Women and Men in the World Religions*. 6th edition. New York: Prentice-Hall.

Foltz, Tanice and Wendy Griffin. 1996. "She Changes Everything She Touches: Ethnographic Journeys of Self-Discovery," in *Composing Ethnography*. Carolyn Ellis and Arthur Bochner, eds. Walnut Creek, CA: AtlaMira Press. Pps. 301–329.

Gage, Matilda Joselyn. 1983. *Woman, Church, and State*. Watertown, MA: Persephone Press.

Gimbutas, Marija. 1974. *The Gods and Goddesses of Old Europe: 7000 to 3500 B.C. Myths, Legends and Cult Images*. Berkeley: University of California Press.

_____. 1989. *The Language of the Goddess*. San Francisco: Harper & Row.

Goldenberg, Naomi. 1979. *Changing of the Gods: Feminism and the End of Traditional Religion*. Boston: Beacon Press.

Gottschal, Marilyn. 2000. "The Mutable Goddess: Particularity and Eclecticism Within the Goddess Public," in *Daughters of the Goddess: Studies of Healing, Identity and Empowerment*. Wendy Griffin, ed. Walnut Creek, CA: AltaMira Press. Pp. 59–72.

Griffin, Wendy. 1995. "The Embodied Goddess: Feminist Witchcraft and Female Divinity." *Sociology of Religion*. Vol. 56, No. 1, Spring. Pp. 35–48.

_____. 2000. "Crafting the Boundaries: Goddess narrative as incantation," in *Daughters of the Goddess: Studies of Healing, Identity and Empowerment*. Wendy Griffin, ed. Walnut Creek, CA: AltaMira Press. Pp. 73–88.

Harvey, Graham. 1996. *Listening People, Speaking Earth*. London: Hurst Company.

Hutton, Ronald. 1999. *The Triumph of the Moon*. New York: Oxford University Press

Jones, Kathy. 1996. *On Finding Treasure*. Glastonbury: Ariadne Publications.

_____. 1997. Taped interview by author. July 11. Glastonbury.

Jorgensen, Danny L. and Scott E. Russell. 1999. "American Neopaganism: The Participants' Social Identities." *Journal of the Society for the Scientific Study of Religion*. Vol. 38, No. 3, September. Pp. 325–338.

Kelly, Aiden. 1991. *Crafting the Art of Magic*. Book One. St. Paul, MN: Llewellyn Publishers.

King, Ursula. 1993. *Women and Spirituality: Voices of Protest & Promise*. 2d edition. London: Macmillan Press.

Komatsu, Kayoko. 1986. "An Empirical Study of Matriarchy Groups in Contemporary Britain and Their Relationship to New Religious Movements." Master's Thesis, University of Leeds.

Lamond, Frederic. 1997. "The Long View," in *Pagan Dawn*, Imbolc. No. 122. Pp. 16, 18.

Leland, Charles G. *Aradia or the Gospel of the Witches*. (1890) 1990. Custer, WA: Phoenix Publishing.

Long, Asphodel. 1994. "The Goddess Movement in Britain Today." *Feminist Theology*. No. 5, January. Pp. 11–39.

_____. 1997. "The One or the Many: The Great Goddess Revisited." *Feminist Theology*. No. 15, May. Pp. 13–29.

Lozano, Wendy Griffin and Tanice G. Foltz. 1990. "Into the Darkness: An Ethnographic Study of Witchcraft and Death." *Qualitative Sociology*. Vol. 13, No. 3. Pp. 211–234.

Matriarch Study Group. 1977. *Goddess Shrew*. London: Women in Print.

McAllister, Pam. 1988. *You Can't Kill the Spirit*. Philadelphia: New Society Publishers.

Monaghan, Patricia. 1997. *The Goddess Path*. St. Paul, MN: Llewellyn Publishers.

Morgan, Robin, ed. 1970. *Sisterhood Is Powerful*. New York: Vintage Books.

NightMare, M. Macha. 1998. "The W Word, or Why We Call Ourselves Witches." *Reclaiming Quarterly*. No. 71, Summer. Pp. 16–18.

_____. 2000. Personal correspondence. Used with permission.

Robertson, Olivia. 1975. *The Call of Isis*. London: Neptune Press.

Roof, Wade Clark. 1999. *Spiritual Marketplace: Baby Boomers and the Remaking of American Religion*. Princeton, NJ: Princeton University Press.

Sjoo, Monica and Barbara Mor. 1981. *The Ancient Religion of the Great Cosmic Mother of All*. Trondheim, Norway: Rainbow Press.

Spretnak, Charlene. 1978. *Lost Goddesses of Early Greece*. Boston: Beacon Press.

_____, ed. 1982. *The Politics of Women's Spirituality*. Garden City, NY: Anchor Books.

Starhawk. 1979. *The Spiral Dance*. San Francisco: Harper and Row Publishers.

_____. 1987. *Truth or Dare*. San Francisco: Harper and Row Publishers.

_____, Macha NightMare, and the Reclaiming Collective. 1997. *The Pagan Book of Living and Dying*. San Francisco: Harper San Francisco.

Stone, Merlin. 1978. *When God Was a Woman*. New York: Harcourt Brace Jovanovich.

Walker, Barbara G. 1983. *The Woman's Encyclopedia of Myths and Secrets*. New York: Harper and Row.

York, Michael. 1995. *The Emerging Network: A Sociology of the New Age and Neo-Pagan Movements*. Manham, MD: Rowman and Littlefield Publishers.

About the Contributors

Mary Gerhart lectures frequently and widely on topics involving religion and literature, and theology and science. A John Templeton Foundation prize-winning professor, she currently teaches at Hobart and William Smith Colleges in Geneva, New York. She is the author of two books, including *Genre Choices, Gender Questions,* and the co-author of *New Maps for Old: Explorations in Science and Religion* and *Metaphoric Process: The Creation of Scientific and Religious Understanding.* She is the past editorial chair of the *Religious Studies Review.*

Wendy Griffin is a professor of Women's Studies at California State University at Long Beach and the author of numerous articles on feminist Witchcraft and Goddess Spirituality. She is the editor of *Daughters of the Goddess: Studies of Healing, Identity and Empowerment* and has been a long-time community activist, having served in leadership positions in the California branch of NOW, the Orange County ERA, and Long Beach's WomanShelter.

Rita M. Gross is a scholar-practitioner and a senior teacher of Shambhala Buddhism. She teaches comparative studies in religion currently at the University of Wisconsin at Eau Claire. One of the early leaders of women studies in religion and in Buddhist-Christian dialogue, she has written many books and articles. Her best-known books are *Buddhism After Patriarchy: A Feminist History, Analysis, and Reconstruction of Buddhism; Soaring and Settling: Buddhist Perspectives on Contemporary Social and Religious Issues;* and *Religious Feminism and the Future of the Planet: A Buddhist-Christian Conversation* (co-authored with Rosemary Radford Ruether).

Riffat Hassan is founder of the International Network for the Rights of Female Victims of Violence in Pakistan (INRFVVP)—an international organization that heightens awareness regarding the scale, degree, and nature of the violence being done to girls and women in Pakistan, provides direct assistance to victims wherever possible, and eliminates the root-causes of that violence. Hassan is one of the pioneers of feminist theology in the Islamic tradition. When she is not teaching religious studies at the University of Louisville, Kentucky, she returns regularly to her native Pakistan.

Susannah Heschel holds the Eli Black Professorship in Jewish Studies at Dartmouth College. She is the author of *Abraham Geiger and the Jewish Jesus* and editor of several books, including *On Being a Jewish Feminist, Insider/Outsider: American Jews and Multiculturalism,* and *Betrayal: German Churches and the Holocaust.* She has been a frequent United Nations contributor to conferences on religion and the environment. She is also co-chair, with Cornel West, of the *Tikkun* Community, and contributes regularly to *Tikkun* magazine.

Vasudha Narayanan is a native of India, and the president of the American Academy of Religion (the largest religious organization in North America). A graduate of the University of Bombay, she currently teaches religious studies at the University of Florida, where she is also the Director of the Center for Women's Studies and Gender Research.

Eva Wong was born and raised in Hong Kong. She is a widely recognized practitioner of the Taoist arts and a well-known translator of Taoist texts. She is the author of 12 books on Taoism and traditional Chinese feng-shui.

Terry Woo grew up in Hong Kong and primarily learned what it meant to be a Chinese Confucian from her father's teachings at home. She currently teaches religious studies at Dalhousie University in Halifax, Nova Scotia.

ABOUT THE EDITORS

Katherine K. Young is James McGill Professor at McGill University. She publishes in the field of South Indian religion, gender and religion, and comparative ethics. She has collaborated with Arvind Sharma on twelve volumes on women and world religions.

Arvind Sharma is Birks Professor of Comparative Religion at McGill University. Along with a steady stream of edited books on women and religion, he has published extensively in the fields of Hinduism and comparative religion.

Index